A 3056
21.95

W9-AVP-512

THIS BOOK HAS EVERYTHING YOU NEED

FOR THE COAST GUARD LICENSE

FROM THE BOTTOM UP

This Book Does Not Tell

You How To Pass The Test.

It TEACHES You How

To Pass The Test.

IF YOU DOUBT THIS STATEMENT

READ THE TABLE OF CONTENTS

AND

THUMB THROUGH THE INDEX

THIS BOOK IS DEDICATED TO THOSE WHO WENT BEFORE YOU.

THE ONES WHO READ THIS TEXT,
SAT THROUGH OUR SEMINARS AND CLASSES
PASSED THE TEST
THEN CALLED BACK.
ONLY WITH THEIR CONTRIBUTIONS HAS THIS VOLUME BECOME
THE BEST SELLING TEXTBOOK ON THE MARINER'S SHELF.

THE COAST GUARD LICENSE

FROM SIX-PAC

TO OCEAN OPERATOR

SAIL AND POWER

Library of Congress Cataloging in Publication Data

Gonder, Budd

   The Coast Guard License - From Six Pac To Ocean Operator

   Includes Index

1. Navigation--Examinatons, questions, etc.

2. Rules of The Road at Sea--Examinations, questions, etc.

I. Title

VK559.5.G66 1984   623.89'076   84-71365

ISBN   0-9613913-0-8

        0-9613913-1-6 pbk.

(for book ordering information, please consult the last page)

Copyright © 1986 by Budd Gonder

All rights reserved. No part of this book may be reproduced or
utilized in any form or by any means, electronic or mechanical,
including photocopying, recording or by information storage and
retrieval system, without permission in writing from the
Publisher. Inquiries should be directed to:

Charters West Publications
P.O. Box 675
Goleta, CA 93116

(805) 964-4555

INTRODUCTION

READ THIS BEFORE YOU TURN ANOTHER PAGE

This is a book of reality. Herein is written the total story of how to acquire the license and what to study to pass the exams. Nothing is left out, no item ignored. The volume was written for self-teaching. Everything is taken from the bottom up. None of the material is insurmountable. This book is a culmination of seven prior editions and numerous changes in the Rules of The Road as well as Coast Guard license policy.

Some will say this is a book for opportunists. Still others will look upon these pages as a sequel to their training with the venerable United States Power Squadron or the Coast Guard Auxiliary...or years at sea. The author hopes the book provides a stepping stone for many who have paid their dues as deckhands on party fishing boats, tourist vessels and the growing fleet of oil patch Mineral and Oil (M & O) vessels.

Here too is a book which could temper the cost factors of boat ownership. Maybe...just maybe, this could be a tax umbrella to shield boat owners from the rain of progressive taxation.

The files of Charters West are resplendent with letters from individual yachtsmen, deckhands and oil patch operators; buyers of the first nine editions who depended on **nothing else** than this book for acquisition of their licenses. For many, the license provided a new lifestyle, escape from the office 8 to 5 job, or the self-esteem garnered from knowing a change of pace can be negotiated at any age. The license is beautiful framed on a cabin bulkhead. Besides, who ever got ulcers from fooling around boats? This is the summit of the "cottage industry".

Having taught the license preparation fundamentals at private classes and seminars since 1968, I know the questions prospective license candidates ask. This book was written to answer all of them.

Nothing in this book should be ignored and it is not packed with useless information. It all counts. Originally written as a text to the Charters West charter skipper classes, the manual was modified for self-teaching. Currently, it circulates throughout the United States. However, you need to spend a few dollars for some equipment if you don't already have these items in stock.

First, go to the appendix and locate the fold-out chart. All of your chart work will be done on this so you will need some spare copies. Razor blade it out and find a copy shop capable of copying 11" x 17". While you are at it, carefully remove the exam answer sheets and have at least five copies made of both sides. Look over the other material in the appendix including the order form. **SAVE THAT FORM.** Sooner or later a friend will want a copy of this book. On the order form we also have available cut-out-and-color-them-yourself flashcards and a complete text of the Rules of The Road. They are both dirt cheap.

Then look up **your** closest U.S. Coast Guard Marine Inspection Office in the Regional Examination Center (REC) list in the appendix. Write them a short letter explaining that you are in training for your Motorboat Operator's License or the Ocean Operator's license and you need: 1) The application, 2) The sea time forms, and 3) a physical exam health form. **Do that today,** because they're busy and you might have to wait a few weeks for delivery. If you are in doubt as to which license to shoot for, read the section under "Licenses".

Next, find your original social security card and your birth certificate. The latter is necessary only for the Ocean Operator's license, not the six-pac. If the original S.S. card is lost, file for a new one right now. Sometimes takes six weeks. These two suggestions are repeated later in the text.

Now head for your favorite stationery store and purchase the following: 1) Felt pens. You need red, green, blue and yellow. 2) Then try to find a pair of dividers. Those are the things with which you measure distance on a chart. They're like a compass you draw circles with, only both ends are pointed and there's no pencil. If you can get one convertible to a compass, do it. There are only two chart problems needing a compass, so keep it cheap. 3) Get a Pentel automatic pencil #P209. The Pentels are color coded. The one you want is buff and the lead diameter is 0.9 mm. It's written right on the pencil. 4) Find a course plotter. The stationery store might have them. They run from three to five dollars. If you have a friend in the U.S. Power Squadrons or the Coast Guard Auxiliary, ask him for one. Those in the chandleries might run a bit more. No moving parts. No rollers. Just a plain plastic course plotter. They're about fifteen inches long by four inches wide. The center looks like a protractor offset by 90⁰. Don't worry about how they work. This book shows you how. There are some pictures of one in the plotting section.

After all this you're committed. Stick with this book two to three hours per day and you'll have that license in six weeks or less. No kidding. A continuous flow of complimentary letters arrives in the office. The choice one lately was from a gent in Alaska who said, "Sitting down to that Coast Guard exam was like sitting down with an old friend. No sweat. Passed the first time out. Took four weeks of evening study and I wasn't hurrying."

Think about that. They might have to call you Captain next month.

Budd Gonder
Goleta, CA
April - 1985

DISCLAIMER

This volume, and all prior editions are not to be considered official Rules of The Road. This volume was published solely as a study guide for the acquisition of pertinent Coast Guard licenses to carry passengers for hire. The reader should be aware that the options and opinions contained herein are for license study purposes only and were not written and published as legal advice or advice on the practical operation of any vessel afloat. A sincere effort has been made to present all of the examination ramifications, but in view of the widely divergent nature of the Coast Guard Regional Examination Centers' policies, the author cannot be responsible for any errors or omissions.

The ability of a new boat owner to navigate his craft within the confines of a harbor is inversely proportionate to the size of his new toy.

CONTENTS

Part I - General Information

Part II - The Rules of The Road

PART III – GENERAL KNOWLEDGE

PART IV – SEAMANSHIP

PART V – LOCAL KNOWLEDGE

PART VI - CHARTWORK

APPENDIX

WHO NEEDS THE LICENSE?

Anyone carrying passengers for hire on the navigable waters of the United States needs the license. It doesn't matter where the waters are, be they inland, in the mountain lakes, down the Mississippi or out to sea. The next question makes hackles stand up on necks. What constitutes carrying passengers for hire?

Don't throw the book across the room when you read this next part. These are decisions handed down by the Coast Guard and the Federal Courts...not me.

1) Anyone accepting money or **gratuities** for taking someone else for a ride on their boat.

Take a friend out and he pays you -you're carrying passengers for hire and should have the license. Towing the neighbor's kids water skiing and they never got into the boat because you were doing step starts off the lake front? If he pays you, you're carrying passengers for hire. Not get this; if he buys the gas, you're carrying passengers for hire.

2) You take a friend out fishing and he buys the beer. You're carrying passengers for hire.

3) You take a friend out fishing and he buys dinner that night after you return ashore. You're carrying passengers for hire. The Coast Guard could fine you and seize your vessel.

4) You are a harbor patrolman working in the harbor master's office. You tow someone in. The person you towed in does **not** pay you. But, the city does because this is in the course of your duties. You're carrying passengers for hire.

5) You are a lifeguard paid by the city or county, just like the harbor patrolman above. You roar out in your city launch and save the life of a beautiful damsel drowning offshore. You are carrying passengers for hire. For example; all lifeguards skippering lifeguard boats in Los Angeles County, have at least the Six Pac ticket.

6) You run the shoreboat in a very small inland harbor. You take people out to their boats in a small outboard. You work only for tips. You are carrying passengers for hire.

7) You are a yacht salesman or broker. You demonstrate a boat with the client on board and he buys the boat. You collect a commission, either from the client or your broker. You are carrying passengers for hire.

Accomplish any of the above on a sailboat, with no auxiliary aboard, or on a boat with no engine (even hidden in the bilges) and you are safe. No license needed. But, remember; no engine on board in any way shape or form.

THE LICENSES

Sometime in 1986 the basic licensing structure **is scheduled** for changes by the Coast Guard to conform to some recent international agreements on the subject. The groundwork for this massive change is already being laid. Most of us expected the changes to occur July 1, 1985, but no such luck. Some of it is very attractive to those already holding licenses referred to in this work. For example, the outer limit for Six-Pac and Ocean Operators could be extended to 200 miles. **Maybe** some with 50 ton Ocean Operator tickets will be grandfathered to 200 tons which could then be the new outer limit for Ocean Operators. There is reason to believe there will be **no more** district restrictions on which U.S. waters a licensed operator chooses to operate carrying passengers for hire. At this writing many decisions were still pending. Thus, if your license examination date should come to fall between say 4-1-86 and 7-1-86, consider contacting this office for **updates**. See page 239.

There is no charge for federal examinations. An unlimited number of retakes is allowed. Licenses must be renewed every five years with a year of grace to stretch it out, but you can't carry passengers during the grace period. The license renewal involves taking an open book test on the rules of the road. If you fail, you can take it over again until you pass. Some do it by mail!

This publication is concerned with only two licenses. The Motorboat Operator's License and the Ocean Operator's License. However there are requirements which the Coast Guard insists you have **before** they will even let you take the exam.

THE SIX PAC LICENSE

The Motorboat Operator's License is the one for which we originated the term "Six Pac." Don't call it "Six Pac" in front of Coast Guard people...some of them don't like the term. They prefer "Motorboat Operator's License". Those holding this license will soon be able to turn in the license for a new type. So let's discuss the new one.

The license permits the holder to carry six or less passengers for hire on an uninspected vessel with the keel having been laid in the United States. You might get away with carrying a crew member as well as yourself and the six passengers, but it had better be a big boat and that crew member should not be among the **paying** guests. The vessel must have a gross tonnage of **less than** 100 tons. Again; that's gross tons. The upper tonnage limit for six passenger "uninspected" vessels use to be fifteen gross tons, but a new decision has been passed down more clearly defining a "small passenger vessel".

The boat should also be up to current legal standards. Any vessel engaging in commercial activities must be documented if in excess of five net tons. It will need life jackets for everyone, a holding tank if it has a marine head, a special little sign by the engine room that states it's a "no-no" to discharge oily stuff into the waters, visual distress signals, etc. These are the same standards required aboard pleasure boats. There is one significant difference. You need a special type of life jacket. If you look carefully on most of the Personal Flotation Devices (PFD's) aboard pleasure craft you will notice they are "approved" by the CG to be used on vessels **not carrying passengers for hire.** Thus, you need a special PFD I. Ask your chandlery. They can show you a catalog. There are other requirements, such as forbidding the use of LPG gases on board, but they are covered in the body of this text, mostly in the quiz sections. Be sure you know them.

Who do you have to be to get a Six Pac? Age-eighteen. Citizenship is not required unless you are operating a vessel of five net tons or more. You must prove 365 days at sea, twenty-five percent of which must have been within the last three years, (that's only ninety days). Ninety days of your time must have been within the general area in which you are going to carry passengers.

Want to extend your license to other areas after you get it? No sweat. Just go there, with your license, log ninety days or twelve round trips then take the "Local Knowledge" quiz. If you wait more than a year after your original issue you may have to repeat the Rules of The Road quiz. Some offices have minor variations in this latter requirement regarding local experience. Washington's Coast Guard Commandant leaves this, for the most part, to the discretion of the local Officer in Charge, (OinC).

Three hundred sixty-five days at sea? How do you prove that? Well, sometimes it isn't easy. Some district offices will let you vouch for your own time by signing the appropriate sea time forms and filling in the blanks. This is generally true if you own your own boat, but again it's up to the discretion of the local OinC. Others insist you cannot vouch for your own time. You must have notarized witnesses' signatures on the government sea time forms the local office will provide. If you are reading this you are seriously considering the long road to the ticket, so write your local district CG office and ask for the appropriate forms. They'll send them right out on the next Snail Express. They will (or should) include some sea time forms for your use. Get some good reproductions made before you mess them up. There are samples in the appendix of this publication if you prefer to use them. Note: There are separate sections on these sea time forms for **each boat** upon which you have served.

You will notice there are three separate forms. One is for military service. Military service is acceptable if the vessel was of the same gross tonnage as the license for which you are applying. Not many of those around which are less than 100 gross tons.

The second form is a Merchant Marine form. This form would more often be used for an Ocean Operator's application than a Six Pac. Use it when you were working for someone else. The CG will generally accept a letter from the company attesting to your sea duty with them if it's written on a company letterhead. However, be sure your company or government agency includes the following:

1) Name of vessel(s) and registration or documentation number(s) as well as the length of the vessel(s) and gross tonnage.

2) Dates of employment **aboard** when **underway**. This can be two inclusive dates but the exact number of days will have to be stated in no uncertain terms.

3) Be sure they include your area of operation. If the area of operation exceeded the boundaries of the CG district to which you are applying that's fine. In fact, that's great. Get two **original** copies of the letter. Later, when you have the license, go to the adjacent district, (or wherever) with the same letter. If you can show ninety days or twelve round trips in the new district they will consider extending your license to that area after you take **their** local knowledge quiz.

4) Aside from the company letter, you should also summarize the time on an official CG form like those in the appendix of this book. For your own time aboard your own vessel, use the one entitled "Small Boat Experience". If you have a company letter, use the one for "Merchant Vessel Service". This latter one should also be used **any time** your sea

time was paid for by the owner or skipper of the vessel.

The third form is for Small Boat Experience. If you owned your own boat or did most of your time on friends' vessels, this is your form. Careful! Some offices might want you to have witnesses to your sea experience. The guy next door or the slip next to yours. Maybe your local harbor master will sign. How about the guy next door who sees you roll your boat out of the driveway every weekend?

The boats. Ah yes, the boats. Just about any old boat will do but we don't recommend small skiffs with outboards or small sailboats used in or very near the harbor. Foreign vessels are O.K., and time spent aboard vessels in foreign waters is also acceptable. But, remember you have to "prove" it. Think about writing to your friends in Yugoslavia and asking them to sign the form and have it notarized regarding the six months you spent together cruising the Greek Isles. Get those letters in the mail today.

And now you're concerned about the official numbers on the boats. These are either the numbers on the bow of the boat, or if documented, the numbers carved into the keel. Six digits for the latter. You say you've forgotten the state registration numbers on the boat you sold eighteen years back? Try the family photograph album.

How big can the boat be? If you are sitting for the Six Pac license your time should be on vessels less than one hundred gross tons and that's not demanding too much. Sail or power...same story. However, if you plan on carrying your passengers on a vessel which will be under way more than half the time under sail, consider having a separate indorsement on your license. This is called the "Sail Indorsement," and isn't much of an exam. Generally, twenty-five questions on a separate exam **after** you acquire your original license. You won't get the sail indorsement just for the asking. You must document time on a sailboat, or auxiliary sailing craft. Check your local office to find out their requirements for the amount of your 365 days time that has to be aboard a sailing craft. Don't phone. **Write** and ask. You need it in writing. **Anything** you are told over the telephone is subject to change without notice and probably will. **Get it in writing.** Now stop and look at page 238.

What if your own boat has a foreign laid keel? You're out of luck! Any foreign vessel cannot carry passengers for hire in the U.S. Ah, you're thinking. But, my boat can carry more than six passengers and do it safely.

Tough! With the Six Pac license you can carry only six passengers for hire. No exceptions. Period. And the boat should definitely be U.S. keel laid. If the craft was originally built to CG specs you have another story.

To **rebuild** a vessel to CG specs means tearing it apart. You would be better off buying a new one already built to C.G. specs. Or build it yourself. A naval architect can clue you in on the basic differences. Here, we're concerned more with licenses than the vessels.

One last thing regarding the Six-Pac. If you **use** this license for a total of 365 days, (not necessarily carrying passengers) you can apply and sit for the Ocean Operator's ticket! This makes you eligible for at least a twenty-five ton ticket even if you have never operated such a large craft. However, that little gem may not last for much longer. Add that to your question list on page 238.

THE OCEAN OPERATOR'S LICENSE.

The Ocean Operator's ticket is another matter. However, if you skipped over the Six Pac License paragraphs above, go back and read them. Especially the part about documenting your sea time.

First of all you must be a U.S. citizen. This license is issued in varying increments up to a point called "less than 100 gross tons". With this you can operate "inspected" vessels. By inspected it is meant that the CG has approved the orginal design, then watched carefully to make sure the builder conformed to those requirements as the vessel was constructed.

Most offices issue the license in increments of twenty-five tons, fifty tons, seventy-five tons and less than 100 tons. If most of your time is on a vessel of say, sixty tons, they will probably give you a seventy-five ton ticket...on a good day.

What if you had two years of good verifiable sea time and you wanted to sit for the Ocean Operator's exam instead of the Six-Pac? How much of that time should be aboard the heavier vessels greater than fifteen tons? That's another REC decision, but generally if you can document twelve months on the larger craft, you could get the Ocean Operator's license. However, OinC's do make exceptions. Be nice and smile. The tests aren't all that different between Six Pac and Ocean Operator. In short, if you **can** go for the Ocean Operator...**do it.**

The number of passengers you can carry on such a vessel is not written on your Ocean Operator's license. **Your** license has nothing to do with the number of passengers allowed aboard. That is determined by the "Certificate of Inspection" which hangs in the pilot house stating the number of passengers permitted on board. This certificate will also tell you how many crewmen must be aboard. If a vessel is underway for more than twelve hours, **two** skippers are required. A few districts permit what has come to be called a "second ticket" to operate in place of a second fully licensed skipper. This "second ticket" man cannot operate the vessel without a fully licensed skipper aboard, but it saves the expense of hiring two licensed skippers. How do you get a "second ticket"? (If indeed your district will even recognize it.) If there's a man on board who has ninety days of sea time with the boat and can pass the exam they will give him the second license.

Want an interesting government publication to read? Get a copy of the one called: **Rules and Regulations for Small Passenger Vessels-(Under 100 gross tons)** and also called just **"Subchapter T"**. It's CG publication #323. Your local CG office might have a copy for you. There is a list of all the U.S. REC's in the appendix of this volume.

SEA TIME DOCUMENTATION.

What's a "day at sea," you ask? There's no clear cut definition. I once heard an OinC say it was "definitely two hours minimum." Then he continued, "If you go out at 2200 and come back in at 0200, that's **two** days." But that was only **one** OinC. Generally, they don't ask you how many hours of each of your declared days you were out at sea. If they do, what do you say? Tell them the truth, whatever it might be. For example: "I don't know. I didn't keep a log. But it was a 'full' day." -Whatever that means-. This definition should become more clear cut after in 1986 if the CG has their way. At that time, the day at sea will undoubtedly be recognized as nothing less than eight hours. Ah, by the way. If you were at sea for two full days...forty-eight hours, that cannot be counted as more than two days.

Area of operation? That gets kind of sticky. The sea time form you fill out should indicate your area of operations afloat. Each REC can only license you for their particular area. After July, 1986, this **may** change. The current proposal before pertinent committees is to let a licensed charter skipper operate throughout any U.S. districts as long as he stays within 200 miles of the U.S. coast. At present, the outer limit is 100 miles. The licenses are undergoing other changes, the leading one seems to be that the Ocean Operator's license will be extended to less than 200 gross tons.

For example; the 11th CG District currently grants licenses from Point Conception to Cabo San Lucas, down Baja California way. O.K., so that's not even U.S. waters, but you could be carrying passengers into Mexican waters sport fishing or sight seeing then return to San Diego. A few even go whale watching at Scammon's Lagoon then return without touching Mexican dirt. The CG likes them licensed and a way to keep a hold on it is requiring sea time in Mexican waters to qualify for a license to carry passengers down there. They don't have a congressional mandate for this so check your local office for their outer boundaries. Again, Washington gives them a wide latitude in deciding on individual situations. Under the new post-July 1986 license, the 200 miles could be defined as 200 miles in any direction. A skipper could get well into Mexican waters by leaving the U.S. coast and sailing south.

When you make out your sea time forms declaring your time at sea, there will be a requirement that you indicate where you've been and the length of the voyage(s). While the Ocean Operator's and Motorboat Operator's licenses are **currently** limited to 100 miles offshore that doesn't mean your experience must be limited to that range.

Some districts have an "Inland" license. With this test you might not have to take the International Rules of The Road test. Just the Unified Rules test. (We'll get to the difference later.) Other districts don't even require a plotting test which would eliminate the latter twenty-five percent of this publication! Once again, when you check, get it in writing.

The question always arises; will my insurance company give me a break in my premium if I have the license? Yes and no. If you're carrying passengers for hire the liability policy will go up. If you have the license and are not carrying passengers for hire you could be in line for a forty percent reduction.

Remember this: **DON'T EVER GIVE THE CG ANY APPLICATIONS OR PAPERS OTHER THAN YOUR PHYSICAL EXAM OF WHICH YOU DO NOT HAVE A COPY YOURSELF.**   There will come a day when you will want to see those papers and the CG keeps everything you give them including the erasure shavings left over from your exam.

GENERAL HEALTH REQUIREMENTS

1) No colorblindness is allowed.   I **think** I know one colorblind captain, but he ran a long gamut of appeals to Washington, D.C. and is restricted to daytime operations.   The red-green blindness is of particular concern to the CG.   Even after your doctor has O.K.'ed your vision, they have a habit of screening applicants for colorblindness right in the CG office.

2) Your corrected vision (glasses) should be 20/20 in one eye with a minimum of 20/40 in the other.   Uncorrected vision requires a minimum of 20/100.   If those numbers are as mysterious to you as they are to me, go check with your doctor.

3) Expect to be in fair physical condition.   That ticker is going to get a pretty fair check out.   They check blood pressure, heart beat, depth of focus, colorblindness and do a urinalysis.

4) Any urine specimen will immediately show use of narcotics.   If you're a user, either cure your habit or forget the license.

5) Your hearing will undergo a test, but many doctors are not equipped with an audiometer for accurate testing.   They all have their own techniques for testing.   I once had a nurse stand at the end of a long hallway and talk to me in a low voice.   Sometimes, it's comical.

> **If God had wanted man to learn to swim he would not have invented Cals, Valiants, Bertrams and the Cape Hatteras.**

When you purchased this little volume you became privy to some very special information and tips. If you weren't told these things here no one would tell you. You would find out the hard way. Take the following any way you wish but remember...it comes from the experience of many people who went before you.

1) Never take your exam on a Monday, a Friday or just before a national holiday. None of the tests are timed, as such, but if you start any one of the tests many offices will insist you finish by lunch, or if you start after lunch you may have to finish by closing time. Lunch in some offices starts at 1130. Quitting time can be as early as 1530. If someone is in the examining room on Tuesday afternoon and still hard at it by 1530, they might let you stay until 1600, or even 1630 to finish while they clean up the day's mess. But, don't bet on it when Friday rolls around. What about Monday? Monday is the day everyone wants cancelled. Do you think the CG personnel are any different? National holidays almost always come on Monday or Friday. Going in on a Thursday before a Friday national holiday might mean you are interfering with a few of the brass getting away early for that three day holiday. Wouldn't your chances be better on Tuesday, Wednesday or Thursday? When you call for your appointment, keep that in mind.

2) Don't go in with a friend. Or, if you do, ignore the friend. CG doesn't like to see two people having lunch together and comparing notes before they come back in for the afternoon session. He travels fastest who travels alone.

3) If you can find one, get a waterfront doctor for your physical. Your own physician might put a check mark in the wrong place. If he does, the CG will send you back to have it done over. There's a waterfront doctor in every town. Ask around. For example, in San Pedro it's William R. Anderson, M.D. 593 West Sixth St. No appointment. Open at 0830 five days a week. Get there early and you'll be out by 0930 or sooner. Cheap. A good seaman's doctor has the medical exam forms on hand.

4) Be humble. Play it dumb. Give them the "I don't know what the hell I'm doing here," grin. Maybe they'll give you the easy form of the test. They hate wise guys and know-it-alls. Be very gracious. "Gee, thanks a lot. Wish I'd known that before. You know, if it hadn't been for you...." Got it?

5) If you fail the exam, say the Rules of The Road part, and you know darn well you're right and they're wrong...**AND IT HAPPENS**...you will probably ask to see what you missed and the correct answer. If it's a big rush that day they'll tell you something to the effect of: "Sorry pal. We're not a training school here and this is an 'institutionalized test'. Can't help you."

It's true they don't owe you a thing as far as help and correct answers go. The Long Beach, California center, when asked by candidates to see the questions they missed, has a standard reply.

"We're pretty busy here. We'll show you the questions you missed and even give you the right answer. However, if we do, you can't come back for the re-examination for ninety days. If you forget about seeing the ones you missed, you can come back in ten days."

Baloney! They're not God. You can challenge any question they have. They **could** ask you to come back another time for the challenge. If you **know** you're right, why not? Make the appointment. The CG **does** make mistakes. If they deny you, ask to see the C.O. If the Lieutenant says, "I'm the C.O," he's fudging. In a Regional Exam Center (REC) there is a commander around some place. Ask to see him. Take the question to him. You might win a reprieve. **But you had better be right.**

6) The exams you are taking were drawn up by the **local** office. That officer behind the desk made most of them up himself. Well, maybe with some basic guidelines and suggestions from Washington, D.C., but it's an in-house thing. It might well be an institutionalized test but you will be looking at the "institution" when he says it. It's not the same in all the offices, but the REC thing is a relatively new concept in examination centers and many offices are still getting their act together.

7) Locate your social security card or send for a new one...quick. Replacement sometimes takes six weeks. The Coast Guard will want to see the original...not some metal or plastic mock-up. Maybe you'd better put that on your want list which is on page 238.

At this writing there are seventeen Regional Examination Centers (REC's) and two monitoring facilities. A complete list can be found in the appendix. For the most part they are crowded and busy five days per week. These "Centers" are charged with administering all the United States maritime exams. This means everything from the Motorboat Operator's License to Master's -Unlimited Oceans and Tonnage. Most offices will require an appointment to take your particular exam. No two are alike.

The various test sections of the Motorboat Operator's (Six-Pac) and Ocean Operator's vary from office to office. They all cover the same basic areas, otherwise this book couldn't be written. Each office is charged with designing their own exams. Few, if any, come from H.Q. in Washington, D.C. Each office is bound only by guidelines from Washington and the requirements as indicated in the Federal Register.

There are several tests and different forms for each one. If you fail the Six-Pac they **can** tell you to come back in thirty days. That's **generally** the max they will keep you cooling your heels at home. For the Ocean Operator they **can** say ninety days. Often, they'll tell you to come back in ten days for either test. Of late, several offices have taken a new tack.

Most offices will give you ninety days to pass the entire test barrage. Careful now. If you can't come back except every ten days, that means you have eight tries left. On the other hand, if your local REC will permit it, why not take the Rules of the Road, then go home and study for the next section? Check out the local policy. With the Coast Guard, you find that nothing is written in stone.

If you have held to the Humble Harry routine then flunk and are told to come back in thirty or ninety days, you might try looking as though you're going to cry. Tell them how bad it is because you have to leave to visit your sick aunt in the Gobi Desert and you might not **ever** be able to come back again unless you can get this thing out of the way soon. You might be milking yaks for the rest of your life. Or try the pitch about that overseas job. However, most offices maintain a cold impersonal professional attitude. Better to be totally prepared than try to fake it.

Don't feel bad if you flunk out the first time around. Most do. The nature of the beast can make a traffic court judge nervous. So **be** nervous. But, give yourself time to calm down before you wade into the exam with a pencil. Thumb through the test. Read the directions. **OH MY GOD...READ THE DIRECTIONS.** Don't laugh. A lot of people miss this point. Breath deep for a while. When the heart beat steadies and the hands stop shaking...go for it.

The cold professionalism comes because they're rushed. For example; some offices will let you take the entire test, even when you flunk several parts along the way. Others will insist you take the Rules of The Road first. If you flunk, you're out on the street looking in. Some offices will let you take the local knowledge part using an open book, probably the Coast Pilot. Another office across the river will make it a closed book exam of multiple choice instead of fill-in answers. Some change their policy overnight. Maybe you should do a little checking when you visit the local office to have your sea time verified and the office policies checked out. Once the sea time is accepted, you can make your appointment and go home to cram.

Here's a breakdown on the tests as they are **generally** administered.

1) International Rules of the Road. If you're after an ocean Six-Pac or Oc. Op. you will probably get the International test first. Generally twenty questions. Since you have to score ninety percent that means you can miss only two. Pass this and they will give you the next one. If you are in an area far from the ocean, they will skip the International Rules test.

2) Unified Rules of The Road. Some offices give a separate test altogether. Again, generally twenty questions and ninety percent perfect required. Some offices attach this one to the International test. You chug along answering International questions, for maybe twenty questions, then a short sentence off to the side tells you the rest are Unified (Inland) and there are perhaps 10 more to answer. Watch for the change. Ninety percent on thirty questions would mean twnety-seven of them correct to pass.

3) Most offices call this one "General Navigation," or sometimes, "General Knowledge," and have reduced the 90% passing requirement to 70%. About forty questions on compass error, buoys, tides, speed-distance-time and chart symbols. Don't start sweating. We cover it all right in this book.

4) Next comes a multi-subject type of thing. Seamanship, weather, marlinspike seamanship, fire, first aid, boat handling, engine maintenance, fueling, rules and regulations, etc. A few offices break this exam down by component subjects. Some throw it all into one exam and it's well mixed. Only lately have they added the two sections entitled "Regulations" and "Safety". **Be careful here.** Some offices allow the "Rules and Regs" to be an open book test but forget to tell you. Make sure you understand which tests are open book.

This is as close to reality as you will come with the CG. The entire test requires seventy percent to pass. The best of common sense should get you through. In this book we call it "Seamanship," then break it down into component parts for your practice exam. Easier to keep things straight that way. No one will take you out and ask you to dock a boat and probably they won't have time to make you tie a few knots. The "Seamanship" test herein covers it pretty well. Most offices should be able to give you some sample questions as well as a memo detailing the various exams and the required percent to pass. Ask for it.

5) Charting could be next. Sometimes they call it plotting. This is the one where you have a chart, dividers, course plotter and calculator attempting to show them how you plan to get from point "A" to point "B". Yes, calculators are allowed in the testing room, but don't try to squeeze one of those mini-computers which will plot set, drift and tell you when the sun comes up on February 29, of every other leap year. You may need ninety percent on this test. A recent suggestion from Washington, D.C., indicated the REC's should lower their standards to seventy percent. Let's hope the officers in your area office read that memo from H.Q.

And how do you calculate seventy percent on a charting test? Some offices give you ten problems -which should take about three hours to solve- and you have to get seven of them correct. Sometimes they even have multiple choice answers. Other offices will assign points to various questions. One office planned to break the test down into two separate sections.

The plan was for a a plotting test first with seven or eight questions then a separate test on compass error, gas comsumption and general math problems linked to navigation. Better plan on ninety percent for **each**.

6) Local knowledge is next. You **can** make this a real easy experience. The CG gets their questions from one of three places for this exam. a) The Coast

Pilot, b) Charts of the area, c) Any popular local publication detailing special features of the coastal area (such as the **Boating Almanac**).

The Local Knowledge section in this book is rather detailed for the California area but be sure to look it over. The examples will give you an idea what to expect in your own area.

7) Then there's a thing for Ocean Operator's called "Rules and Regulations" for Small Motor Vessels. A more common name for this quiz is "Subchapter T". Briefly, there are certain rules for inspected vessels detailed in a CG publication. (See page 16). This is almost always an open book and you should plan on getting them all correct. It details specific requirements -among other things- for vessels carrying more than six passengers for hire. Basically, it's a guideline for "S" and "L" vessels. "S" vessels are those carrying more than six passengers and less than sixty-five feet in length. "L" vessels are over sixty-five feet carrying more than six passengers. If your exam is to be open book, (see page 238) remember to use the index. If it's to be closed book, ask for a copy to study. More later on this one.

8) Oil Pollution is another open book everyone has to take. The popular questions are cited in this publication. Nothing to worry about. If you miss any, most OinC's will send you back into the exam room until you get them right.

For the entire exam, plan on two days. When you're flush with information brimming over and ready to spill it out on their IBM type multiple choice answer sheets, get your sea time together and take it to the REC. As you have your sea time approved and accepted by the OinC, start going down your question list as to what's open book, percentages to pass, etc. And you would do well to start your question list on page 238 right now. It's going to get lengthy.

When the OinC O.K.'s your sea time, make the appointment to come in. Try to stretch it ahead to about ten days from the time you turn in your sea time. It's quite a motivating force driving you to study and review your plotting techniques.

When someone says "Rules of The Road" they're not just talking a list of specs you're suppose to memorize and spit out when told.   The Rules come in several sections...all interrelated, yes, but individual within their own scopes. Consider the following arbitrary subdivisions.   It might help you keep things straight.

1) The correct maneuvering procedures based on which vessel has the right-of-way.
2) The correct signals when executing these maneuvers.
3) The signals in restricted visibility.
4) The visibility of lights.   How far they should be seen on a dark and clear night.
5) The pecking order as regards rights-of-way.
6) The required lights and dayshapes to be shown on vessels underway, at anchor and aground.

One way to appreciate the following simplification is to acquire your own copy of the Rules.   Charters West has published them and the five annexes for $4.95.   The government copy runs about $6.50.   Use the ordering form in the appendix.

Similar to our flashcards, you will need to color the section on lights and dayshapes.   It's a good exercise and kind of fun.   The lights and dayshapes on the sketches have been exaggerated so they stand out.

Don't dwell continuously on the Rules.   Take a break and move to the charting section to start honing your navigation skills.   After a few days, go back to the Rules.   Alternating these sections will keep you current on both.

METRIC CONVERSION TABLE.

Metric Measure	U.S.
1000 Meters (M)	3280.8 feet
500 M	1640.4 feet
200 M	656.2 feet
150 M	492.1 feet
100 M	328.1 feet
75 M	246.1 feet
60 M	196.8 feet
50 M	164.0 feet
25 M	82.0 feet
20 M	65.6 feet
12 M	39.4 feet
10 M	32.8 feet
8 M	26.2 feet
7 M	23.0 feet
6 M	19.7 feet
5 M	16.4 feet

RIGHTS OF WAY

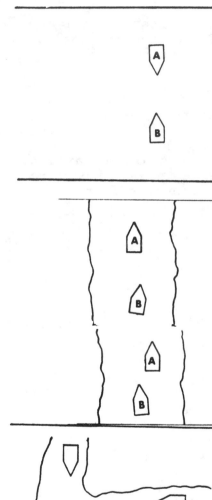

Note that vessel "A's" sidelight arcs are shown. This is indicated by the small arrows which are pointing to the aftermost range of the arc. This is known as "22.5° abaft the beam". Farther aft of this point the sidelights cannot be seen. Thus, if the sidelights disappear the sternlight shows up immediately and hence vessels "D" and "E" are in an overtaking situation. Vessel "F" is crossing and has the right-of-way over "A". No vessel, even a sailboat overtaking a power-driven craft, has the right-of-way when overtaking. "B" has the right-of-way over "A" as "B" is a sailboat, but not "C". "G" has the right-of-way over "A" as would any vessel approaching "A's" starboard side.

When two vessels meet head-on there is no right-of-way conferred, but each should take the **preferred course** by directing her respective course to starboard so as to pass port-to-port with appropriate signals. International rules state vessels shall give signals when within sight of each other. Inland states signals shall be given when within sight of each other **and** when within a half-mile of each other. International signals are given only when a change of course is necessary.

Passing in a narrow channel requires special signals in International waters. See whistle signals in this section. Narrow channels in International waters may sound strange, but many countries do not have Inland rules and are using International Rules for everything. "Narrow channels" in U.S. Inland waters do not merit special signals. However, downbound river craft have the right of way over upbound craft and are responsible for initiating passing and/or crossing signals as well as choosing the method and location of passing. Here, "A" has the right-of-way. If "A" does not return the O.K. signal to pass, or if she sounded a "danger" signal, then "B" would have to wait and try again later.

Note that sound signals in Inland waters mean a vessel **intends** to make a given change of course. She then waits for a return signal. In International waters the signal infers **action** as the maneuver is currently being undertaken.

Both Inland and International rules require vessels approaching a bend or channel obstruction give one prolonged blast.

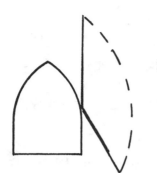

Vessels approaching from within the range of another's starboard sidelights have the right-of-way in any crossing situation. Thus, any power boat's starboard side, within this arc, is considered the "danger zone". A lookout is posted, with a keen eye to this side when in restricted visibility and when water traffic is heavy. The helmsman **cannot** be considered a lookout. In International waters, a flashing one second white light visible for five miles can **supplement** the sound signals. Inland, the light can be white **or** yellow, visible for two miles. One flash equals a short blast, two are given for two blasts, etc. Inland rules allow maneuvering agreement via radiotelephone. International does not.

Sailboats have their own rights-of-way rules when encountering each other. First, a vessel on the starboard tack, (wind coming over starboard side-so mainboom is over port side) has the right of way over a sailboat on the port tack. Second: A sailboat on the same tack as another but down wind of the other sailboat has the right-of-way. Also, if in doubt as to the other's tack-assume you are the give-way craft. In this diagram: "D" has the right-of-way over "A". "C" over "D", "B" over "A", "C" over "A", "E" over "A", and "D" over "B".

Definition of a sailboat's tack. A sailboat's tack is called on the basis of the **opposite** side over which the mainboom is extended. Mainboom over port side-starboard tack. Mainboom over starboard side-port tack.

Note diagram to the left. "A" is on a port tack, "B" on a starboard tack. If "B" suddenly decided to come right, "A" would have to move...fast. And; "D" has the right of way over "C" as "D" is to the lee of "C"...downwind of "C". Then "B" has the right of way over "E" even through "E" is to the lee. Tack takes precedence as it is called out first in the Rules. But, "E" has the right-of-way over "A".

The Rules of The Road **seem** to indicate that sailboats sound maneuvering signals in International waters...but not Inland.

MANEUVERING SIGNALS

Short Blast=About 1 Second.   Prolonged Blast=About 4-6 Seconds.

Vessels Are Considered Underway When: Not tied up, not at anchor and not aground.

INTERNATIONAL   **UNIFIED**

HEAD ON

One Short Blast – I **AM** altering my course to starboard. The intent is to pass port side to. No return signal required.

One Short Blast – I **INTEND** to leave you on my port side. Same as International within the meaning of the maneuver. Both vessels give the same signal.

Two Short Blasts – I **AM** altering my course to port.

Two Short Blasts – I **INTEND** to leave you on my starboard side. Both vessels signal.

Three Short Blasts – I **AM** operating in astern propulsion.

Three Short Blasts – I am operating astern propulsion.

CROSSING

One Short Blast – Initiated by the give-way craft indicating she **IS** altering course to starboard to pass astern of the on-coming craft or is slowing down to allow other vessel to maintain course & speed **which is the duty of the stand-on craft.**

One Short Blast – Same as International except for one important difference. The signal is **returned** by the stand-on craft.

OVERTAKING

One Short Blast – Altering course to starboard to overtake vessel ahead. No return signal unless stand-on craft signals at least five short blasts indicating "doubt" or "danger", whereupon overtaking vessel must abort, wait & try again later.

One Short Blast – Same as International except the vessel ahead returns the signal indicating agreement for the maneuver.

Two Short Blasts – Same as above but vessel overtaking intends to do so by coming left to pass vessel ahead.

Two Short Blasts – Same as International except the vessel ahead returns the signal indicating agreement for the maneuver.

OVERTAKING IN A NARROW CHANNEL

Two Prolonged – One Short. Initiated by the overtaking vessel in a narrow channel when the overtaking craft wishes to pass the vessel ahead by coming **right** and passing to the other vessel's starboard side.

There are no special "Narrow Channel" overtaking signals in Inland waters.

Two Prolonged – Two Short. Same as above but coming **left** to pass.

One Prolonged–One Short–One Prolonged–One Short – An agreement signal given by the stand-on vessel in a narrow channel. The same signal applies to either option indicated by the give-way craft.

RESTRICTED VISIBILITY SIGNALS

* * * * * * * * * *

SIGNALS WHICH ARE GIVEN AT LEAST ONCE EVERY TWO MINUTES

One Prolonged Blast – Given by vessels underway "in or near" any area in which the visibility is restricted for any reason or in any way.

Two Prolonged Blasts – Underway, but stopped. No way on.

One Prolonged – Two Shorts – To be given **INLAND** in restricted visibility underway **and** at **anchor** (every minute) by:
Fishing vessels fishing, or any craft restricted in ability to maneuver.
The same signal is also given **only** when underway by sailboats, vessels not under command and tugs pushing or towing.

In **International** waters one prolonged and two shorts are sounded by any craft underway **and** at anchor (every minute) when fishing or working vessels restricted in ability to maneuver. Also to be given by craft underway when: constrained by draft, restricted in ability to maneuver, not under command, sailboats, tugs pushing or towing and fishing vessels when fishing.

One Prolonged – Three Short - Signal to be given by ANY vessel when being towed IF MANNED.

Four Short Blasts – Identity signal for a pilot vessel. Pilot vessel must also give one prolonged blast when underway, and any other signals for a vessel of their respective size.

* * * * * * * * * *

SIGNALS WHICH ARE GIVEN AT LEAST ONCE EVERY MINUTE.

One Short–One Prolonged–One Short – Given by a vessel at anchor. This is an optional signal to give extra warning of one's position.

Five Second Ringing Of A Bell – Given by vessels at anchor. In Inland waters some vessels do not need to give this signal if anchored in special designated anchorage areas. This includes vessels less than 20 meters in length, barges, canal boats and scows plus other "non-descript" craft.

Five Second Bell – followed by – **Five Second Gong in Stern Area.** Given by vessels at anchor of 100 meters or more in length.

Three Distinct Strokes on the Bell – followed by – **Five Second Ringing of the Bell** – followed by – **Three More Strokes on the Bell** – is the signal for a vessel aground. And if you think that's funny; if the vessel is 100 meters or more in length, the above signal must be followed by a **Five Second Ringing of the Gong** in the stern area.

VESSELS LESS THAN 12 METERS IN LENGTH: Not required to give the above bell signals but must have ready at hand some sound producing signal which can be used every two minutes.

INTERVENING OBSTRUCTIONS - OBSCURED CHANNELS AND FAIRWAYS

One Prolonged Blast — Given when approaching a blind bend or ANY obstruction making it difficult to observe on-coming traffic. The same signal is given in answer by any approaching vessel. **Inland Rules state** this signal must be given when leaving a dock or berth. Some CG tests have indicated this signal is valid even if **backing** out of the berth or dock.

Five Short Blasts — Doubt or danger signal. The rule says "at least" five short blasts. Officially, the rules call it the "doubt" signal. Unsure of intention of other vessel. Used only when vessels are within sight of each other. Not used in restricted visibility.

MANEUVERING SIGNAL TIPS TO REMEMBER.

1) Except for #8 below, the maneuvering signals are always initiated by the "give-way" craft.

2) In Inland waters maneuvering signals can be agreed upon via radiotelephone between two vessels thus eliminating the necessity for sound signals. This is not the case in International waters.

3) In International waters signals are sounded when a change of course is necessary and only when vessels are within sight of each other.

This is an interesting implication and leads to a tough rules of the road question. Consider: If maneuvering signals are given...the assumption is that there is danger of collision present. Otherwise, they wouldn't be given.

4) In Inland waters signals are sounded when vessels are within sight of each other **and** when within one half-mile of each other.

5) If operating in restricted visibility when vessels were not within sight of each other, the maneuvering signals are not appropriate!

6) Special emphasis should be placed upon the fact that in International waters the maneuvering signals indicate **action**. You ARE coming right, coming left, or whatever. Again; if no change of course is necessary in International waters, no maneuvering signals are necessary.

7) In Inland waters the signals indicate you **intend** to come right, left, etc. The object being to await agreement of the stand-on craft before executing the maneuver.

8) When a vessel is operating on the Great Lakes, Western Rivers or any narrow passage inland and proceeding "downbound" with a following current, this vessel shall initiate the maneuvering signals proposing the manner and place of passage and has the right-of-way.

9) Any vessel 100 meters or more in length at anchor should illuminate her deck area.

The following is a one page condensation of the required arcs of visibility required on various power and sailing craft.   While initially the memorization appears impossible, please bear with it while we establish some memory crutches enabling you to answer the questions encountered in the Coast Guard exam.   In the entire Rules quizzes you might get two on visibility.   The questions is; which two?   As you read this page, glance at the diagrams on the next page.

Upon close scrutinty of the arcs of visibility one notices first that:

1) All sidelights show an arc from dead ahead to 22.5º abaft the beam.   For **each** sidelight that's 112.5º.   Total arc of both sidelights is therefore 225º which is the same **total** arc required on masthead lights.

2) All masthead lights show an arc of 225º.

3) All stern lights show an arc of 135º.   Add the masthead arcs and the sternlight arcs together and you have 360º.

While it might not appear so at first, there is a quasi-pattern to the distance these lights must be seen.   Grouping them horizontally across the page they look something like this:

Vessel	Sidelights	Sternlights	Masthead Lights
Less than 12 meters...	1 mile.........	2 miles..........	2 miles.
Greater than 12....... but **less than** 20 meters.	2 miles........	2 miles..........	3 miles.
20 meters, but........ **less than** 50 meters.	2 miles........	2 miles..........	5 miles.
50 meters or greater..	3 miles........	3 miles..........	6 miles.

Examine the characteristics of the pattern.   Those requiring two miles of visibility show up six times out of the twelve and never on vessels 50 meters or greater.

Now read **down** the column under masthead lights.   Progressive, but there's no 4 miles.   In fact, there's no "4 miles" anyplace!   Then read **across** the "50 meters or greater" line.   Think 3 + 3 = 6.

All the rest are "2" except the "1" and the "5" which show up only once.

Out of four types of vessels that's not bad.   Now study the number group below then see if you can reproduce it on a separate piece of paper without looking.   If you can you can do the same in the exam room.

    1-2-2
    2-2-3
    2-2-5
    3-3-6

32

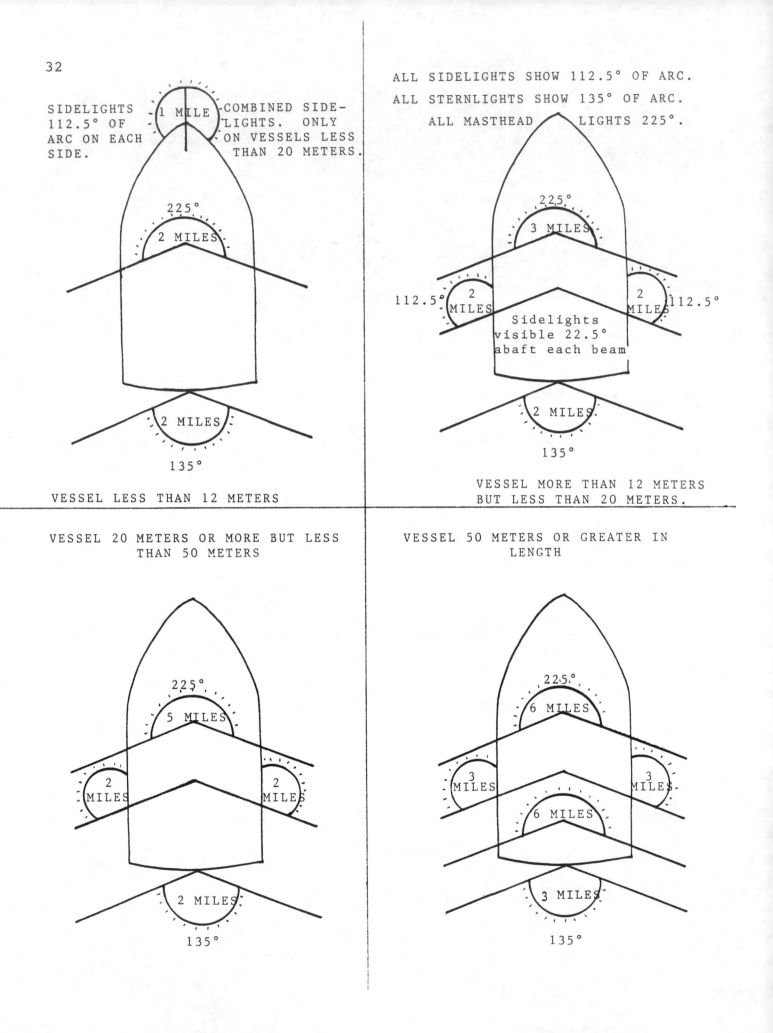

SIDELIGHTS
112.5° OF
ARC ON EACH
SIDE.

1 MILE

COMBINED SIDE-
LIGHTS. ONLY
ON VESSELS LESS
THAN 20 METERS.

225°

2 MILES

2 MILES

135°

VESSEL LESS THAN 12 METERS

ALL SIDELIGHTS SHOW 112.5° OF ARC.
ALL STERNLIGHTS SHOW 135° OF ARC.
ALL MASTHEAD LIGHTS 225°.

225°

3 MILES

112.5°

2
MILES

2
MILES

112.5°

Sidelights
visible 22.5°
abaft each beam

2 MILES

135°

VESSEL MORE THAN 12 METERS
BUT LESS THAN 20 METERS.

VESSEL 20 METERS OR MORE BUT LESS
THAN 50 METERS

225°

5 MILES

2
MILES

2
MILES

2 MILES

135°

VESSEL 50 METERS OR GREATER IN
LENGTH

225°

6 MILES

3
MILES

3
MILES

6 MILES

3 MILES

135°

Below is a simplified version of the so-called "pecking order". Vessels in group #1, have the right of way over vessels in group #2. Vessels in group # 2 have the right of way over those in group #3, etc. The new Unified rules (they used to be called Inland) and International are very much alike with one exception in #3 below. However, the Unified rules are very clear as regards craft travelling in traffic patterns or rivers, fairways and channels. All special lights below should be visible for 360°.

VESSEL	NIGHT SIGNALS	DAYSHAPES
1) Not Under Command: No steerage, no power or perhaps underway with no way on. "Red over red, the captain's dead."	® ®	
2) Restricted In Ability To Maneuver: Underwater operations, surveying, fueling at sea, recovering aircraft, transferring cargo, fuel or personnel, servicing aids to navigation, dredging.	® Ⓦ ®	
Towing-severely restricted in maneuverability. Note:this requires TWO separate signals: One indicating towing, + restricted maneuverability.	Ⓦ ® Ⓦ Ⓦ Ⓦ ®	
Minesweeper. No other restricted in ability signal required, but needs masthead light(s).	Ⓖ Ⓖ Ⓖ	
3) Vessel Constrained By Draft: A deep draft vessel in a narrow or shallow channel. No such signal Inland.	® ® ®	
4) Fishing or Trawling: Fishing is using "lines, nets or trawls" but NOT trolling. Note separate signals for "fishing" vs. "trawling".	® Ⓖ Ⓦ Ⓦ	
5) Sailing: Sailboat under sail. Red over green masthead lights optional. Sailboats must display inverted cone when under sail with engines running.	® Ⓖ	
6) Powerboats: Low end of totem pole. Only lights required are those specified in regular rules section on lights and dayshapes. Note that towing is included here unless the skipper indicates otherwise by hoisting signals indicated in #2 above.	Ⓦ Ⓦ Ⓨ Ⓦ Ⓦ Ⓦ Ⓦ Stern View	Dayshape if tow 200 meters or more astern

INTERNATIONAL - Power vessel less than 50 meters in length. Needs one 225⁰ masthead light forward. If less than 12 meters **may** exhibit an all-round (360⁰) white light & sidelights. **All** sternlights are 135⁰ of arc.

INLAND - If less than 12 meters can use 360⁰ light in lieu of masthead light and sidelights. See #5 below. If less than 12 meters can use the combined sidelights. ①

INTERNATIONAL - Example of power vessel 50 meters or greater in length. The after masthead light is added and must be higher than the one foreward. Both are 225⁰ arcs. Due to length, sidelights are now split and the usual sternlight is required. The after masthead light is optional for vessels less than 50 meters in length.

INLAND - Almost the same. On the Great Lakes, any craft can opt for a 360⁰ light aft to replace the after masthead light and sternlight. ②

③

INTERNATIONAL - If less than 7 meters in length sailboats can use electric torch (flashlight) or lantern to show in time to prevent collision...if sidelights are impractical.

INLAND - Same.

④

INTERNATIONAL - Rowboats can light up like sailboats. The white "lantern" (flashlight) is required when sidelights are not available or impractical. Collision prevention is the whole key. Or, as Thucydides put it: "A collision at sea can ruin your entire day."

INLAND - Same.

⑤

INTERNATIONAL - If less than 7 meters and making less than 7 knots the 360⁰ light aft can be used in lieu of the masthead light forward. Sidelights to be used if practicable. If less than 12 meters, the 360⁰ light can be used, but the combined sidelights **must be** used.

INLAND - If less than **12 meters** the 360⁰ light can be used in lieu of the masthead lights. The sidelights **must be** used.

⑥ & ⑦

INTERNATIONAL - Sailboats have a special option. They can exhibit 360⁰ red over green lights at the masthead. When this option is used the sidelights must be split regardless of the vessel's length.

INLAND - Same.

⑧

INTERNATIONAL - A Special arrangement for masthead lights on sailboats less than 20 meters in length.

INLAND - Same.

⑨ & ⑩

A sailboat shown head-on. Note that no white light can be seen. **Number 10** is the sternview showing the required 135⁰ sternlight. This is the case both **International** and **Inland**.

⑪

INTERNATIONAL - Day-shape for sailboat with sails up but also with engine running. She is no longer considered a sailboat, but a power vessel.

INLAND - Not required on sailboats under sail with engines running if less than 12 meters in length.

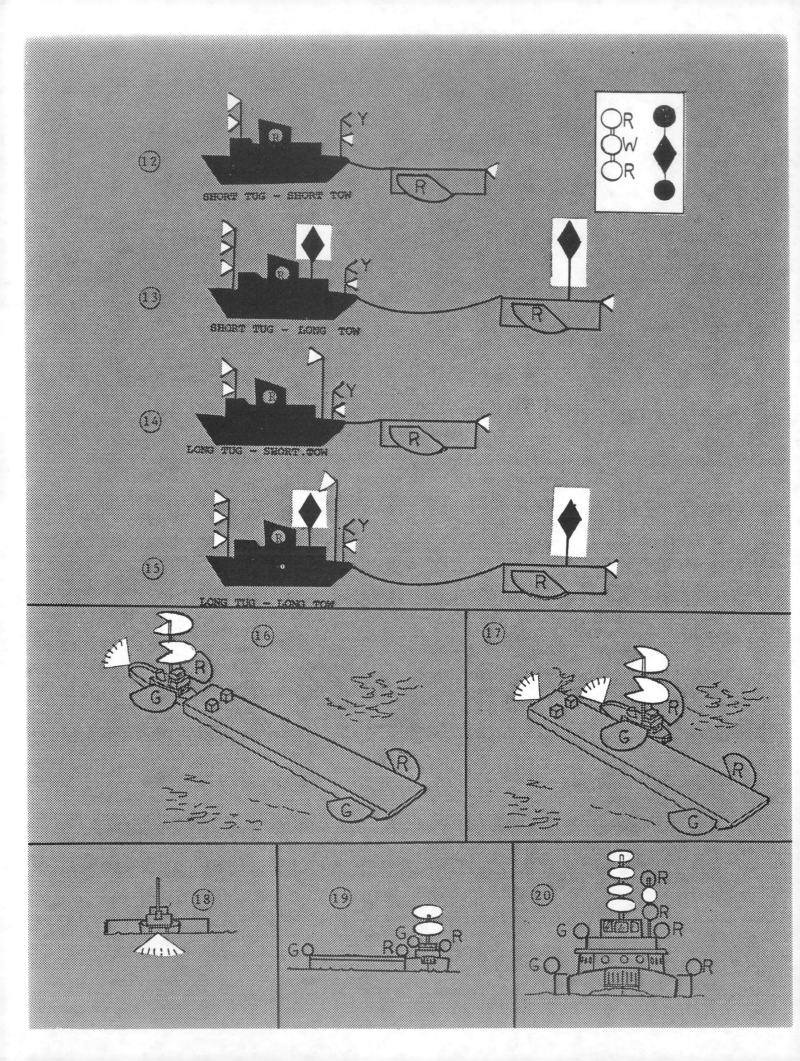

SHORT TUG — SHORT TOW

SHORT TUG — LONG TOW

LONG TUG — SHORT TOW

LONG TUG — LONG TOW

INTERNATIONAL TUGS

Develop this memory crutch for the International Tugs:

If the tug is less than 50 meters in length it's a "short tug".

If the tug is 50 meters or greater in length it's a "long tug".

NOW THE BARGES THEY ARE TOWING BEHIND.

If the barge is less than 200 meters astern it's a "short tow".

If the barge is 200 meters or farther, it's a "long tow".

Now read the next column on your right.

COMPARE THE DESCRIPTIONS BELOW WITH THE TUGS ON THE FACING PAGE

(12) Short tug-short tow. Two 225° masthead lights forward.

(13) Short tug-long tow. Three 225° masthead lights forward. The diamond dayshape for the daytime.

(14) Long tug-short tow. Same as #12 above but add a 225° after masthead light. Thus, viewed head-on you would see three white lights coming right at you.

(15) Long tug-long tow. Same as #13 above but add a 225° after masthead light.
And don't forget the diamond dayshape. It's only needed when the tow is more than 200 meters astern. Required on both tug and tow.

Did you notice the sternlights? Yellow over white. Both 135° arc. But careful here. The yellow one is called a "**towing** light", but the white is still a "**stern**light".

(16) This is a short tug pushing her barge. Note the yellow towing light is eliminated-she is not "towing", she's "pushing". This is the one rare occasion when the barge does not need a sternlight. Note that tug and barges **ALWAYS** need sidelights. All vessels or barges towed behind or alongside always need stern & sidelights. In #16, if the tug were a "long tug" she would need an after masthead light.

(17) Short tug with her barge alongside. Note that now sternlight is required on barge.

(18) Tug pushing her tow as seen from astern. No yellow towing light necessary.

(19) Tug with barge alongside.

(20) Long tug with her barge and coming right at you! Also note the dayshape for "restricted in ability to maneuver". The barge's sidelights are visible on each side of the tug, but probably not so in reality.

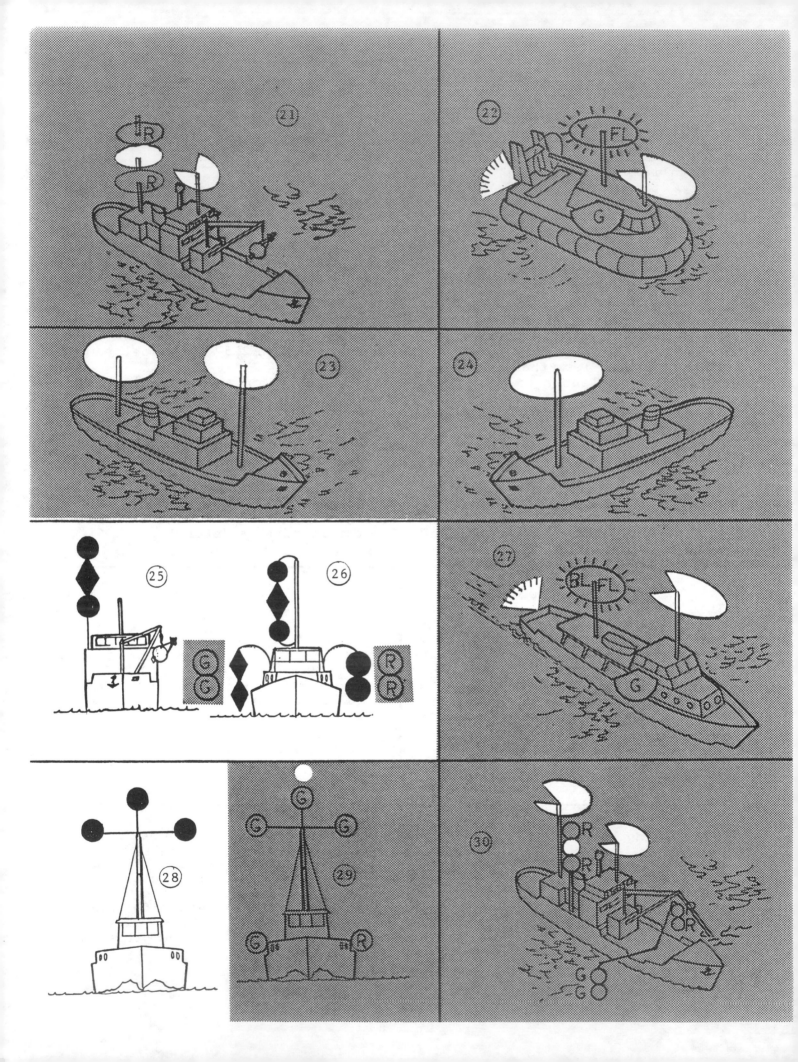

INTERNATIONAL - Coast Guard Buoy Tender. The 360° vertically arranged red-white-red -offset from centerline- indicates restricted in ability to maneuver. Since the vessel is not actually making way the sidelights are extinguished. Anchor lights are not required as technically, she is not anchored. (21)

INLAND - Same.

INTERNATIONAL - A "non-displacement" craft. Here, a hovercraft. Needs all the usual lights PLUS a "flashing light". A flashing light on a vessel is one which always flashes at 120 fpm and is **always yellow.**

INLAND -Same. (22)

INTERNATIONAL - Vessel 50 meters or more in length and at anchor. Note that both lights are 360°, **atop** masts and are reversed in position from those viewed on a vessel underway. Not like masthead lights which are lower than tips of masts. The stern anchor light is LOWER than the forward one. Vessels 100 meters or more in length must **also** illuminate their decks at night. Black ball is the dayshape for being at anchor. See the dayshapes on the back outside cover and the key sheet on the reverse side. All dayhapes are black, except flags. (23)

INLAND - Same.

INTERNATIONAL - Vessel less than 50 meters in length and at anchor. Only one 360° white light required. Vessels less than 7 meters in length need not show the light if not anchored in area normally used by other vessels.

INLAND - Same except vessels less than 20 meters are exempt in approved anchorage areas.

(24)

INTERNATIONAL - Number 25 is the dayshape for a vessel restricted in her ability to maneuver.
Number 26 is engaged in some form of underwater work. Passing side is denoted by the black diamonds over the side. The night counterpart is #30 below. Note: Underwater work could include having a hardhat diver down. Diver's cable is attached to the vessel. (25) & (26)

INLAND - Same, except vessels less than 12 meters need not signal unless diving operations are in progress.

INTERNATIONAL - Minesweeper. Considered restricted in ability to maneuver without having to use the signal. The three black balls or three green lights are reserved for minesweepers only. You must stay clear of the vessel by 1,000 meters.

INLAND - Same, except stay clear of sides 500 meters, stern by 1,000 meters. (28) & (29)

INTERNATIONAL - No special law enforcement lights are indicated under International Rules of The Road.

INLAND - Flashing Blue Light. Law enforcement. Federal or local. (27)

(30)

INTERNATIONAL - Underwater operation. For example, dredging. Favorite on CG exams. Red 360° lights mark the non-passing side. Stay away. Pass on the green light side. Excusing the perspective of the sketch, these lights are always higher than the sidelights.

Note absence of side and sternlights. He is not making way. "Underway" is defined as not at anchor, not aground and/or not tied to a pier or dock.

INLAND - Same.

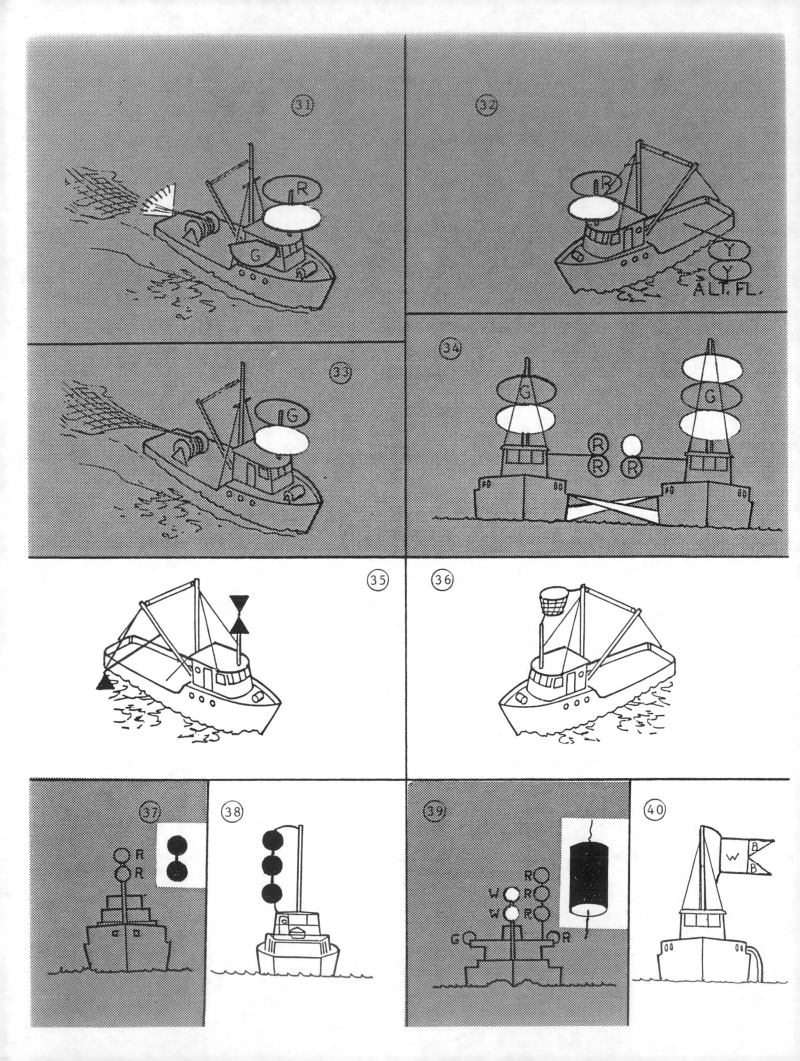

INTERNATIONAL - A fishing vessel is considered fishing only when using lines, nets or trawls. Trolling is not considered fishing! "Red-Over-White,Fishing Tonight." Side and sternlights displayed only when underway. Special lights and day-shapes for fishing shown only when actually engaged in fishing. Fishing in navigable channels or fairways is illegal.

INLAND - Same.   (31)

INTERNATIONAL - A trawler has different lights than the other fishing vessels. Green over white. Very common test question! Trawling means she is dragging the bottom as opposed to the fishing vessel above with nets or lines. The net shown here is weighted and on the way to the bottom.

INLAND - Same.   (33)

INTERNATIONAL - Dayshapes for fishing vessels. Two cones apex to apex and up high. Small cone over side -higher than sidelights- indicates nets on that side horizontally out 150 meters or more. At night this is a white 360° light in the direction of the gear. Cone over side is NOT used by trawlers...nor is the 360° light.

INLAND - Same   (35)

INTERNATIONAL - Not under command. Two red lights, each 360° and arranged vertically. "Red-over-red, the captain's dead." Engine down, prop fell off, drifting. Dayshape is two black balls. **Special note:** If a vessel is aground this same signal is used but a white anchor light is added if less than 50 meters long, or two white anchor lights (see #23) if 50 meters or greater. (37) & (38)

Dayshape for being aground is three black balls as indicated in #38. Vessels less than 12 meters in length do not need these special signals.

INLAND - Same.

41

INTERNATIONAL - Purse seiners can show a special signal of two 360° vertically arranged flashing yellow lights when hampered by their fishing gear. They flash alternately every second.

INLAND - Same.   (32)

INTERNATIONAL - Special lights for trawlers when fishing in fleet or as a team. They can shine searchlights on each other's hull. Separate signals to indicate current maneuver: Vertically arranged - two white lights=shooting the nets; white-over-red=pulling the nets; red-over-red=nets hung up on some obstruction in water. Special masthead lights green over white. If less than 50 meters in length the top white masthead light is optional. Only when actually underway would the sidelights and sternlight be lighted.   (34)

INLAND - Same.

INTERNATIONAL - The only standard dayshape which is not black. This is the dayshape for a fishing vessel less than 20 meters in length. The two cones shown in **number 35** can be used instead.

INLAND - **Same.**   (36)

INTERNATIONAL - The cylinder shape describes a deep draft vessel in a narrow channel. Cargo vessel or very large craft. Cannot deviate from course. At night, three vertically arranged 360° red lights.   (39)

INLAND - Technically, no such signals yet. However, smaller vessels may not impede the passage of any craft, especially large cargo-type craft, in a traffic pattern.

SPECIAL NOTE: - **The Alfa Flag** means there is a diver down. Rigid construction to show all around. No mention is made in the rules concerning the more traditional red flag with the diagonal white stripe. Note night signal.   (40)

INTERNATIONAL - See International Tugs in this section. ㊶

INLAND - Note the big difference between Inland and International is two towing lights when towing alongside or pushing ahead as on the next panel. BOTH are yellow and recall they are called "towing lights"...not sternlights. The masthead light arrangement is same as International.

INTERNATIONAL - See International Tugs - this section. ㊷

INLAND - Tug is less than 50 meters in length. Only a pushed barge shows that "special flashing light." Light is yellow and flashes 50-70 fpm. Arc of that light can be anything from 180° to 225°. **Used Inland and only when pushing.**

And note the tug still has two yellow "towing" lights instead of merely the stern light as used when pushing or towing alongside in International waters.

㊸

INTERNATIONAL - Note the **solid** attachment of the tug to the dredge. This is an example of a **composite unit.** Thus, both are treated as one vessel. In this case the dredge shows the masthead and sidelights while the tug fills in with the sternlight. Also restricted in ability to maneuver.

INLAND - Same.

INTERNATIONAL - A dredge under her own power. In this case she is actually underway and moving...see the sidelights? If she becomes stationary the sidelights are extinguished. Restricted in ability to maneuver. She can show two 360° red lights over the bow, stern or either side to indicate side **not** to pass. Similarly placed dual green lights for side to pass. See #'s 26 & 30. ㊹

INLAND - Same.

㊺

INTERNATIONAL - See numbers 12-15.

INLAND - The Inland tug shows the same as the International tug **when towing astern.** Since tow is less than 200 meters astern only two 225° masthead lights forward. The tug shows an after masthead light as she is 50 meters or greater in length. If barges are towed in tandem or abreast all outer barges show respective sidelight and end barge(s) show stern light(s).

INTERNATIONAL - "White-over-red, pilot ahead." He uses these lights ONLY when on duty which could include being at anchor. If at anchor this would add another 360° white light to his array but would extinguish his sidelights and sternlight. ㊻

INLAND - Same.

INTERNATIONAL - International Rules have only recently employed a rule regulating lights on submerged or partially submerged vessels under tow. Basically, they are the same as the Inland light spacing required on the tow. International and Inland both require the diamond dayshape on the tow, but International insists on one at each end if 200 meters or more astern. The light spacing is indicated on the panel to your right.

㊼

INTERNATIONAL - No such dredge-pipe line navigable openings exist in the International Rules. ㊽

INLAND - The yellow lights mark the pipeline. The vertical red lights mark the navigable opening. All 360° lights.

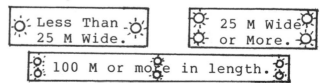

DISTRESS SIGNALS

DYE MARKER (ANY COLOR)

CODE FLAGS NOVEMBER CHARLIE

SQUARE FLAG AND BALL

WAVE ARMS

RADIO-TELEGRAPH ALARM

RADIO-TELEPHONE ALARM

POSITION INDICATING RADIO BEACON

SMOKE

RED STAR SHELLS

CONTINUOUS SOUNDING

FLAMES ON A VESSEL

GUN FIRED AT INTERVALS OF 1 MIN.

SOS

SOS

"MAYDAY" BY RADIO

PARACHUTE RED FLARE

ORANGE BACKGROUND BLACK BALL & SQUARE

So far you have covered the Rules of The Road, Lights and Dayshapes, Maneuvering Signals, Signals In Restricted Visibility, not to mention a small dissertation on the license requirements. Now let's go through a general overall view of the types of questions the CG will ask you. This is a tip sheet indicating CG emphasis on the tests. For the Rules, you will probably get two separate tests, each requiring 90% accuracy. Some offices will combine the two tests into one, i.e., International and Unified. If you are working the rivers, inland waters or the Great Lakes, chances are you will receive only the Unified test.

CAUTION HERE. If you work the offshore route you just might get a combined test. Maybe the first part will indicate "International Rules", then a short way down the test will be a separate quiz for "Unified". If you're not watching carefully, you will find the change escapes you and you will keep on answering questions as though they were International. Above all else, **READ THE DIRECTIONS.** Take along a 3 x 5 card. Each question will be multiple choice. Cover up the choices and read the question carefully. Decide on an answer then move the card and look for the answer you want. If the answer isn't there, **pick the best answer,** which is what the directions will say anyway. Try this technique with the first test in this book. You will surprise yourself to discover you didn't really **read** a good many of the questions.

DON'T MUCK UP THE TESTS.

Don't make marks in your book indicating your choice of answer. Make some copies of the blank answer sheets in the appendix and use those. That way the next time you take the same test, the answers won't be automatic or influence your decision.

Careful of the tests in the CG office. You will most likely receive a test booklet and told not to write in it. The test booklet might be covered in loose plastic. You will also receive an IBM answer sheet to indicate choices A,B,C, or D. If the test booklet appears to have some choices indicated beneath the plastic cover...ignore them. You could be the victim of a set up! Use your own brain...not what someone else indicated.

Now let's run through some emphasis. We call these "Test Tips". Read them carefully before taking the next two tests. By the way, if someone should ask you, the following tips, tests and previous artwork, took into consideration that the 1972 COLREGS had 55 amendments attached to them effective June 1, 1983.

Show me a man who has ulcers from messing around boats and I'll show you an unlicensed charter skipper. Someday, a long time from now, he will laugh again and tell you how his boat was seized and auctioned.

---

1) If you are reading this book more than a year after its' publication, be advised there could have been some changes. At this date the government publication of the Rules of The Road runs about $6.50. If you feel you would like to have a copy of the Official Rules, Charters West publishes one for $4.95. Use the order form on the last page. **If** anything changes an update will be in your order. No one is safe when the legislature is in session.

2) The Western Rivers are rivers which empty into the Mississippi River. There is no mention, in the new Rules of The Road, of the Red River of The North.

3) Many Western Rivers have their own "Vessel Traffic Control" centers. The VTC rules differ by the area. You should check with the local CG in the area of your operation to determine how they differ from the regular Rules.

4) An Inland Rule (Unified) permits Western River vessels to operate without masthead lights due to low bridges!

5) A vessel bound down-river has the right of way over a vessel bound up-river.

6) A tug with tow, bound up-river, does not have the right of way over a non-towing vessel coming down-river. However, if the up-bound tug displayed the signals for being "restricted in ability to maneuver" then the up-bound tug would **seem** to have right of way. Boat-for-boat, the down-bound vessel has the right of way.

7) A vessel crossing the river, channel or fairway or traffic lane must give way to any vessels ascending or descending said river, channel or fairway or traffic lane.

8) Keep to the right.

9) Keep a proper lookout. The helmsman is NOT considered a valid lookout!

10) The Rule of Good Seamanship says: a) Keep proper lookout, b) Use the Rules to avoid collision, c) Use the proper lights and dayshapes, d) Use radar properly.

11) When navigating by radar, especially in restricted visibility, any change of course necessary for safety should be a "substantial" change of course. Easier to detect on radar by other nearby vessels.

12) The radiotelephone can be used Inland to designate maneuvering intentions. There is no such mention of this in the International Rules.

13) Sailboats in Inland waters are not required to sound maneuvering signals. Sailboats **do** sound maneuvering signals in International waters.

14) Maneuvering signals can be **supplemented** by flashing lights. One flash, of about one second duration supplements a short blast. There is no supplemental light signal for a prolonged blast! Inland you can use a yellow OR white 360° light visible for at least two miles. International permits only the use of a white light visible for at least five miles.

15) You may not determine if a risk of collision does or does not exist based on scanty information...especially scanty radar information.

16) If, in restricted visibility, you detect a vessel forward of your beam you

17) All vessels, Inland and Interntional, shall travel at a **safe speed.** And just what is a "safe speed"? That is, what constitutes "safe"? Read the conditions outlined in Rule 6. If you include operating with radar, there are twelve conditions to consider.

18) If a collision situation exists and you are in "extremis" you should make any move necessary to avoid the collision. To hell with the Rules. The term "extremis" still shows up in some REC tests, but the term is no longer used in the Official Rules.

19) It is the duty and requirement of the stand on vessel to maintain course and speed.

20) In Inland waters, signals are given when vessels are within sight of each other **and** within a half mile of each other.

21) Giving signals and maneuvering your vessel upon the approach of another, infers that unless you did maneuver, there would be a collision. If no maneuvering is necessary in International waters, the inference is that there is no need for a signal. If a signal needs to be given in International waters it is because the vessels are within sight of each other and a course change is necessary. Inland Rules insist that signals be given when meeting or crossing within a half-mile of each other (as well as within sight).

22) Inland Rules insists that there be **agreement** before a maneuver is made. You are supposed to wait until the other vessel returns the signal before commencing your maneuver.

23) Note the difference in the technical meanings of blasts given Inland and International.

Inland: one blast; I **intend** to leave you on my port side.

International: one blast; I **am** altering my course to starboard.

24) Maneuvering signals are instigated by the give way craft.

25) In Inland waters, maneuvering signals are returned by the stand on craft when meeting, crossing or overtaking.

26) Maneuvering signals in International Waters are not returned by the stand on craft when crossing, or overtaking unless overtaking in a narrow channel.

27) Be sure you know and understand the signals for **International Narrow Channels** when one vessel is overtaking another. There is a return signal.

28) The traditional "danger signal" of at least five short blasts infers **doubt** when maneuvering. The danger-doubt signal is not used in restricted visibility.

29) One prolonged blast, Inland or International, is given when approaching an obstruction which might inhibit visibility of on-coming vessels. Also given by sailboats. There is an Inland Rule (#34g) stating you must sound one prolonged blast when leaving a dock or berth. No such rule exists in International Rules. However, the CG tests insist that this is the case when leaving a berth, pier or dock due to the obstructed visibility caused by the

48

dock or berth.   While the rule doesn't exist in International Rules the CG tests insist that this is the case when leaving a berth, pier or dock due to the obstructed visibility caused by the dock, pier or berth! One Long Beach test insisted the prolonged blast be given even when **backing** away from your slip, pier, berth or dock. They regarded three blasts as a wrong answer.

30) A vessel is underway when NOT tied to a dock, at anchor or aground. So, keep in mind that you could be "underway", but with no way on. Drifting.

31) ANY vessel overtaking another vessel is considered the give way craft. Even a sailboat passing a powerboat is burdened to give way.

32) A minesweeper, by the nature of her duty, is considered "restricted in ability to maneuver". The three green lights indicate this. No other lights or dayshapes are necessary to indicate this impairment.

33) Avoid speeding up to avoid collision. Slow down. Instead, if possible, change course and make it "substantial".

34) There are no special signals for "passing in narrow channels" in Inland waters.

35) What is the difference between overtaking and crossing? If a vessel bears **aft** of 22 1/2^O abaft the beam of another vessel, it's an overtaking situation. **Forward** of 22 1/2^O abaft the beam of another vessel is considered crossing. Obviously, the third alternative is head on.

36) If, upon approaching another vessel at night, and you see the sternlight, it's an overtaking situation. If you see either of the sidelights, it's a crossing situation.   Theoretically, it's impossible to see both the sternlight and the sidelights simultaneously.

37) One cutie seen on a test asked who had the right-of-way when a sailboat approached a fishing vessel fishing in a fairway. Ans: Sailboat. It's illegal to fish in a fairway when you obstruct traffic! Does this mean if the other guy is doing something illegal, you have the right-of-way?

38) The preferred course change to avoid collision when meeting head on, is to change course to the right.

39) Ordinarily a fishing vessel, engaged in fishing, has the right of way over a sailboat, but he has to be engaged in fishing at the time.

40) All Six-Pac and Ocean Operator candidates should know the rules for sailboats vs. sailboats whether they plan on doing sail charters or not.

41) Sailboats under sail do not use white masthead lights. Recall, there is a special 360° red over green mast top light indicating a sailboat underway at night, but no white masthead light.

42) **Fog signals** are required when operating within a half-mile of an area of restricted visibility...e.g., a fog bank.

43) Every vessel is required to have some form of sound producing device aboard to indicate position in restricted visibility. Even when at anchor if not anchored in an "approved anchorage".

44) There is no such thing as a **fog horn** on a vessel. Sail or power. Now

they're called whistles, "fog signals", or "sound producing appliances". Foghorns are situated ashore in lighthouses, or such. Beware of the question using the term "foghorn" when referring to a ship at sea.

45) The Old Rules used to make repeated reference to the "points" of the compass. A point is 11 1/4° of the compass. There are 32 points. Divide 32 points into 360 degrees to get the 11 1/4°.

46) Concerning yellow lights:

   a) Yellow lights which are on constantly -fixed- are only found Inland on dredge pipelines.

   b) "Flashing yellow lights" means 120 fpm. Hover craft.

   c) "Special flashing yellow light" means 50-70 fpm. This is found only on the bow of a barge being pushed ahead by a tug in Inland waters. It has an arc ranging from 180° to 225° meaning it could be mounted below the deckline.

   d) A towing light is a yellow stern light on a tug which is towing astern. Inland or International, the towing light is vertically above the usual white stern light and has the same arc of visibility; 135°. Only Inland tugs when pushing their tow or have it alongside, are required to show two vertically arranged "towing" lights.

   e) There are alternately flashing yellow lights on purse seiners. See pp. 40-41, picture #32

   f) Submarine. Careful here. This is dictated by the Sec. of the Navy and changes on every other national holiday. At this writing, three one second yellow flashes, dark for three seconds, then a repeat cycle. 360° lights.

47) Catch question: What vessel displays a blue light? Ans: None. Law enforcement displays a "flashing" blue light.

FOG SIGNALS-A SUMMARY

Technically, the term "restricted visibility" is used. This means **any** kind of visibility restriction: fog, haze, rain, hail, sleet, snow or a bad hangover. The Rules indicate these signals should commence when you are within a half-mile of any fog bank or area of restricted visibility. Some signals are sounded underway, some when at anchor and even special ones when aground. Some are sounded every minute, some every two minutes. The CG loves these, so get them straight.

48) Powerboats underway, every two minutes...one prolonged blast.

49) Powerboats underway, but stopped, every two minutes, **two** prolonged blasts.

50) There are some special **Inland** restricted visibility signals. Study this next part carefully. One prolonged and two short are given every two minutes in restricted visibility by the following vessels **whether underway or at anchor**. And careful here. **If at anchor-signal is given every minute.**

   a) Any vessel restricted in ability to maneuver,
   b) All fishing vessels...when fishing.

The following sound one prolonged and two short **when underway**:

    a) Vessels not under command,
    b) Sailboats under sail.
    c) Tugs pushing or towing.

51) Now let's look at the International counterpart to the above. One prolonged and two short are given every two minutes in restricted visibility by:

    a) Any vessel not under command,
    b) Any vessel restricted in ability to maneuver, **also when working at anchor**, (as of 6-1-83).
    c) A vessel constrained by her draft,
    d) Sailboats,
    e) Fishing vessels, **also when at anchor, fishing**, (as of 6-1-83).
    f) Tugs pushing or towing.

52) The one prolonged and two short signal is also given by **Inland and International** tugs, when pushing or towing in restricted visibility. If the barge being towed, (or the last one in the tow if there are more than just one) gives one prolonged and **three short**, but only if said barge is **manned**.

53) Bells and gongs are never used when underway. What **are** bells and gongs used for? Glad you asked. Listen up 'cause this applies to both Inland and International.

    a) A five second bell is sounded **every minute** by vessels at anchor in restricted visibility.

    b) If vessel is 100 meters or greater the five second bell is rung in the forward part then a gong for another five seconds near the stern.

    c) If aground, an additional bell signal is given: Three "distinct" strokes, the usual five second ringing, then another "distinct" three strokes. And if you are unfortunate enough to be 100 meters or greater, don't forget the gong right after the last three "distinct" strokes. If you're the only man on watch you have a lot of jogging to do on a vessel over 100 meters in length.

    d) You don't think that's enough? Still afraid of getting run over? Tell ya what's ya do. Sound one short, one prolonged, one short. It's an optional signal anyone can give when at anchor. Frequently on CG tests.

    e) The above are all **one minute** interval signals...Inland and International. There's one exception. Any vessel less than 12 meters can, instead, "make some other efficient sound signal at intervals of not more than **two minutes**".

    f) Then, of course, there's the pilot vessel when engaged in duty who **may** sound four short as an identity signal. However, Pilot still has to abide by all of the others above.

    g) Inland waters permit the use of an adjunct to the maneuvering signals in the form of a white **or** yellow light. The light is used in conjunction with the maneuvering signals...one flash, one blast, etc. International allows only a white light...no yellow.

    h) We save one of the most important for last because it leads to trick questions on exams. The usual maneuvering signals are given "when vessels are within sight of each other". Thus, ordinary maneuvering signals **are not used in restricted visibility**!

54) Nobody, but nobody, anchors in a fairway, channel, shipping lane or traffic pattern.

55) Small craft, under 20 meters, do not have to sound fog signals all night if anchored in an "approved anchorage," but that exception is only stated in the Inland Rules!!

56) Fishing means fishing with lines, nets or trawls. If you have trolling lines stringing from astern, you're not considered fishing and have no special rights of way.

57) Trawling is "green over white". Regular fishing boats show "red over white". If you don't know what that means, go back to the boat pictures and look up the fishing boats and trawlers. Very important.

58) "Notice To Mariners," is published by the Secretary of The Department of Transportation in Washington, D.C.

59) "**Local** Notice to Mariners," is published by the CG in each district.

60) A man standing on the beach, with his hands straight out at his sides is signalling the semaphore letter "R". This means "affirmative" and nothing more.

61) A man on a vessel moving those outstretched arms up and down is signalling for help. See "Distress Signals" in this volume.

62) In the following exams: if the statement says a "sailboat" you may assume it's under sail alone. If it states "fishing vessel" assume it's fishing.

ON TAKING THESE TESTS

1) Do not mark up the tests. Use the blank numbered test sheets in the appendix. If you haven't done so already, get some copies. You'll need them.

2) Take the entire test before checking the answers which are at the end of each test. You'll be glad you did.

3) If you get better than 60% the first time, you're genius material and shouldn't even waste your money on silly books like this.

4) Use a 3 x 5 card. Cover up the multiple choice answers and try to figure YOUR answer before looking at the choices offered. You might think about doing this on the real CG quiz when your day comes. Makes you really **read** the questions.

5) Never accept ANY answer until you have read all of the choices.

6) CG directions generally state, "Choose the best answer." Now their idea of the best answer is frequently questionable, but you'll get the idea.

7) While grading your answers, don't memorize them. Try to grasp the concept of **why** that was the correct answer.

8) Don't waste your time, temper and attitude arguing with the answer. Instead, consider trying to find why the answer was so strange. Look for a

tricky word or phrase.   Mo bettah you get caught herein than in the exam room.

9) Some questions describe various boats under certain circumstances when underway, prior to asking a right-of-way question.   It helps to slow down and sketch a picture.   It could become very clear what's going on.

10) Your first test is on the "Unified" or Inland Rules.   The next will be on the International.   Keep your mind on the differences.

DISCLAIMER

This book was written for those boaters trying to pass a test. The information contained herein is to be used solely for that purpose and that purpose alone.   Any similarity between statements made in this publication and that of empirical law, safety afloat or common sense is purely coincidental.

This volume is not a legal document and not intended as such.   The author specifically disallows any assumption on the part of the reader that rules, suggestions, hints or advice can be utilized legally while operating any vessel afloat sail, power, or otherwise.

Well, O.K., so it's not easy. Maybe you haven't been back to school in the last ten years or more and stuffing things into the brain isn't easy. Especially when you have to remember them, then feed them back on an impersonal piece of paper. To make life easier, here's some suggestions.

1) Don't muck up the tests. In the appendix there's a sheet of paper with numbers on both sides. These are unmarked "key sheets" to record your answers to the various tests. Razor blade it out and have some copies made. Lots of them. That way you can take the test over and over again without messing up the original leaving clues behind the next time you take it.

2) The Coast Guard has some directions with their tests. Generally, it's something like, "Pick The Best Answer". While the best answer to you might not mean the same thing to the CG, it's **their** test and you have to go along. Some of these answers you won't agree with. For example, in the First Aid and Engine Maintenance parts, there are real doozies that should leave you in stitches. Thus, remember this is a **test** and any resemblance to reality is purely coincidental.

3) If you score 60% or better on **any** of the quizzes the first time out, you're doing fantastic. Really!

3) Don't get mad at the answers. Some of them are pretty sneaky, but mo' betta' you screw them up here than someplace else when it really counts.

4) Take the entire test, **then** correct it. No matter how curious you are, skip the answer key which follows each quiz until you complete the entire test.

5) Don't try to memorize the answers. That's dumb. The tests you get from the CG will bear the same concepts, but not the exact wording. Learn the "concept" of **why** the answer is what it is.

6) Use a 3 x 5 card. Cover up the multiple choices and try to figure out the answer before you look at the choices.

7) Study for the test **before** you take it. True, the tests are excellent

"teachers", but you need a lot of special know-how before wading in. This may not be true for portions of the Seamanship test, but it is for the rest. You'll see.

8) You will find a few strange words...vocabulary, in many places. Don't hesitate to check the glossary in the back. The glossary is an excellent test in itself. You should know all the definitions found there before you make your exam appointment with the CG.

9) As mentioned earlier, these questions came from those who went before you. They're real. They came from Florida, Maine, Hawaii, Seattle, California and all over the U.S. Somewhere, someplace, some CG test contained them...one and all. When you take **your** test and find something unusual or peculiar to your area...we'd like to hear about it. Sorry, we haven't any T-shirts to mail out as rewards. This volume was first conceived as a textbook for my own classes, but soon became a marine national best seller. If we dedicated this volume to those who made it possible, we would need a second volume.

10) Again: These tests have nothing to do with the practical situation out there at sea. The only value is in helping you to pass a test. No one is trying to teach you first aid or how to handle a boat in the legal or practical sense of the word. This is all theory and admittedly, some of it is warped by necessity.

SEMINARS IN YOUR HOME TOWN?

Yes, it could happen. Not everyone is one of those "dedicated" beings who can plow through a morass like this without motivational forces behind them. Charters West is always on call for three day seminars. We will come to town and do a Friday evening three hour thing, then reappear Saturday morning for three hours plus an additional three hours Sunday morning. We cover the rough spots, iron out the charting and rules of the road then stage a question-answer session that reveals more than any book could ever accomplish. We never fail to exit leaving everyone with a smile knowing it has been money well spent.

If you are interested, the charge is $199 for each student plus the cheapest round trip super-saver flight fare available. The meetings are given in a local lodge or community meeting place. Even a large living room works out nicely. If you can find nine friends who are interested, write for details.

1) A vessel at anchor, not in an approved anchorage or navigable area, is required to show an anchor light or ball at what minimum length listed below?

   a) 5 meters, b) 6 meters, c) 7 meters, d) 11 meters.

2) Which vessel underway need not show a white masthead light at night?

   a) A powercraft 10 meters in length, b) A sailboat under sail, c) A dredge, d) A law enforcement craft.

3) Two sailboats are on a collision course. Which vessel signals her intent first?

   a) The vessel off the starboard bow of the other, b) The vessel off the port bow of the other, c) The vessel on a port tack, d) None of these.

4) One short blast from a stand-on powercraft in a crossing approach means:

   a) I am altering my course to port, b) I intend to alter my course to port, c) I intend to alter my course to starboard, d) I will maintain course and speed.

5) Referring to the sketch at right, which should vessel "A" not attempt?

   a) To come right, b) To come left, b) To stop, d) All of these.

6) A vessel approaches you from your starboard side. You should first:

   a) Wait for him to signal intent, b) Blow one short blast, c) Maintain course and speed, d) Come right slowly.

7) When approaching a blind bend in a river or an intervening obstruction one prolonged blast need not be given by which of these vessels?

   a) A sailboat, b) A powercraft propelled by an outboard, c) A taxiing seaplane, d) None of these should avoid giving the signal.

8) In a crossing situation the right-of-way stand-on vessel is obligated to:

   a) Maintain course and speed, b) Return the crossing signal, c) Refrain from coming left, d) All of these.

9) The weather is restricted in visibility and you detect a vessel forward of your beam. You should:

   a) Come to a full stop until a bearing on the other vessel is substantiated, b) Keep sufficient headway to maintain steerage way, c) Increase the frequency of your fog signal, d) Post two lookouts, one on each bow.

10) In crossing and overtaking situations appropriate signals are initiated by:

   a) The stand-on vessel, b) The give-way craft, c) Either vessel, d) The skipper who observes the other vessel first.

11) On which of the vessels below would you not find a yellow navigation light?

   a) A barge, b) A law enforcement craft, c) A submarine, d) A tug.

12) A black diamond dayshape would most likely be found on a:

   a) Barge, b) Purse seiner, c) Trawler, d) A fishing boat 20 meters in length or more.

13) An black cone, apex pointing down, would be found on a:

   a) Fishing boat, b) Sailboat, c) Barge, d) Trawler.

14) Masthead lights are situated on a vessel's:

   a) Bow, b) Stern, c) Truck, d) Forward and/or after masts.

15) A vessel unable to maneuver out of the way of on-coming vessels due to some exceptional circumstance is considered which of the following?

   a) Restricted in ability to maneuver, b) Not under command, c) A large tanker moving down a river or channel, d) All of these.

16) Which vessel is considered underway?

   a) Aground, b) Not under command, c) Anchored, d) Secured to a mooring buoy.

17) Which of the following is not considered restricted visibility?

   a) Darkness, b) Sandstorm, c) Smoke, d) Mist or fog.

18) Your engine is jammed in neutral, but you are drifting astern. You should signal:

   a) Three short blasts, b) Five or more short blasts, c) A rapid ringing of the ship's bell, d) None of these.

19) You are backing out of your slip. You should sound:

   a) Three short blasts, b) One long blast, c) One prolonged blast, d) None of these.

20) The night is foggy and you detect another vessel closing fast with no sound signals, You should sound:

   a) Five short blasts, b) One short blast every two minutes, c) One short blast every minute, d) One prolonged blast every two minutes.

21) As regards underway signals in restricted visibility; which vessel below does not belong in the group?

   a) Tug with tow, b) Sailboat, c) Fishing vessel, d) Powerboat.

22) When a tug is pulling barges in a multiple line and in tandem in restricted visibility, the restricted visibility signal is situated on and sounded from:

a) None of the barges, b) The two outermost barges in front, c) The last barge in the center-rear, d) The barge closest of the center of the string.

23) Which vessel below does not sound a prolonged and two shorts when anchored in a fog?

a) A sailboat, b) A fishing boat, fishing, c) Both of these, d) Neither of these.

24) A 30 meter tug is pushing her tow. On a dark and clear night approaching her starboard beam forward of 22.5° abaft her beam, which light would you see first?

a) Flashing yellow light, b) Masthead light, c) Sternlight, d) Green sidelight.

25) A white 360° light would be seen in what position on a powercraft underway?

a) Aft, b) Forward, c) Midships, d) Cabin top.

26) You observe, at sea, a man standing on the bow of his craft slowly raising and lowering his outstretched arms. He is:

a) Asking for a radio contact, b) Requesting you stand clear, c) In distress, d) Indicating he is short on beer.

27) In restricted visibility all vessels shall travel:

a) At a moderate speed, b) At a speed enabling them to stop in half the distance of their visibility, c) A safe speed, d) At a speed substantially less than that travelled in clear weather.

28) Among other criteria, safe speed in Inland waters can be determined by:

a) The proximity of land, b) Traffic density, c) Stability of your craft, d) All of these.

29) A potential collision situation is deemed to exist when:

a) The relative bearing of an on-coming craft does not vary, b) When the other craft displays the November-Charlie flags, c) When a stand-on vessel fails to return a maneuvering signal, d) When the other vessel makes a radical change of course.

30) Detecting a vessel on radar, you cannot see the side lights until you are 2,000 yards off his beam. His length is therefore at most:

a) 7 meters, b) 12 meters, c) 19 meters, d) 20 meters.

31) Which of the following lights is not authorized?

a) Steering light, b) Towing light, c) Sternlight, d) Sidelights

32) Annex I of the Rules of the Road is concerned with:

a) Technical details of signals for fishing vessels, b) Technical details of sound signal appliances, c) Distress signals, d) Technical details of positioning of lights and shapes.

33) Annex II, of the Rules of the Road is concerned with:

a) Technical details of signals for fishing vessels, b) Technical details of sound signal appliances, c) Distress signals, d) Technical details of positioning of lights and shapes.

34) Annex III of the Rules of the Road is concerned with:

a) Technical details of signals for fishing vessels, b) Technical details of sound signal appliances, c) Distress signals, d) Technical details of positioning of lights and shapes.

35) Annex IV of the Rules of the Road is concerned with:

a) Technical details of signals for fishing vessels, b) Technical details of sound signal appliances, c) Distress signals, d) Technical details of positioning of lights and shapes.

36) Navigation lights are required to be lighted:

a) Between sunrise and sunset, b) Twenty minutes before sunset, c) In any restricted visibility & from sunset to sunrise, d) Only at night or when foggy.

37) The arc of visibility of lights aboard vessels is measured:

a) By points of the compass, b) From dead ahead to two points abaft the beam, c) In a variety of ways, d) In degrees only.

38) Two powercraft are approaching each other as indicated at right:

a) Vessel "A" should keep clear of "B", b) "B" should maintain course and speed, c) "A" should sound one blast, d) All of these.

39) In which case does the sailboat not have the right-of-way over the powerboat?

a) When overtaking, b) When crossing a fairway, channel or river, c) When approaching a fishing vessel, fishing, d) All of these.

40) Four vessels meet in a narrow channel. Which has the right-of-way?

a) Minesweeper on duty, b) A vessel not under command, c) A vessel aground, d) Deep draft vessel in a narrow channel.

41) Four sailboats meet. Which has the right-of-way?

a) Close hauled on a port tack, b) Running down wind, c) Sailing on a starboard tack, d) Sailing to the windward of the other three.

42) Which vessel would have the right-of-way over a vessel which can navigate safely only in a channel or fairway?

a) Sailboat, b) Fishing vessel fishing, c) An 18 meter tug with tow, d) None of these.

43) Designated traffic lanes should be crossed:

a) At a right angle, b) At an oblique angle to the lane, c) As narrow an angle as is prudent, d) In compliance with applicable regulations.

44) A vessel approaching a blind bend in a river sounds:

a) One long blast, b) One short blast, c) One prolonged blast, d) Four or more short blasts.

45) Changes of speed and/or course to avoid collision situations should be:

a) Slowly and with great care, b) Substantial, c) Radically, d) In close quarters situations, when vessels are within a half mile of each other.

46) A sailboat is approaching the port bow of your powerboat. The sailboat is flying an inverted black conical shape, apex down. You should:

a) Stand-on, b) Slow down, c) Blow one blast, d) Come left.

47) Consider a close quarter situation with collision a distinct possibility. You should:

a) Not relinguish your right-of-way, b) Maintain course, but slow down, c) Maintain speed, but make a substantial course change, d) Take action to avoid collision by maneuvering.

48) An 18 meter power vessel should have a masthead light visible for a minimum of:

a) 1 mile, b) 2 miles, c) 3 miles, d) 5 miles.

49) The Pilot Rules are found in:

a) The Coast Pilot, b) Annex V, c) The Light List, d) The Pilot's Handbook.

50) Which statement regarding signals in restricted visibility is true?

a) Underway signals are sounded every two minutes, b) Anchored vessels sound the signal once every minute, c) Vessels aground sound their signal every minute, d) All statements are true.

51) A vessel is deemed to be overtaking another vessel when approaching the other vessel:

a) Aft of 22.5° abaft the beam, b) Any point aft the beam, c) At least 45° abaft the beam, d) Within sight of the arc of the sidelights.

52) Two vessels are approaching each other head-on. The most desirable course of action is:

a) To change course before closing to less than a half-mile apart, b) Come left, c) Come right, d) Vessels bound closest to east or north have the right-of-way.

53) You are approaching a vessel underway off your port bow. The short blast sounded by the other vessel means:

a) I have the right-of-way, b) I am altering my course to port, c) I am leaving you on my port side. d) I intend to come right leaving you on my port side.

54) Which of the following would be considered operating in restricted visibility?

a) Dark moonless night, b) A very cloudy day, c) Within a half-mile of a fog bank, d) On a winding river with heavy traffic.

55) A "flashing light" is one which flashes:

a) At regular intervals at a frequency of 120 fpm or more, b) Flashes from 60 to 120 fpm, c) Flashes yellow at 90 fpm, d) Flashes 90 fpm.

56) The sternlight of a vessel 50 meters or more in length would become visible within:

a) 2 miles, b) 3 miles, c) 4 miles, d) 5 miles.

57) Three masthead lights on a tug means:

a) The tow is over 200 meters astern, b) The tug is 50 meters or more in length, c) a & b, d) a or b.

58) Which 18 meter vessel below is improperly lighted? Assume arcs correct.

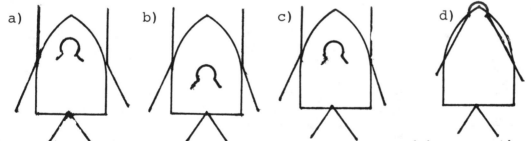

59) When a tug is towing several barges abreast, each barge on the outermost side should have sidelights plus sternlight(s) must be displayed:

a) On each barge b) On the lead barges, c) On each tailing barge, d) Only on the outermost tailing barges.

60) Sailing vessels underway and under sail at night never show:

a) Split sidelights, b) Sidelights and a sternlight on the top of the main mast, c) Vertically arranged 360° lights, red over green, d) A masthead light.

61) Departure from the Rules of The Road would most likely occur:

   a) In restricted visibility, b) In a overtaking situation once the overtaking craft is clear, c) In extremis, d) Never.

62) A rowboat may exhibit:

   a) The same lights as a sailboat, b) A flashlight, c) A lantern, d) Any of these.

63) Upon approaching a vessel with a black conical shape, apex up, and extended over the side, you should conclude it is:

   a) A dredge, pass on the side opposite the cone, b) a purse seiner with a net over the cone's side, c) A fishing vessel with nets out on the cone side over 150 meters, d) A minesweeper maneuvering.

64) A working dredge at night shows two vertically arranged green 360° lights over the port side. This indicates:

   a) There is an obstruction off the starboard side, stern or bow, b) She is dredging off the port side, c) The dredgepipe is over the port side, d) It is safe to pass as the dredge is not dredging at that moment.

65) Which vessel underway would never show a ball-diamond-ball dayshape?

   a) Fishing vessel, b) Tug, c) Harbor patrol, d) Minesweeper.

66) A vessel displays a basket from one of her yards. She is:

   a) Greater than 50 meters, b) Greater than 20 meters, c) Less than 20 meters, d) Less than 50 meters, but greater than 20 meters.

67) An anchored vessel at night is engaged in underwater operations which restrict her ability to maneuver. She would show which lights:

   a) An anchor light, b) Red-over-white-over-red vertical lights, c) Green and red lights over the sides, d) All of these.

68) Any vessel may display the red-over-white-over-red restricted in ability to maneuver signals if:

   a) The circumstances warrant, b) The channel is heavy with traffic, c) When conforming to one of the ten Rules criteria for this signal, d) She is one of 5 types of ships so authorized.

69) Which of the following dayshapes would you see on a working dredge not underway?

   a) One black ball, b) Two cones, apex to apex, c) A black diamond, d) Two black balls.

70) Which of the following is a distress signal?

   a) The alfa flag, b) The November-Charlie flags, c) The ensign flown upside down, d) A green flare.

71) A pilot vessel underway and on duty would not show which light?

a) Two vertically arranged 360º lights, white-over-red, b) A sternlight, c) Sidelight, d) A 225º masthead light.

72) How many degrees of arc of light are visible on each side of a sternlight?

a) 67½, b) 135, c) 112.5, d) 225.

73) Visibility is restricted and you hear a whistle signal of one short-one prolonged-one short. The vessel sounding this signal is:

a) Anchored, b) Underway, c) Aground, d) In distress.

74) A vessel over 20 meters in length, anchored in fog, would sound:

a) A fog horn, b) Whistle, c) Bell, d) Gong

75) Which moored barge below is improperly lighted?

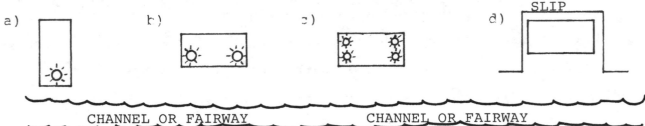

76) Which vessel below sounds the whistle signal every minute in restricted visibility?

a) Deep draft vessel, b) Underway but stopped, c) Restricted in ability to maneuver, d) At anchor.

77) A barge being towed shall give one prolonged and three short blasts on the whistle in restricted visibility when:

a) Entering congested waterways, b) When manned, c) When two or more barges are towing from the same tug, d) All of the above.

78) A vessel making a stern approach with intent to pass another vessel need not sound a signal when:

a) No change of course is necessary to pass, b) Overtaking is already in progress, c) The passing vessel is over 1,000 yards astern, d) The lead vessel is approaching a wide harbor mouth.

79) Vessel "A" has just sounded a passing signal indicating desire to pass vessel "B" on vessel "A's" starboard side. Vessel "B", if in agreement, should sound:

a) No signal, but maintain course and speed, b) Two short blasts, c) One prolonged-one short-one prolonged-one short, d) One short blast.

80) Maneuvering signal lights can be:

a) White, b) Or yellow, c) Visible for two miles, d) Any of these.

81) An acceptable substitute for maneuvering signals is:

a) Radio telephone communications, b) Visual hand signals, c) Semaphore communications, d) None of these are permitted as substitutes.

82) A vessel departing a slip, dock, pier, wharf or berth shall sound:

a) No signal required, b) One short blast, c) One prolonged blast, d) Three short blasts.

83) Five or more short blasts means:

a) Danger, b) Doubt, c) Change your current maneuver, d) Wait for return signal.

84) Which vessel below is not properly equipped with sound producing appliances?

a) A vessel over 100 meters with a bell, gong and foghorn, b) A rowboat with a loud rattling device, c) A vessel less than 12 meters carrying a freon horn, d) A vessel 22 meters in length carrying a whistle and a bell.

85) Which vessel below is not required to carry a sound producing device in restricted visibility?

a) Rowboat, b) Vessel less than 20 meters, but greater than 12 meters, c) A vessel less than 12 meters, d) None of these.

86) Your radar indicates you are in a close-quarter situation with another vessel and the fog is very dense. You should sound:

a) One prolonged blast every two minutes, b) Three short blasts and back down, c) Five short blasts every minute, d) A siren or other radical sound to attract attention.

87) A fishing vessel at anchor, fishing in restricted visibility sounds:

a) One prolonged-two shorts, b) One prolonged, c) One short, d) None of these.

88) Which vessels below do not sound one prolonged-two short blasts when anchored in restricted visibility?

a) A fishing vessel, fishing, b) A sailboat, c) A vessel not under command, d) A hovercraft.

89) Two short blasts mean:

a) I intend to leave you on my port side, b) I intend to leave you on your starboard side, c) I intend to leave you on my starboard side, d) I am coming left.

90) Sailboat "A" is approaching sailboat "B" off "B's" starboard bow. Both are under sail. Sailboat "A" will have the right of way:

a) When "B" sounds one blast, b) When "B" is on a port tack, c) When "A" is on a starboard tack and "B" is on a port tack, d) When "B" is to the lee of "A".

91) A strong northerly is blowing offshore. Sailboat "A" is close-hauled and both vessels are on starboard tacks. "B" is south of "A":

a) "B" has the right-of-way, b) "B" is to the lee of "A", c) "A" must give-way, d) All of these.

92) Two sailboats are approaching each other under sail and at risk of collision. Vessel "X" is sailing downwind with her mainboom over the port side and her jib over the starboard side. Vessel "Y" is close-hauled with her mainboom over the starboard side and her jib parallel with the main:

a) "X" is on a port tack and must give way, b) "X" is on a starboard tack and has the right-of-way, c) "Y" is to the lee of "X" and has the right-of-way, d) "Y" is on a starboard tack and has the right-of-way.

93) A pilot boat on duty in restricted visibility:

a) **Must** sound only four short blasts, b) **Must** sound regular signals, but **may** sound her own four short as well, c) **Can** substitute the four short blasts for any underway signals in restricted visibility, d) **Can** opt for any combination of the above.

94) As of March 1, 1983, which of the following is not mentioned as being Inland waters in the Rules of the Road?

a) Old River, b) Atchafalaya River, c) Great Lakes, d) Red River of The North.

95) You are a stand-on craft in an approach situation. The other craft does not initiate proper signals. You should:

a) Initiate the signal yourself, b) Take decisive avoidance action, c) Maintain course and speed, d) Come left.

96) Which vessel performing their function has the right-of-way over all of the others indicated?

a) Deep draft vessel in narrow channel, b) Fishing vessel, c) Buoy Tender, d) Sailboat.

97) Which vessels listed below shall not impede the passage of vessels operating in a traffic pattern?

a) A vessel less than 20 meters in length, b) A fishing vessel fishing with lines nets or trawls, c) A sailboat, d) All of these.

98) Which vessel below need not sound a prolonged blast when nearing a blind bend in a river?

a) A sailboat, b) A fishing vessel fishing, c) A vessel less than 20 meters. d) None of these.

99) A 14 meter craft needs a minimum of sound producing appliances aboard. They are:

a) A bell, b) A whistle, c) A whistle and a bell, d) Any sound producing appliance will suffice.

100) A vessel less than 20 meters in length and sailing vessels shall not impede power-driven craft when the power-driven craft are:

a) Operating under adverse conditions, b) In a traffic lane, c) Operating in an area of restricted visibility, d) Travelling up-river.

101) Which statement is false as regards signals which must be given when overtaking in Inland waters?

a) Sailboats do not have to give the signal, b) Must be given by power-driven craft when within sight of each other c) This signal is given only when a change of course is necessary, d) The signal is returned by the vessel ahead.

102) A power-driven vessel is defined by the Rules as any vessel afloat which is:

a) Equipped with an outboard, b) Propelled by machinery, c) Propelled by steam, d) All of these.

103) The lights shown at the right indicate a:

a) A purse seiner pulling her nets, b) A dredge, c) A trawler, d) A dredge pipe opening.

104) Which is the correct signal for coming right at night?

a) One short blast and two flashes of a white light, b) One short blast and one flash from a yellow light, c) Two short blasts, d) One flash from a white light.

105) What is the signal for making way in a dense fog?

a) Two prolonged blasts every minute, b) One short blast every two minutes, c) One prolonged blast every minute, d) One prolonged blast every two minutes.

106) Visibility is restricted and you are adrift with no way on. You sound:

a) Two short blasts every minute, b) One prolonged blast every minute, c) One short-one prolonged-one short every minute, d) Two prolonged blasts every two minutes.

107) Two vessels are approaching head-on. The preferred maneuvering signal is:

a) Two short blasts, b) One short blast, c) One prolonged blast, d) Two prolonged blasts.

108) Which of the following is not a distress signal?

a) A black circle and a black square on an orange background, b) The vertical motion of a white flag, c) Flames aboard a vessel, d) A red parachute flare.

109) Vessel "B" is pushing a barge. Vessel "A" should:

a) Alter course to port, b) Alter course to starboard, c) Signal for a stand-on exchange, d) Sound a cross-signal.

110) You have the right-of-way in a crossing situation, but are closing fast on what appears to be an immediate collision situation. You should:

a) Assume an extremis situation exists, b) Vary your course rapidly to port, c) Make a substantial speed decrease, d) Maintain course and speed.

111) Cross signals are:

a) Used only on the Great Lakes, b) Used only on Western Rivers, c) Forbidden, d) Used only on International waters.

112) A fishing vessel is fishing a fairway and is approached by a sailboat. The right-of-way belongs to:

a) The sailboat, b) The fishing vessel, c) Either, d) Neither.

113) Dense fog and you detect a vessel forward of your beam. Who has the right-of-way?

a) You do, b) The other vessel does, c) Neither vessel, d) Both vessels.

114) Navigating on a western river when do you have the right-of-way?

a) When the other vessel is running up-river, b) When the other vessel is running down river, c) When no VTC is in effect, d) Never.

115) On a harbor approach you detect an obstruction blocking part of the entrance. You choose the opening which is marked on each side by:

a) Two sets of yellow blinking lights, b) Two sets of green lights marking the opening, c) Two vertical red lights, d) A vertical string of white lights.

116) Which vessel, when working, is assumed to be restricted in ability to maneuver?

a) Minesweeper, b) Dredge, c) Buoy Tender, d) All of these.

117) A tug is pushing a barge. What lights do you expect to see on the barge?

a) Sternlight, b) Sidelights, c) Sternlight and sidelights, d) Mastlight and sidelights.

118) A ten meter powercraft must have the following minimum lights:

a) A 360° white light aft, b) Sternlight and sidelights, c) 360° white light aft and sidelights, d) Sidelights.

119) Vessels restricted in their ability to maneuver except a diveboat must show the prescribed lights indicating this condition unless they are:

a) Less than 20 meters, b) Greater than 15, but less than 20 meters, c) Less than 12 meters, d) Greater than 12 meters but less than 20 meters.

120) A fishing vessel fishing uses side and sternlights only when:

a) Underway with way on, b) Anchored, c) Drifting, d) Underway.

121) Five short blasts:

a) Could mean abort your planned maneuver, b) Infers doubt, c) Should not be used in a fog, d) All of these.

122) A barge towed alongside shows:

a) Sternlight, b) Sidelights, c) Masthead light, d) Side and sternlights:

123) A barge being pushed does not have to show:

a) Sidelights, b) Masthead light, c) Sternlight, d) Must show all of these.

124) When passing you hear 5 short blasts. You should:

a) Pass with extreme caution, b) Wait for the vessel ahead to signal you to pass, c) Keep trying your passing signal until you hear the same signal you have sounded, d) Answer and pass.

125) Night, and you see a red light NW of you. The other vessel is heading:

a) North, b) South, c) East, d) West.

126) When towing astern which is proper arrangement for the lights showing aft?

a) A towing light over a sternlight, b) A sternlight over a towing light, c) A towing light over a towing light, d) A sternlight over a sternlight.

127) Which vessel 50 meters or more need not show an after masthead light?

a) A sailboat under sail, b) A pilot boat on duty and underway, c) A fishing vessel fishing while underway, d) All of these.

128) Regarding the visibility of special masthead 360º lights. For vessels less that 50 meters, the visibility should be _____ miles and for vessels over 50 meters, the visibility should be _____ miles.

a) 3 and 4, b) 2 and 3, c) 1 and 2, d) 4 and 5.

129) Anyone found guilty of negligence or failing to conform to the Bridge to Bridge Radiotelephone Regulations can be fined not more than:

a) $500, b) $1,000, c) $15,000, d) $2,000.

130) The River and Harbor Act of 1899 imposed a maximum fine of how much for dumping refuse into harbors and rivers?

a) $500, b) $1,000, c) $1,500, d) $2,500.

131) Indicate which of the following is a distress signal:

a) A flashing yellow light, b) A flashing white light, c) A red parachute flare, d) All are distress signals.

132) The ones aboard any vessel exonerated from neglecting to comply with the Rules are:

a) The Captain,, b) The Owners, c) The Crew, d) None of these are exonerated.

133) "Inland Waters" in the Rules means;

a) Navigable water of the United States, b) Waters shoreward of the demarcation lines, c) Bays, Sounds, Rivers and Great Lakes, d) All of these.

134) Inconspicuous, partly submerged vessels or objects being towed must have attached an all-round white light visible for:

a) One mile, b) Two miles, c) Three miles, d) Four miles.

135) The diving signal for a boat with divers down on a night dive is:

a) The same as restricted maneuverability, b) An anchor light in accordance with the size of the vessel, c) Two red vertically arranged all-round lights over the side the divers are down, d) A flashing strobe light above the cabin top.

136) Which type of vessel listed is not required by law to have a radio aboard?

a) A dredge, b) A vessel 300 gross tons, c) Any vessel carrying passengers for hire, d) Vessels of less than 100 gross tons carrying passengers for hire.

137) Two vessels are within sight of each other and approaching. Which signal does not apply?

a) Five short, but rapid flashes of a white light, b) Two short blasts on the whistle, c) Four short blasts on the whistle, d) Five short blasts on the whistle.

138) You detect a vessel on the radar one-quarter off your port bow. What action do you take first?

a) Slow down, b) Go around, c) Sound five short blasts on your whistle, d) Sound one short blast on your whistle.

139) Power-driven vessels operating on the Great Lakes may substitute an all-round white light in place of:

a) A forward masthead light, b) The after masthead light, c) The sternlight, d) The after masthead light and sternlight.

140) A power-driven vessel bound down river on the Great Lakes or Western Rivers:

a) Has the right-of-way, b) Shall initiate passing signals, c) Chooses the manner and place of passage, d) All of these.

Indicate the give-way craft in each case below.

141) A or B, 142) C or F, 143) D or F, 144) G or H, 145) I or J, 146) E or I, 147) E or J, 148) K or I, 149) C or D.

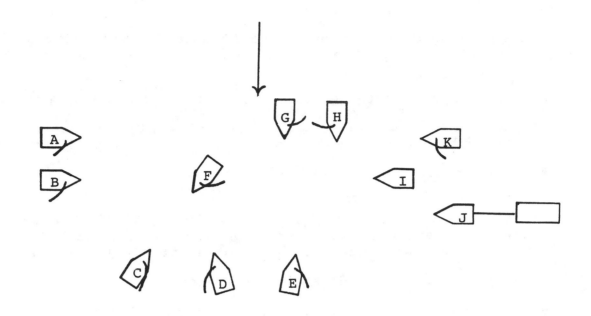

150) A power-driven vessel bound down river on the Great Lakes or Western Rivers:

   a) Has the right-of-way, b) Shall initiate passing signals, c) Chooses the manner and place of passage, d) All of these.

151) In a crossing situation, a single blast by either vessel means:

   a) I intend to alter my course to starboard, b) I intend to leave you on my port side, c) I will maintain course and speed, d) Any of these.

152) The Rules of The Road consider a "vessel" as:

   a) Boat, b) Non-displacement craft, c) Sea plane, d) All of the above.

153) A partially submerged tow displays which of the following?

   a) A black ball, b) A black diamond, c) A yellow around light, d) Red all around light.

154) A towing light is:

   a) An all around light, b) A light over the stern, c) A white light, d) A yellow light.

155) Which of the following vessels does not show sidelights?

a) A vessel not under command, b) A becalmed sailboat, c) A fishing vessel with no way on, d) A dredge.

156) Which of the following signals can you use when you see another vessel head-on in restricted visibility?

a) One prolonged followed by two short blasts, b) Two prolonged followed by two short blasts, c) One short blast, d) One short, one prolonged, one short blast.

157) If you hear one prolonged followed by 4 short blasts, you assume:

a) A manned barge under tow, b) A return signal by a vessel in a narrow channel, c) A pilot vessel on duty, d) Two trawlers, fishing as a team.

158) A vessel restricted in ability to maneuver must, in addition to the restricted visibility lights, show which of the following?

a) Masthead lights, side lights, stern light, b) Side lights, identity lights and stern light, d) Stern light and identity lights, d) Masthead lights, side lihts, stern light, and identity lights.

159) A safe speed shall be determined by which of the following?

a) Experience of the crew, b) Maneuverability of the vessel, c) Construction of the hull, d) All of the above.

160) Which of the following is not a distress signal?

a) A yellow-orange smoke signal, b) A hand held flare, c) A continuous raising and lowering of outstretched arms, d) Green star shells.

161) Maneuvering lights flash:

a) Two seconds apart, b) A minimum of 15 seconds between signals, c) Flash simultaneous with the whistle signal, d) All of the above.

162) A 110 meter vessel anchored in a fog would display which signals at night.

a) Two anchor lights-one forward and one aft, b) One anchor light, c) Two anchor lights one each fore and aft and deck lights, d) Anchor lights fore and aft and yellow fog lights fore and aft.

163) Meeting situation in Rule #14 covers:

a) Only motor driven vessels, b) Vessels on reciprocal courses, c) Risk of collision, d) All of the above.

164) Which is not a legal distress signal?

a) Red parachute flare, b) Green stars, c) Pyrotechnic rocket, d) A flag with a black square and ball.

165) Which of the following would be considered Inland Waters:

a) Within one mile of any ocean shoreline, b) Lakes in any state, c) Within one mile of any islands, d) The Great Lakes Boundary between U.S. & Canada.

166) In an inland narrow channel, which of the following apply?

a) Avoid anchoring in the channel, b) Keep channel on your port side, c) Do not restrict the passage of vessels restricted in their ability to maneuver, d) All of the above.

167) A vessel is considered restricted in ability to maneuver:

a) By the nature of their work, b) With a deep draft, c) Extraordinary circumstances, d) All of the above.

168) A tug pushing or towing alongside on Western rivers must show a minimum of which lights?

a) Towing light, stern light and side lights, b) Towing lights, side lights and masthead lights, c) Side lights and towing lights, d) Masthead lights, sternlight, towing light and sidelights.

UNIFIED TEST KEY

1) B	28) D	55) A	82) C	109) B	136) D
2) B	29) A	56) B	83) B	110) A	137) C
3) D	30) C	57) D	84) A	111) C	138) D
4) C	31) A	58) B	85) D	112) A	139) D
5) D	32) D	59) C	86) A	113) C	140) D
6) B	33) A	60) D	87) A	114) A	141) A
7) D	34) B	61) C	88) B	115) C	142) C
8) D	35) C	62) D	89) C	116) D	143) F
9) B	36) C	63) C	90) C	117) D	144) H
10) B	37) D	64) A	91) D	118) C	145) J
11) B	38) D	65) D	92) B	119) C	146) I
12) A	39) D	66) C	93) B	120) A	147) J
13) B	40) B	67) D	94) D	121) D	148) K
14) D	41) C	68) A	95) C	122) D	149) C
15) B	42) D	69) A	96) C	123) C	150) D
16) B	43) a	70) B	97) D	124) C	151) D
17) A)	44) C	71) D	98) D	125) B	152) D
18) D	45) B	72) A	99) C	126) A	153) B
19) C	46) A	73) A	100) B	127) D	154) D
20) D	47) D	74) C	101) C	128) B	155) A
21) D	48) C	75) A	102) B	129) A	156) C
22) A	49) B	76) D	103) B	130) D	157) C
23) A	50) D	77) B	104) B	131) C	158) A
24) B	51) A	78) C	105) D	132) D	159) B
25) A	52) C	79) B	106) D	133) D	160) D
26) C	53) D	80) C	107) B	134) C	161) C
27) C	54) C	81) A	108) B	135) A	162) C
					163) D

164) B	
165) B	
166) D	
167) A	
168) C	

THE INTERNATIONAL QUIZ

True or false.

1) Approaching a 25 meter vessel from the stern, you could not tell if it was a tug towing or a power-driven vessel.

2) An 11 meter pleasure boat engaging in a towing operation need not show special towing lights.

3) Tug boats show two vertically arranged towing lights when towing astern.

4) A sidelight shows an arc of 112º.

5) The day signal for being aground is three black balls.

6) In a crossing situation, sailboats have the right-of-way over powerboats.

7) White masthead lights have an arc of 225º.

8) A vessel displaying 360º vertically arranged lights of red-white-red could be servicing aircraft.

9) A basket on the yard of a fishing vessel indicates she is less than 50 meters in length.

10) Flashing yellow lights, flashing at 60 fpm, are used only by purse seiners and hover-craft.

11) Trawlers never use yellow lights.

12) Sailboats under sail never use white masthead lights.

13) Sailboats must sound maneuvering signals.

14) A black cone with the apex pointing up is used exclusively by fishing vessels.

15) Two cones, apex-to-apex, are used as dayshapes by fishing vessels in excess of 50 meters in length.

16) All fog signals in International waters are given every two minutes.

17) A tug boat, restricted in ability to maneuver, does not have the right of way over a deep draft vessel in a narrow channel.

18) Two black balls are the dayshape equivalent of the night signal of two 360º vertically arranged red lights.

19) The only light needed in a rowboat at night is a flashlight.

20) Hit and run at sea can cost you $1,000 fine and a year in jail.

21) Trawlers and purse seiners show green over white 360º vertically arranged night signals when fishing.

22) Navigation lights are never used between sunrise and sunset.

23) Two short blasts means you are coming left.

24) Towing lights on tugs are used only when the tow is being pushed, or is alongside.

25) A 5 meter sailboat and small rowboats do not need sidelights.

26) A sailboat utilizing the masthead option of red over green 360° vertically arranged special lights cannot use combined sidelights.

27) Sailboats can use sidelights and sternlights totaling 360°.

28) A stand-on vessel, upon hearing one blast from a vessel off her port side, returns the one blast and maintains course and speed.

29) A sailboat in restricted visibility and on a starboard tack, sounds one short blast every two minutes.

30) Vessels anchored in a fog must sound their respective signals every minute.

31) Vessels underway, but stopped in a fog must sound two prolonged blasts every minute.

32) Two prolonged blasts followed by two short blasts is the signal of a vessel wishing to overtake a vessel in a narrow channel.

33) The corresponding night signal for three black balls, is three red 360° vertically arranged lights.

34) A black diamond shape is used only on tugs when the tow is 200 meters or more astern.

35) A cone, apex down, is an optional signal for a sailboat with sails up but engine running.

36) Vessels should cross traffic patterns at a right angle to the pattern.

37) Joining and departing a traffic pattern should be done at a narrow angle.

38) Black diamonds are found only on tugs and barges while underway.

39) A black cylinder displayed at the forepart of a vessel gives that vessel the right of way over buoy tender.

40) There is no signal in International waters called a "special flashing light".

MULTIPLE CHOICE

41) Masthead lights have an arc of:

   a) 225°, b) 112.5°, c) 135°, d) None of these.

42) The masthead light of a 25 meter sailboat would become visible within:

   a) 1 mile, b) 2 miles, c) 3 miles, d) None of these.

43) Masthead lights on a tug showing four white lights from dead ahead would have masthead lights which are visible at least:

   a) 3 miles, b) 4 miles, c) 5 miles, d) 6 miles.

44) Approaching from aft of 22 1/2° abaft the beam of a 19 meter craft the light you see should be visible for:

a) 1 miles, b) 2 miles, c) 3 miles, d) 4 miles.

45) A five meter sailboat underway may show minimum lights of:

a) A stern light, b) An electric torch, c) An electric torch and sidelights, d) All of these are required.

46) A six meter outboard making 6.5 knots must show at least:

a) Sidelights, b) A sternlight, c) A 360° white light aft, d) An electric torch.

47) Air cushion vessels underway show a special 360° light which is:

a) Yellow, b) Blue, c) Red, d) Flashing yellow.

48) Tugs must have a sternlight and towing light when:

a) Pushing, b) Towing astern, c) Towing alongside, d) All of these.

49) A black cylinder at the forestay of a vessel indicates:

a) Not under command, b) Deep draft in narrow channel, c) Aground, d) A sailboat underway with engines running.

50) A black cone, apex up, means the vessel is:

a) Towing, b) Sailing, c) Fishing, d) Tending buoys.

51) A rapid ringing of the gong is a type of restricted visibility signal required:

a) On small craft, b) On vessels of 100 meters or more, c) On all buoy tenders, d) On some large vessels, and then only when aground.

52) To which of the following vessels would a sailboat not be obligated to give way?

a) Trawler, b) Purse seiner, c) A vessel trolling, d) Buoy tender.

53) A vessel showing three vertically arranged 360° red lights has the right-of-way over:

a) A CG Buoy Tender, b) A survey vessel, c) Both of these, d) Neither of these.

54) A vessel laying a submarine cable would show the dayshapes of:

a) Black balls, b) Black diamonds, c) Black cone(s) d) Both a & b.

55) Visibility is restricted and you hear two prolonged blasts. This could be:

a) A trawler, b) A dredge, c) A Buoy Tender, d) Any of these.

56) A heavy fog closes in. You should travel:

   a) At a safe speed, b) At a moderate speed, c) At a speed enabling you to stop in half the distance of visibility, d) With lookouts posted fore and aft.

57) A fishing vessel is anchored and fishing in a fog. She sounds the same signal as what other anchored vessel:

   a) A sailboat, b) A vessel restricted in ability to maneuver, c) A vessel not under command, d) All of these.

58) Which two vessels sound one prolonged and two short when working at anchor.

   a) Fishing and restricted in ability to maneuver, b) Restricted in ability to maneuver and not under command, c) Not under command and fishing, d) Any of these.

59) Restricted visibility and you detect a vessel forward of your beam:

   a) Maintain course and speed, b) Slow down, but maintain steerage way, c) Stop and wait until your intended path is clear, d) Back down.

60) One prolonged and two short blasts in a fog would indicate:

   a) A minesweeper, b) A vessel aground, c) Pilot vessel on station and on duty, d) Power vessel underway with way on.

61) Five vertically arranged 360o white lights is the signal for:

   a) A tug over 50 meters in length, b) A tug showing optional towing lights, c) An oil platform, d) A series of mooring buoys.

62) Aft of 22 1/2o abaft your starboard beam you hear one short blast. Without looking you assume:

   a) A sailboat on a starboard tack, b) Someone is sounding a crossing signal, c) A vessel intends to come right, d) Someone wants to pass.

63) When determining safe speed in restricted visibility which of the following conditions should be considered:

   a) State of the current, b) Background lights from shore, c) Traffic density, d) All should be considered.

64) Flown from the forward mast or stay, which code flags indicate distress?

   a) Alfa-bravo, b) November-Charlie, c) Delta-Tango, d) Hotel-Lima.

65) A minesweeper on duty has the right-of-way over:

   a) A tug with tow, b) A CG buoy tender, c) A survey vessel, d) A vessel repairing a submerged marine railway.

66) Trawlers fishing have the right-of-way over:

   a) Sailboats, b) CG buoy tender, c) Vessel constrained by draft, d) A fuel tanker transferring cargo.

67) A swallow-tailed blue and white flag could claim:

a) Scuba divers from a dive boat, b) A hard-hat diver working, c) An abalone boat or crew harvesting, d) All of these.

68) You hear a short whistle blast about 12 times. You suspect:

a) Danger signal, b) Doubt signal, c) Distress signal, d) A whistle is stuck.

69) Visibility is severely restricted. You can see only the lower deck of a vessel ahead which has two vertically arranged 360° white lights over the side. You infer:

a) A trawler shooting her nets, b) A mooring buoy, c) A vessel 50 meters or more aground, d) A vessel, less than 12 meters, underway.

70) A composite unit is lighted at night:

a) With special yellow flashing lights, b) With yellow lights, c) As any vessel her size, d) With applicable towing lights.

71) A ten meter powerboat may show which minimum lights when operating at night?

a) Anchor light, b) Sidelights, c) 360° light aft & sidelights when available, d) 360° white light aft and sidelights.

72) A 10 meter sailboat must show which of the following?

a) A sternlight, b) A 360° masthead light, c) A range light, d) A flare-up light.

73) Regarding the diagram at the right, vessel "A" should sound:

a) One short blast, b) Two short blasts, c) Three short blasts, d) None of these.

74) You detect a vessel on your radar during a heavy rain storm. You should:

a) Sound one prolonged blast, b) Stop and proceed with caution, c) Take early action to avoid close quarters situation, d) Sound five short blasts.

75) The restricted visibility signal involving three distinct strokes on the bell, followed by a rapid ringing of the bell, then another three distinct strokes is associated with what type of vessel?

a) A vessel of 100 meters or more in length, at anchor, b) A vessel of 100 meters or more in length underway in restricted visibility, c) A vessel aground, d) A vessel of 100 meters or more, aground.

76) The lines of demarcation are indicated by:

a) Applicable aids to navigation, b) Nearest breakwater, pier or jetty, c) Lines drawn across harbor entrances, d) Notice to Mariners.

77) A give-way vessel overtaking a stand-on vessel sounds two short blasts then passes the vessel ahead:

a) Port side to, b) Starboard to starboard, c) Port to port, d) starboard side to.

78) Restricted visibility and you hear one prolonged blast forward of your beam. What action do you take?

a) Stop engines, b) Refrain from changing course, c) Commence plotting by radar, d) All of the above.

79) One short blast from an overtaking vessel means:

a) I am coming right, b) When can I pass? c) I am going to pass you, d) Request permission to pass.

80) Note the diagram to the right and indicate which the give-way vessel should not do:

a) Make stern-way's b) Come to port, c) Come right, d) Decrease speed.

81) You sight a vessel lights, all of which are 360°. One high white light is forward, two red vertically arranged lights amidships and a lower white light aft. This vessel is:

a) Towing a submerged object, b) Aground, c) Servicing buoys, d) Moored over a wreck.

82) A sailboat is towing another vessel in a heavy fog. The signal the sailboat should sound is:

a) Two prolonged and one short, b) Whatever a sailboat should sound as a sailboat, c) One short-one prolonged-one short, d) One prolonged blast.

83) A white light flashes three times on a vessel. This means the vessel:

a) Is attempting to pass in a narrow channel, b) Sailboat flare-up claiming right-of-way over power craft, c) Vessel backing down, d) Vessel leaving a pier, dock, berth or wharf.

84) A vessel trolling would avoid which type of craft?

a) Sailboat, b) A tug restricted in ability to maneuver, c) Trawler with nets down, d) All of these.

85) A vessel approaching you at a relative angle of 210° avidences which of the following situations?

a) Overtaking, b) Crossing, c) Head-on, d) Collision.

86) Certain vessels are encouraged to use inshore traffic zones at all times. These are:

a) All small craft, b) Sailboats and vessels less than 20 meters in length, c) Only sailboats, d) Only vessels less than 20 meters.

87) Inshore traffic zones are not normally used by:

a) Through traffic, b) Large cargo vessels, c) Vessels bound for distant ports, d) All of these.

88) Which type of vessels would normally enter a separation zone or cross a separation line?

a) Crossing traffic, b) Down-bound traffic, c) Inshore traffic, d) None of these.

89) A vessel approaching you at a relative bearing of 115°:

a) Is a stand-on vessel, b) Is a give-way craft, c) Could see your green sidelight at night, d) Could not see your sternlight at night.

90) Vessels pushing or towing alongside could show a maximum of how many masthead lights?

a) one, b) two, c) three, d) four.

91) The dayshape for a submerged or partially submerged vessel being towed greater than 200 meters astern is:

a) None, b) A black diamond, c) Two black diamonds, d) The Bravo flag.

92) Vessels restricted in their ability to maneuver, when underway and making way, must also display which lights?

a) Masthead lights, b) Sternlights, c) Sidelights, d) All of these,

93) A working minesweeper underway must exhibit which lights in addition to her special three green lights?

a) Masthead, stern and sidelights, b) Stern and sidelights only, c) Masthead lights according to her length, d) No additional lights are needed on a minesweeper.

94) How far should a vessel on approach stand clear of a minesweeper?

a) 500 meters, b) 1,000 meters, c) 1500 meters, d) 1 mile.

95) A diveboat must be less than how many meters before being exempt from displaying the dive flag?

a) 7 meters, b) 12 meters, c) 16 meters, d) No length is an automatic exemption.

96) A pilot vessel underway, on duty and lighted as a pilot vessel is exempted from displaying:

a) Side and sternlights, b) Masthead lights according to her length, c) Both of these, d) Neither of these.

97) All vessels aground are required to display proper signals indicating their dilemma except vessels less than:

a) 12 meters, b) 20 meters, c) 50 meters, d) All must show the signal.

98) Which one of the vessels below, when anchored away from channels, fairways and anchorages is exempted from displaying an anchor light?

   a) 6 meters, b) 11 meters, c) 19 meters, d) None of these are exempt.

99) Backing out and/or getting underway from a dock, berth, pier or wharf you sound:

   a) One short blast, b) One prolonged blast, c) Three short blasts, d) None of these are required.

100) When a tug is pushing a rigidly connected tow in restricted visibility the tug shall sound which signal every two minutes?

   a) One prolonged blast, b) Two short, one prolonged, c) Two prolonged, one short, d) One prolonged, two short.

101) When attempting to attract attention, what type of light should be avoided?

   a) Alternately flashing yellow lights, b) Spot lights, c) Strobe lights, d) Flares.

102) Which vessel is not considered restricted in maneuverability?

   a) Severely restricted tug, b) Carrier launching aircraft, c) Minesweeper, d) Not under command.

103) Maneuvering signals are not sounded when two vessels:

   a) Are within sight of each other, b) Are obscured from each other by intervening obstructions, c) Are sailboats, d) Do not have to change course.

104) A seaplane navigating on the water is considered:

   a) Restricted in ability to maneuver, b) Equal in rights-of-way to any water-craft, c) Must remain within traffic patterns, d) Has right of way over water-craft.

105) Which of these dayshapes could be extended over the side of a fishing vessel?

   a)   b)   c)   d)

106) A small pleasure boat is crossing a shipping channel. To the right, the small craft skipper sees a cargo vessel approaching. The cargo vessel has the right-of-way because:

   a) The small craft is smaller, b) The small craft is crossing an inshore traffic zone, c) The small craft is more maneuverable, d) Small craft should not hinder large vessels in traffic lanes.

107) A black ball is the dayshape for:

   a) Anchored, b) Distress, c) Adrift, d) A buoy tender.

108) A 55 meter tug without a tow needs how many masthead lights?

   a) 1, b) 2, c) 3, d) 4.

109) A fishing vessel is working her nets in fog. She sounds:

a) One prolonged blast, b) Two prolonged blasts, c) One prolonged, two short blasts, d) One short, two prolonged blasts.

110) A rowboat can show which lights at night?

a) The same as a sailboat, b) A flashlight, c) Either of these, d) Neither of these is required.

111) The dayshape of two black diamonds could be seen on:

a) A dredge, b) A tug with tow over 200 meters astern, c) A fishing vessel, d) A vessel 100 meters or more in length, at anchor.

112) Vessel "A" in a narrow channel signals the vessel ahead, "B", with two prolonged and one short blast. "B" replies with five short blasts. "A" should:

a) Wait for "B" to reply with one prolonged-one short-one prolonged-one short, b) Keep signaling for permission to pass, c) Try a signal to pass on the other side, d) Try contacting by radiotelephone.

113) You are in charge of a motor vessel and off the starboard side at night you see a green light and masthead lights. The highest masthead light is to the left of the lower one. What action do you take?

a) Stop, b) Maintain course and speed, c) Come right, d) Come left.

114) A fishing vessel, with no way on, and fishing, does not show which lights listed below?

a) Sternlight and sidelights, b) Masthead lights, c) Both (a) and (b) is correct, d) Neither (a) nor (b) is correct.

115) What is the maximum length a power vessel can be and still use combined sidelights?

a) Less than 7 meters, b) Less than 12 meters, c) Less than 20 meters, d) Less than 26 meters.

116) The stand-on vessel shall deviate from course and speed when:

a) The other vessel's action is not sufficient to prevent collision, b) The other vessel's actions are erratic, c) The give-way craft has sounded no signals, d) The other craft has sounded the wrong signals.

117) A disabled vessel towed alongside shall exhibit which lights?

a) No lights are required, b) Masthead lights, sidelights and sternlights, c) The outboard sidelight and sternlight, d) Sidelights and sternlight.

118) Restricted visibility and you detect another vessel forward of your beam. Who has the right-of-way?

a) You do, b) He does, c) Assume he does because you are in doubt, d) Neither vessel has the right-of-way.

119) When you see a vessel displaying a ball-diamond-ball dayshape in vertical order it means you should:

a) Stay out of the way, b) Be restricted in maneuverability, c) Recognize the vessel is claiming special right-of-way, d) Any choice is correct.

120) What is the basic difference between maneuvering lights on International waters and those of Inland waters?

a) International does not use the white light, b) The rules are reversed, c) Inland uses yellow or white, International only white, d) There are no differences.

121) At night you observe a red light northeast of you.   That vessel is heading:

a) North, b) West, c) South, d) East.

122) You are in charge of a motor vessel and off the port side at night you see a red light and masthead lights.   The highest masthead light is to the right of the lower one.   What action do you take?

a) Stop and back down, b) Come right, c) Come left, d) Maintain course and speed.

"An excursion to the offshore islands, Mam? Certainly, and have no fear. All the way over we won't be more than a half-mile from land." Straight down.

INTERNATIONAL QUIZ KEY

1) F	28) F	55) D	82) B	109) C
2) T	29) F	56) A	83) C	110) C
3) F	30) T	57) B	84) D	111) A
4) F	31) F	58) A	85) A	112) B
5) T	32) T	59) B	86) B	113) B
6) T	33) F	60) A	87) D	114) C
7) T	34) F	61) C	88) A	115) C
8) T	35) F	62) D	89) B	116) A
9) F	36) T	63) D	90) C	117) D
10) F	37) T	64) B	91) C	118) D
11) T	38) F	65) A	92) D	119) A
12) T	39) F	66) A	93) A	120) C
13) T	40) T	67) D	94) B	121) B
14) T	41) A	68) C	95) D	122) B
15) F	42) D	69) A	96) B	
16) F	43) D	70) C	97) A	
17) F	44) B	71) D	98) A	
18) T	45) B	72) A	99) B	
19) T	46) C	73) D	100) A	
20) T	47) D	74) A	101) A	
21) F	48) B	75) C	102) D	
22) F	49) B	76) C	103) D	
23) T	50) C	77) D	104) B	
24) F	51) B	78) C	105) C	
25) T	52) C	79) A	106) D	
26) T	53) D	80) B	107) A	
27) T	54) D	81) B	108) B	

GENERAL KNOWLEDGE

This is the section wherein you prove your basic skills of navigation without resorting to a chart. You must demonstrate your ability to solve speed-distance-time problems, compass error and esoteric things like doubling the angle on the bow and computing deviation by utilizing a range. Also included is the U.S. buoyage system, tides, publications, and a little on weather.

As indicated earlier, this is a 90% quiz. While there is a substantial amount to master, the subject matter itself is not difficult. Probably less than 10% fail this part of the quiz the first time through the REC. You can expect a quiz from the Coast Guard containing approximately forty questions.

Yes, some does come under common sense. This means you might learn more from the quiz than from the text itself. The old adage still applies; if all else fails, read the question.

One big problem is the new International Association of Light House Authorities, (I.A.L.A.). This is not exactly a group of little old men wearing baseball hats and driving around in pickup trucks. Rather, this is an attempt to instill some form of standardization for buoys on an international basis. Unfortunately, the entire system is not scheduled to be completed until 1989. This is more than merely painting the black buoys green. The point is, you need to know which one the CG is going to use in their exam. The "old system" seems easier to many of us because we are accustomed to it. In short, as indicated in the introduction to the system, check with your local office to see what their pleasures are. Maybe you won't have to master both the old and the new.

That's right...**time**. Everything goes by the 24 hour clock. You know, military time...navy time, or whatever. This means the clock doesn't start over again at noon. Each one of the 24 hours in the days has its' own special number. Compare these.

These first	Then these
0200 = 2:00 A.M.	1235 = 12:35 P.M.
0230 = 2:30 A.M.	1259 = 12:59 P.M.
0615 = 6:15 A.M.	and one minute later
0900 = 9:00 A.M.	we have
1000 = 10:00 A.M.	1300 = 1:00 P.M. which
1159 = 11:59 A.M.	is really correct
and two minutes	because that's the
later we find:	13th hour of the day.
1201 = 12:01 P.M.	2000 = 8:00 P.M.
don't forget	2359 = 11:59 P.M.
1200 = 12:00 A.M. (noon)	2400 or 0000 = 12:00 P.M. (midnight)

All of which leads to a thing called elapsed time. How long it takes to get from point "A" to point "B". Here are a few for practice. First whip out your trusty 3 x 5 card and cover up the answers in the right column and try to figure how much time has gone by from Column #1 to Column #2.

Col #1	Col #2	Col #3
DEPARTURE	ARRIVAL	ELASPSED TIME
0400	0700	3h
0230	0530	3h
0315	0545	2h 30m
0345	0515	1h 30m

Right! That last one is still a subtraction problem, but you have to borrow. Watch.

84

The catch is to be aware that the first two columns on the left are reserved for hours only. The two columns on the right are for minutes. If you do any borrowing, you must borrow one of the hours on the right and convert it to sixty minutes. Then add the sixty minutes you borrowed to the minutes you already have on the right. Regarding the last example above. From 0345 to 0515 means you line them up like this:

```
            0515

            0345

            ---------
```

However, you can't take 45 minutes from 15 minutes. So, you borrow one hour from the five hours on the **top left**. Take that hour, convert it to 60 minutes, then add it to the 15 minutes you already have on the top in the minutes column. That makes for 4h 75m. Now you can subtract.

```
            0475

            0345

            ----------
```
0130....or more appropriately, 1h 30m...length of time which has elapsed since, you got underway.

Before going any farther, try these. **And forget your calculator on this.** The calculator goes by tenths, hundredths, thousandths, etc. Time goes in units of 60. Again, cover up column 3.

#1	#2	#3
0630	0728	58m
0630	0732	1h 02m
1130	1330	2h
1159	1442	2h 43m
1000	1658	6h 58m
2300	0100	2h
2250	0210	3h 20m
2009	0308	6h 59m

DISTANCE ON A CHART

This is the simple one. Pull out the big book chart and grab your dividers. On the **right** side of the chart near the bottom is 34° of latitude. From 34° to 34° 10' is ten nautical miles. There! Wasn't that simple?

Go ahead. Count them. Ten spaces. Ten miles. What's the catch, you ask? Well, so maybe there's a couple. 1) You have to be able to measure the distance to the nearest **tenth** of a mile. Something like using an old fashioned slide rule. With a little practice you'll be surprised at how adept you can become. 2) On a regular large chart you must be sure to use what is called the "mid-lat" to take your measurements. This means you should use that part of the chart closest to the distances you are measuring.

In other words, if you're going to measure from the Anacapa Light to the Bunny Isle Light, use the measurements in that general area. Don't go to the top of the chart to measure this particular distance. Spread the dividers so they stretch from Anacapa to Bunny. Right on the respective dots. Without opening or closing the dividers, slide them gently over to the right side. Place one point on the 34° mark and notice where the other point falls on the small grid. How many miles? Would you buy 12.2 miles? Try another one.

How about Cavern Point to Anacapa Light? Spread dividers between them then make your camparison on the side of the chart. Either side-just so you don't budge the dividers and keep in the general area of the bottom of the chart when you take the measurement. Did you get 10.3 miles? You don't have to indicate "nautical miles". If you are measuring on a **chart**, everyone understands you are talking about nautical miles. If it's on a **map**, that's statute miles.

Curious? O.K. A statue mile is 5,280 feet. A nautical mile is 6,076 feet.

Here's some more for limbering up. No fair standing on your head to read the answers before you've completed them all. And don't get sore because you have to look for most of these fictitious places. You will have to become acquainted with this chart and know it as well as your own. Might as well start now.

1) Try a long one first.   Draw a line from Santa Barbara Point Light to the West Point Light on Santa Cruz Island. Then spread your dividers on the **side** of the chart to equal ten miles.   Walk off the ten mile increments, counting as you go, then measure the remaining small distance and add everything together.

Or you can do what I do.   I don't trust dividers, so I use a metric ruler. This particular distance came out 21.4 centimeters (cm).   Then I measured off that much on the side of the chart to get the answer.

2) Try from Spa Rock Light to Brockway Point Light on Santa Rosa.

3) Go from Brockway Point Light to West Point Light.

4) Santa Barbara Bell Buoy (Fl G) to Bunny Isle Light, **thence** to West Point
   Light.   State the total distance.

5) Now try something more like what you find on a regular coastal chart.   Go
   from the Spa Rock Light to the Anacapa Light.

> **Required reading for victims of death at sea due to collision: The Rules of The Road.**

ANSWERS
1) 21.4 M, 2) 19.8 M, 3) 11.9 M, 4) 43.6 M, 5) 42.8 M.

SPEED, DISTANCE AND TIME

How accurate should answers be in the CG exam as regards speed, distance and time? The traditional standard of accuracy says you should have speed to the nearest tenth of a knot, distance to the nearest tenth of a nautical mile and time to the nearest minute.

Don't hesitate to use your trusty hand-held calculator, but make sure you don't show up for the test with weak batteries.

If you are to know the **speed** the boat is going and assuming no fancy electronic gear is aboard to give you an automatic read-out, then you must first know the distance covered and the length of time taken to cover said distance.

For example: if your boat makes 6 miles in 30 minutes, then you're travelling at a **speed** of 12 knots. Or: Speed = 60 x the distance divided by time. The 60 is used to make things come out to the nearest minute of time. As a formula it looks like this:

$$S = \frac{60 \times D}{T}$$

Then, we replace the letters with numbers which apply to this particular case:

$$S = \frac{60 \times 6 \text{ (miles)}}{30 \text{ (minutes)}}$$

The rest is arithmetic which is where your calculator comes in:

$$S = \frac{360}{30} = 12 \text{ (knots)}$$

If this is so simple it's insulting please keep in mind we're starting from the bottom here and not all of us remember everything learned in eighth grade math. Besides, we're using whole numbers. Let's mix it up a little.

Here is the same problem, only this time assume that "time" is the missing factor. The equation for **time** is:

$$T = \frac{60 \times D}{S}$$

Again, we replace the formula letters:

$$T= \frac{60 \times 6 \text{ (miles again)}}{12 \text{ (knots)}}$$

The last step looks like this:

$$T= \frac{360}{12} = 30 \text{ (minutes)}$$

That takes care of finding **time** which assumes you know the distance travelled and the time underway.   We have also covered **speed**-which assumes you know the distance covered and the time underway.

There's only one left. This time assume we know how long under way and the speed of the boat.   Now, we're looking for **distance**.

Formula looks like this:

$$D= \frac{S \times T \text{ (speed times time)}}{60}$$

Numbers replace the letters:

$$D= \frac{12 \times 30 \text{ (minutes)}}{60}$$

$$D= \frac{360 \text{ (12 times 30)}}{60}$$

$$D= 30 \text{ (miles)}$$

We now have three formulas:

Now all you have to do is remember the formulas!

Not easy? Like you might get "tied up" in the exam room and pull a big fat blank? Try this:

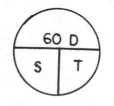

Suppose you were missing...say, "time". Put a finger over the "T" in the diagram above and look what's left. 60D written **over** the "S", right? The term 60D means multiply 60 by the distance. Since the 60D is "over" the "S" that means multiply sixty times the distance **then** divide by the speed of your craft. Your answer will come out in minutes. You need to express the answer in hours and minutes, so divide the answer (the minutes) by 60. Don't divide it on your calculator. Do it on paper. Your answer will be in hours. The remainder is the minutes left over.

Maybe you will have to measure the distance on your chart first, but the assumption is that you know your departure point and your destination.

If you need to find speed, cover up the "S". What's left? 60D **over** "T". Multiply the two factors 60 and your distance, then divide by the time. **Before you divide by time, make sure time is expressed in minutes...**not hours and minutes.

What if the "distance" was missing? Just cover up the upper portion of the circle leaving "S" and "T" next to each other. Letters next to each other infer multiplication. After you have multplied the value given for "S" and "T" **don't forget to divide by 60.** Then round off your answer to the nearest tenth. In other words, if your final answer came out: 45.67, you would round off to 45.7, because the numeral in the hundredths column (7) is more than 4. If the final answer was, say 45.64, then drop the four to get 45.6

Don't scoff at using the numeral "60" all the time. If you try reducing hours to fractions or decimals without using the 60, sooner or later one of your rounding off items wouldn't jibe with the "pure" answer and the Coast Guard will be waiting for you.

Time for the big trial. Try this one: Assume your boat speed to be 10 knots. You have been underway for 2 hrs. and 15 minutes (after this time will read like 2h 15m) so the question is how **far** have you travelled? Now, don't look any further down the page until you have at least tried.

Multiply speed (10) by the time-135 (minutes), then divide by 60.
    22.5 nautical miles, right?

Now try one when you're trying to find the speed of your boat. The assumption is you know how far you have travelled and how long it took. Make the distance 78.6 miles and the elapsed time 6h 14m.

That makes for something like this: 60 x 78.6, (4716) then divide by your time underway which was 374 minutes. 4716 divided by 374 = 12.61. Since the last numeral, the one in the hundredths column is less than 4, you drop it, rounding off to 12.6 knots.

Go for one on time. Assume underway at a speed of 13.6 knots having travelled a distance of 34.6 nautical miles.

That means you must multiply that distance of 34.6 miles by 60, which yields 2076. That number gets divided by your speed of 13.6, producing an answer stating 152.65. Now what?

That 152.65 is an answer in minutes. Your answer has to be to the nearest minute. So round off. You should get 153 minutes. Now break it down into hours and minutes. **Not on your calculator.** Do it the long hard way...you know, with one of those things called a pencil. Dividing 60 into 152 yields an answer of 2 hours with a remainder of 32. The 32 is the minutes remaining. Hence, a final answer of 2h 32m.

Here's three of each kind. All mixed up. The answers are at the bottom of the page. Do them **all** before you look up any answers. You will learn more that way and reveal any weak spots. There are plenty more in the test.

1) Distance is 15.2 miles on your chart and the time to make the run is 2hr 10m. How fast were you going?

2) The distance covered is 47.9 miles and you're making 13.2 knots. How long did it take you?

3) You have 3h 2m to cover 55.8 miles. How fast must you go?

4) You're hauling it out at 18.6 knots for a distance of 74.8 miles. How long did it take you to make the trip?

5) Underway for 4h 19m at a speed of 12.5 knots. How far?

6) Travelling at 14.6 knots for 3h 47m. How far?

ANSWERS

1) 7.0 knots, 2) 3h 38m, 3) 18.4 knots, 4) 4h 01m, 5) 54.0 miles, 6) 55.2 miles.

The Coast Guard will not expect you to define the physics of tides...you know, interaction of sun and moon, etc. However, you will be expected to know the basic vocabulary and how to read a tide table.

On the west coast of the U.S., we have four "tides" per day; two lows and two highs. The highs are seldom equal within a day's span. The lows are also different each time hence, they are called **mixed tides**. There are also two round trip tides on the east coast, but they are more consistent in the highs and lows each day, hence the term **semidiurnal** is used. Examine the tide sketches on the next few pages. They will stick in your mind better than mere words.

The term "Datum Level" is the depth you find written on the charts. The tide doesn't get much lower than this. That's handy to know. The depth indication on a chart means anything dangerous will be indicated at what is **almost** the lowest tide. When the tide **does** get lower than the charted depth, it's called a "minus" tide. Datum level also means "charted depth". The term **Datum Level** is the one used in the Tidal Block of all charts. Pick up one from your own area and study the writing in the Tidal Block which is found in the Title Block of charts.

East coast chart tidal blocks state the depth of the water is computed from "Mean Low Water", which is a way of saying someone took the **daily** lows from the last **nineteen years** of data and averaged them up. "Mean" is another way of saying average. The Charted Depth, or Datum Level -the numbers on the charts- is thus established for any given year. The few low tides falling below the datum level are called **minus tides** and are indicated by a minus sign "-". If higher than the datum level, a plus sign "+" is **sometimes** used. Look again at the next two pages of diagrams before continuing. If no sign is used, assume a "+".

On the west coast the lowest of the two lows is used to compute the averages. In west coast chart tidal blocks you will therefore find the words; "mean lower low water."

Now for some more vocabulary. The **range** of any tide is from one high to the next low, or vice-versa. When the tides are extremes (higher highs and lower lows) you have what is termed **Spring Tides**, which has nothing to do with March,

●DAILY TIDES●

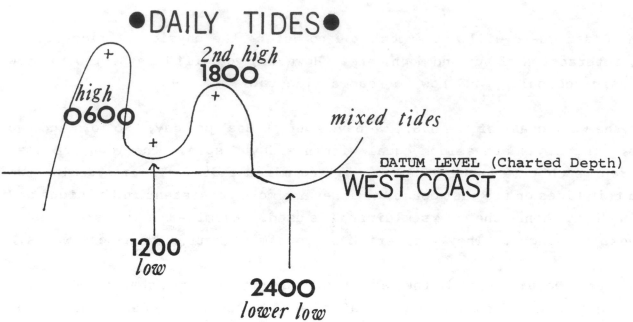

high
O6OO

2nd high
18OO

+

+

mixed tides

DATUM LEVEL (Charted Depth)

WEST COAST

1200
low

2400
lower low

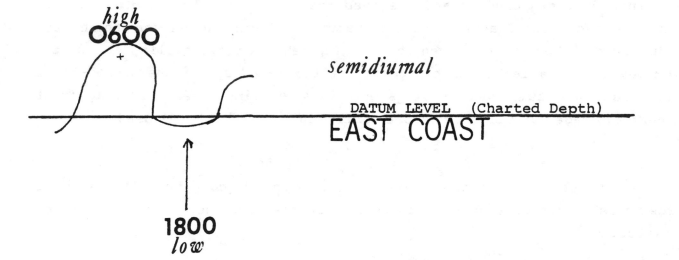

high
O6OO

+

semidiurnal

DATUM LEVEL (Charted Depth)

EAST COAST

1800
low

•TIDE DIAGRAMS•

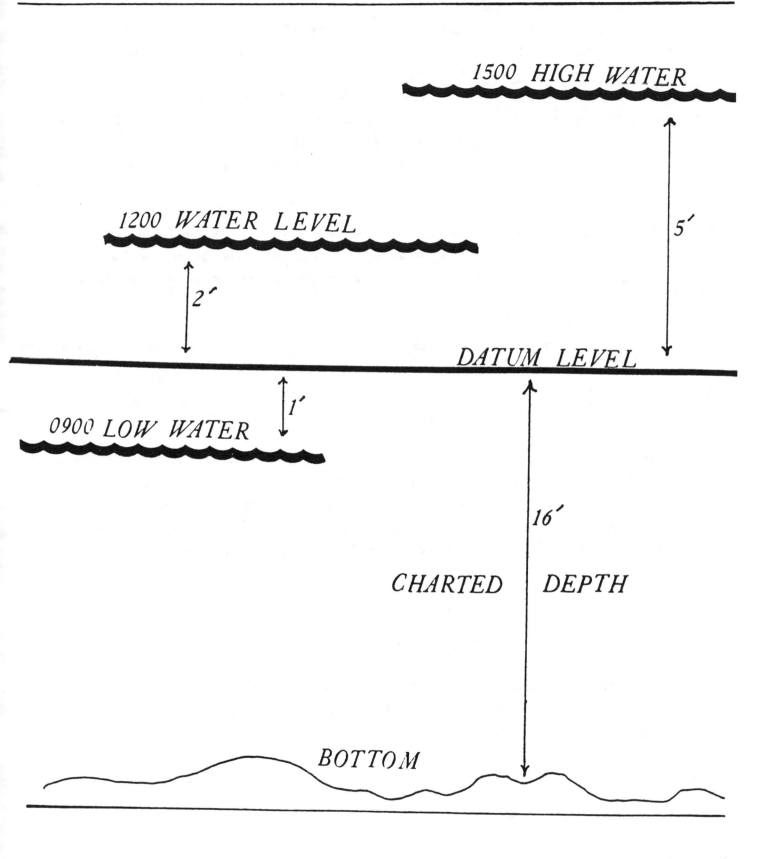

April or May. When the range between high and low tides is minimal, they are called **Neap Tides**. If you like mind benders, lower highs and higher lows!

To publish tide tables containing every port along any given coast would require a wheel barrow to carry them around. Instead, local commercial tide tables, the kind with a lot of advertising in them, are acquired from the local bait shop. The CG won't stand still for this. It means someone looked up Portsmouth, Maine and made an interpolation for Kittery. The CG will often want you to be able to read an official Tide Table; the kind published by the NOS. This means you have to make the interpolations by yourself. No big deal.

First, there is a major port listing the times and heights of the tides which are expected to occur there each day. These major ports are called **Reference Stations**. Pick out the applicable reference station to your harbor and apply a few simple computations to your **own** harbor which is listed as a **Subordinate Station**.

Glancing at our tidal abstract at the top of the next page containing **only** subordinate stations, find #949 which is Stellacoom. Stellacoom is a subordinate station based on tides found in **Seattle**. The reference station of Seattle is **not quoted** on this page. Instead, we'll make them up.

If Seattle experienced a high tide of 6.2 feet, at 0815, Stellacoom's high tide could be determined by (look at Stellacoom on the table) adding 22 minutes - which would make it 0837 in Stellacoom- and +1.8 feet making it 8.0' at 0837. **CAREFUL:** The CG delights in leaving off the "+" mark in their exams which confuses some people into believing they should subtract. Careful-subtract only when the "-" sign is indicated.

Do it again. (1) Give the time and height of Stellacoom's low tide when (let's say) Seattle's **low** tide occurs at 1430 and -1.5.

(2) Then try the times and heights for **both** high and low tides on #967, Sheltor, Oakland Bay, based on the Seattle's high (let's say) of 4.9 at 1935, and her following low of -1.2 at 0135.

Answers: (1) 1505 with a low of -1.5

(2) Hi of 7.7 at 2047 - Low of -1.4 at 0329.

No.	PLACE	POSITION		DIFFERENCES				RANGES		Mean Tide Level
		Lat.	Long.	Time		Height		Mean	Di-urnal	
				High water	Low water	High water	Low water			
		° ′ N.	° ′ W.	h. m.	h. m.	feet	feet	feet	feet	feet
				on PORT TOWNSEND, p.94						
	WASHINGTON—Continued									
	Admiralty Inlet—Continued			Time meridian, 120°W.						
897	Port Townsend (Point Hudson)--------	48 07	122 45	-0 04	-0 04	+0.3	+0.1	5.3	8.6	5.2
899	Marrowstone Point--------------------	48 06	122 41	+0 09	+0 07	+0.5	0.0	5.6	8.8	5.3
901	Oak Bay------------------------------	48 01	122 43	+0 15	+0 29	+1.0	+0.1	6.0	9.4	5.6
	Puget Sound									
913	Point No Point-----------------------	47 55	122 32	-0 16	-0 16	*0.92	*0.92	6.7	10.4	6.1
915	Port Madison-------------------------	47 42	122 32	-0 08	-0 08	+0.1	0.0	7.7	11.4	6.6
917	Poulsbo, Liberty Bay-----------------	47 44	122 39	+0 02	+0 08	+0.6	+0.1	8.1	11.9	6.9
919	Brownsville, Port Orchard-----------	47 39	122 37	+0 02	+0 08	+0.4	0.0	8.0	11.7	6.8
921	SEATTLE (Madison St.), Elliott Bay--	47 36	122 20	Daily predictions				7.6	11.3	6.6
923	Eighth Ave. South, Duwamish River---	47 32	122 19	+0 05	+0 07	-0.1	0.0	7.5	11.1	6.5
945	Home, Von Geldern Cove, Carr Inlet--	47 16	122 45	+0 27	+0 39	+2.3	+0.2	9.7	13.6	7.8
947	Wauna, Carr Inlet--------------------	47 23	122 38	+0 20	+0 36	+1.8	0.0	9.4	13.1	7.5
949	Steilacoom--------------------------	47 10	122 36	+0 22	+0 35	+1.8	0.0	9.4	13.1	7.5
951	Hyde Point, McNeil Island-----------	47 12	122 39	+0 23	+0 41	+2.1	+0.2	9.5	13.4	7.7
953	Sequalitchew Creek, Nisqually Reach-	47 07	122 40	+0 24	+0 42	+2.1	+0.1	9.6	13.4	7.7
955	Longbranch, Filucy Bay--------------	47 13	122 45	+0 26	+0 39	+2.2	+0.1	9.7	13.5	7.7
957	Henderson Inlet---------------------	47 09	122 50	+0 27	+0 45	+2.6	+0.2	10.0	14.0	8.0
959	Vaughn, Case Inlet------------------	47 20	122 46	+0 35	+0 47	+2.8	+0.2	10.2	14.1	8.1
961	Allyn, Case Inlet-------------------	47 23	122 49	+0 27	+0 46	+2.8	+0.2	10.2	14.1	8.1
963	Walkers Landing, Pickering Passage--	47 17	122 56	+0 35	+0 47	+2.9	+0.2	10.3	14.3	8.1
965	Arcadia, Pickering Passage----------	47 12	122 56	+0 35	+0 54	+3.0	+0.2	10.4	14.4	8.2
967	Shelton, Oakland Bay----------------	47 13	123 05	+1 12	+1 54	+2.8	-0.2	10.6	14.2	7.9
969	Burns Point, Totten Inlet-----------	47 07	123 03	+0 36	+0 54	+3.6	+0.2	11.0	15.0	8.5
971	Rocky Point, Eld Inlet--------------	47 04	123 01	+0 34	+0 52	+3.3	+0.3	10.6	14.7	8.4
973	Dofflemyer Point, Budd Inlet--------	47 08	122 54	+0 29	+0 47	+3.1	+0.2	10.5	14.4	8.2
975	Olympia, Budd Inlet-----------------	47 03	122 54	+0 31	+0 46	+3.1	+0.2	10.5	14.4	8.2

On #1, the addition factor under Seattle is 0.0, so the low will be the same as for Seattle.   On the time, we added 35 minutes.

On #2, the addition factor to Seattle's high of 4.9 is 2.8 to give you 7.7 feet.   The time difference is 1 hr 12 min.   Add the 1h 12m to Seattle's time of 1935 and you should get 2047.

On #2 for the low tide, add -0.2 (under Shelton's low tide) to Seattle's low of -1.2.   That should produce a low of -1.4.   The time difference for the low (between Seattle and Shelton) is 1hr 54m.   Add this 1hr 54m to Seattle's low tide time of 0135 and you get 0329.

Now this.   A Reference Station indicates a low of 0.8 feet at 2305.   The subordinate station indicates the difference to be -2.2 with a time difference of one hour three minutes.   Give the time of the low and the height of the tide.

Solution: Not yet...try it yourself first.   Add 1h 03m to 2305 giving a time of 0008.   (There's no such thing as 2408, dummy.)   Take -2.2 from 0.8 for low tide. And just how in #@%$&)* do you do that, you ask? Stand by.

Draw a horizontal line on a piece of paper. That's the Datum Level.
Charted Depth, if you like. Put a smaller line just above it to indicate the 0.8
of the Reference Station. If you go from 0.8 just above the line, to the line
below it-the first line you drew-you have travelled 0.8 of a foot. That's **part**
of the -2.2 you need to cover. How much farther do you have to go? Forget the
"-" sign for a minute. Subtract 0.8 from 2.2. 1.4, right? Now put the minus
sign back and you get -1.4, because there isn't room here to teach algebraic
addition, subtraction and integers.

- - - - -

We call her Tadpole because of the wiggling tail piece. When she showed up in
the Charter Skipper class the first night I knew I wouldn't have to worry about
absenteeism. By then, she was a regular around the harbor, but not for long.
She's a short girl with tight brown curls all over her head. She has an
exceptionally small waist and things get neat and curvy going both ways from
there. She barely avoids arrest by wearing two pieces of string around the
harbor and that mahogany tan is flat out vulgar. I later learned she was
educated to be a school teacher, but after a year of the heebie jeebies she
landed in Santa Barbara with a few saved dollars and decided to stay. A short
time later she had come a long way from starting out with paint and varnish work
and putting names on boats. Now she's licensed.

Tadpole works a scalene triangle and does it with real panache. Late spring and
summer finds her in Santa Barbara working the charter boats. Dive, fish or
sight-seeing; she doesn't seem to care. When fall rolls around she stuffs things
into a deep straw bag and pushes it under the seat of a jet heading for Hawaii.
Sometimes she works the Cats off Kona, sometimes Oahu or Kauai's north shore.
Before leaving she unwinds for a few weeks on Kauai by hiking over the Kalalau
trail to her favorite beach. That beach is like a lot of Santa Barbara beaches;
no one calls the cops if you forget the strings. In late December, after the
hurricane season, she heads for Mexico or the Virgins.

Down there she works those Vacation Clubs where everyone is always smiling and
only one string is required even during working hours. Tadpole loves smiling
people. She runs a boat and teaches water skiing to N.Y. and L.A. refugees. I
asked her once why they hire U.S. licensed skippers in those foreign places.
She explained that those Clubs have to carry liability insurance and only the
U.S. or G.B companies will underwrite it. One of their requirements is the use
of licensed skippers. I can't help feeling she makes a nice ornament for the
Clubs.

I learned that Tadpole works her triangle on a declared income the government
would consider poverty level. She keeps her needs as slim as her waistline and
saves a lot of money doing it. She likes to be paid in cash and generally is.
We won't talk about her tips. Last year she paid cash for her own thirty footer
to charter and live aboard while in California. When away, she bare boats it
through a boat rental agency. She's a girl you could easily hate. Or emulate.
Now get back to work.

PUBLICATIONS WE KNOW AND LOVE

1) Tide Tables   Dept. of Commerce
                                  National Ocean Survey

2) Current Tables   NOS

3) Light List   USCG

4) Coast Pilot   NOS

5) Notice to Mariners(Nat'l.)   Defense Mapping Agency
                                  Hydrographic Center
                                  (DMAHC)

6) Local Notice to Mariners   USCG

7) Sailing Instructions   DMAHC

This may seem silly, but frequently on the tests the CG asks who publishes what. Better know them just in case. Oh yes! Almost forgot. The Government Printing Office **prints** publications. However, the above agencies are the ones who **publish** the books and phamphlets.

Congratulations. You have just finished laboring through another section. Get through and understand the next quiz and the rest is duck soup. Here's your next teaching aid. Otherwise known as the General Knowledge Quiz. Like the others, go slow. Don't be discouraged with your score the first time around. It's what you **learn** from the test and how you do in subsequent tries that really counts.

WEATHER ADVISORIES

Pennants are red.   Large outer squares are red.   Inner squares are black.

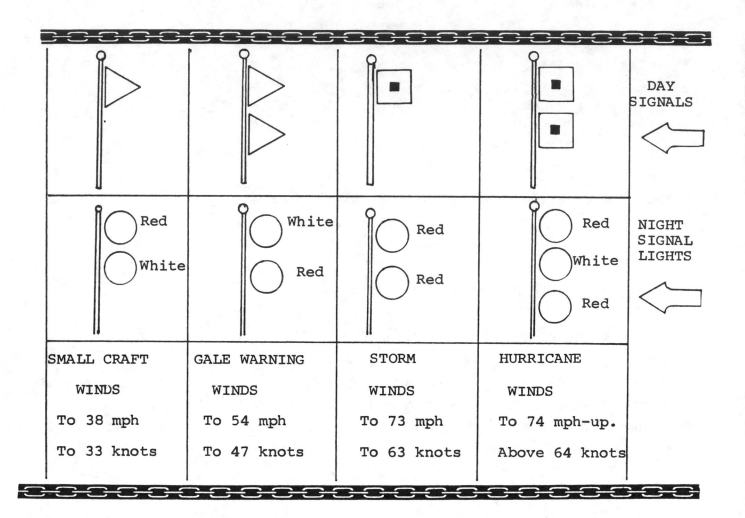

SMALL CRAFT	GALE WARNING	STORM	HURRICANE
WINDS	WINDS	WINDS	WINDS
To 38 mph	To 54 mph	To 73 mph	To 74 mph-up.
To 33 knots	To 47 knots	To 63 knots	Above 64 knots

Don't try to memorize all of the wind forces.   Commit the mph to memory.   If they ask for **knots,** multiply the appropriate mph wind speed by 0.88

THE LATERAL BUOYAGE SYSTEM

That's a fancy term for buoys marking channels.   They are maintained by the U.S. Coast Guard.   The emphasis here will be on the important points that are incorporated into the CG tests.   Since no two REC's are alike, it is difficult to pinpoint the emphasis in **every** area.   However, all of them stress certain facts.   That's what you will find here.   Unfortunately, the so-called "Lateral Buoyage System of the U.S." is on the way out.   The new I.A.L.A. (International Association of Lighthouse Authorities) commenced replacing the "old" system in 1983 and the CG says this will be completed by 1989.   The Great Lakes, at this writing, are due to be completed very soon.   In short, you have another dilemma.

Are they going to examine you on the "old" system or the new I.A.L.A. or both?   Here's another entry for page 238.   Write it down now.

The first impulse is to call and ask.   That's not always wise.   An answer over the phone -which can be denied or revoked- isn't half as good as a letter. Amazing what you can do when something's written on paper.   Incidentally, that goes for **any** questions you may have for the CG.   **Get it in writing.**

The cautious candidate will wish a copy of a government publication entitled, "Chart Number One" obtainable at any chandlery.   It would be presumptuous of us to try to match the artwork therein, but we can sure put an extra dent in the explanations.   The CG feels the same about the art so they seldom have pictures of the buoys in their exams.   **The tests use the standard chart symbols for the buoys.**   You might get one or two hasty sketches at the most.

| White | Black | Red | Green | Blue |

This is the color code for the buoys following

Whip out your feltips.   It will help.

1) The nun.   Red in color, of conical shape.   This buoy is numbered evenly (2,4,6,etc.) and is passed starboard side to when entering from sea.   Thus, it marks the right side of the fairway when entering from sea.   "Red right returning."   The numbers progress evenly from the fairway entrance.   The closest one would probably be "2", the next a "4", etc. on up the channel.   Note examples to the left on this page.   Remember, **anything in quotation marks means that is what is printed right on the buoy.**

2) The can.   Black in color and looks like a large tin can. Odd numbered.   Pass to starboard when **LEAVING** the harbor. It marks the right side of the channel when leaving port. A nautical way of putting it sounds a bit different.   The black buoys are on your **starboard hand** when bound towards the sea.   Inference is that you should be between the red and black buoys favoring the right side of the channel.

3) The third type of **unlighte**d buoy is little more than an upright telephone pole afloat and sticking out of the water.   Like the others, it's anchored on the bottom by a block of cement and a long chain reaching to the bottom of the buoy.   These are almost always upstream in shallow water.   Upstream, in the shallows, nuns and cans can be dragged under by swift river currents so these long poles are more visible.   They are called spar buoys and denoted by the letter 'S' on charts. Unlike the nuns and cans, spar buoys are used on either side of the channel.   However, they are red if on the right when returning from sea and black on the left.

C "7"

N "4"

C "7"
Ref

N "6"
Ra Ref

Anything denoting a buoy, that is a floating navigation marker, is indicated by a diamond shape. The dot beneath the diamond is the exact location of the buoy. Again, the chart symbol will show quotation marks for anything written on the buoy. Therefore, the first one is a can with the number "7" printed thereon. The second is a nun with a "4" on it, the third one is a can with a "7" and a reflector. On black buoys, this reflector will be green in color, but could be white. Never red. A red reflector would appear only on a red nun. But, a red nun could sport a white reflector. Hence; cans-green or white reflectors; nuns-red or white reflectors. Number four is a red nun with a "6" printed on it and has a radar reflector attached.

RB
N

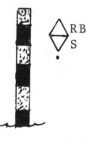

RB
C

RB
S

4) There's something else about nuns, cans and spars with which you should be familiar. They can be banded, that is, horizontal stripes. Among other things, this means they will have **no numbers**. When banded, they mark a channel junction where vessels crossing might collide. They are also used to indicate there is an underwater obstruction in the area. You should consult your chart immediately to determine the obstruction. These buoys are not directly over the obstruction. On the contrary...they mark the **preferred channel**. Hence, if banded, leave them on your port hand. Look closely at the diamond used to denote a floating aid to navigation. Notice the **horizontal** line across the center of the diamond? This means it's banded.

When a nun is banded, the top band is always red. If it's a can, the top band is black. If a spar is banded, it's on the side of the channel indicated by the top band. Red - right side going up. In all cases, the buoy will be banded its entire length with black and red bands. Remember - no numbers when banded. Sometimes the CG calls these, "bifurcation" buoys.

When a nun, can or spar has **vertical** black and white stripes, it marks the middle of the navigable channel. Appropriately enough, it's called a "mid-channel buoy".

LIGHTED BUOYS

When located in a harbor, fairway or channel the color implication is the same. Upon returning from seaward, reds are on the right, blacks are on the left. Except these are larger buoys, lighted either white, green or red and have certain varying light characteristics.

The chart symbol for any lighted buoy is different than an **un**lighted buoy. Remember the dot beneath the diamond indicating the exact location of the buoy? When the buoy is lighted, this dot will have a circle around it and colored magenta on your chart. At night, on many large military and civilian craft, the bridge is kept dark to preserve night vision. The only lights allowed are red. Frequently called "battle lights", these red lights turn the magenta color on a chart to black. Easier for the navigator to see.

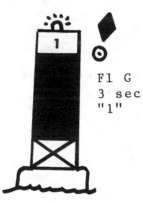

1) Black buoys, when lighted, have either green or white lights. If the light is white, the color is **not** indicated on the chart! You must assume it's white. Black buoys with lights are numbered odd, like cans. The numbers will become progressively greater up the channel. These buoys, because they have battery or gas power, are frequently equipped with fog horns or some other audible signal. Some have bells or whistles which are activated by a surging sea.

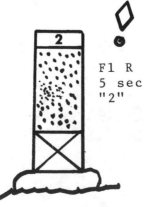

2) Lighted red buoys are pretty much the same. The light is either red or white. If the color of the light is not mentioned on the chart, again, assume white. They are numbered like the nuns; even only. Because lighted buoys are so large (due to the power plant) they are sometimes called "sea buoys" but not all are located at sea. Many are a long way up river.

3) Black and white **vertically striped** buoys, whether nuns, cans, spars or lighted sea buoys, are used to mark the middle of the channel. Like their nun, can or spar counterparts, which can also be striped black and white, they are called mid-channel buoys. The lighted mid-channel buoy is assigned an exclusive flashing signal. The chart symbol indicates an **Mo A**, meaning it flashes the morse code "A" signal. Dit-dah, dit-dah, dit-dah, or if you like, short long, short long, short long. This buoy will also have a letter printed on it, as indicated by the quotation marks on the chart symbol. This one has an "L". Now inspect the diamond on the chart symbol. Notice this time the line through the diamond is **vertical**, indicating vertical stripes. Guess what the BW stands for.

4) Interrupted quick flash means they flash at least 60 times per minute. You might see five quick flashes, then a pause and then another five quick flashes. This is somewhat attention getting and meant to be. This means you are facing either a fairway junction where other craft may be approaching or there is is a dangerous obstruction in the channel. Sound familiar? Right, this is the lighted counterpart to the nun, can or spar obstruction and channel junction buoy described above under **un**lighted buoys. The lighted buoy is also banded, hence the initials RB in the chart symbol. The **RB** on the chart is sometimes used even when the top band is black. Notice the diamond on the chart symbol? There's that horizontal line across the middle of the diamond. Banded horizontally.

Summarized: Vertical black and white bands with MoA (if lighted) means mid-channel. This buoy, in the lighted version, would have an identifying letter, e.g. "L" or "Q". This letter would be in quotation marks on the chart symbol for the light.

Black and red bands (horizontal) with Int. Qk. Fl. means junction or obstruction or maybe even both. Only letters if banded. No numbers.

6) There are also **five can-type** unlighted buoys for special designations. These buoys are maintained by local governments rather than the CG.

C
WOr

a) White and orange indicating special purpose. WOr Horizontally banded and special purpose is written right on this buoy. For example: 5 knots; No Swimming; Water Skiing; Nude Beach ... things like that and these are generally tended by the local city, harbor force, country, etc. Not the CG.

C
Y

b) An all yellow can buoy is a quarantine area where incoming ships anchor to be cleared by the port captain or a physician. Keeps the incidence of leprosy and bubonic plague down to a minimum!

C
W

c) An all-white buoy is an mooring buoy, and may have a letter or something written on it. Generally these are private permanent moorings.

C
BW

d) Black and white **HORIZONTALLY BANDED** is a marking for a fish net area. Don't go between two of these or your prop will chop things up. Don't confuse this beauty with the mid-channel buoy described above which is black and white **VERTICALLY STRIPED.**

C
GW

e) Green and white horizontally banded can buoys are to be found in a dredging area. Stay clear.

7) Now comes the upriver daymarkers. These daymarkers are little more than pilings driven into the river bottom. On the pilings are mounted small signs. On the right side going upstream you will find they are shaped in the form of triangles. On the far left side-for people coming downstrean-they are square. These are double-faced so they can be seen going both ways.

The ones on the right-going upstream-have a red color and are numbered even. The squares on the left side (going up) are black... with a green border and are numbered odd.

Figures. They are replacing the nuns and cans.

Funny thing about the **chart symbols** used to represent
these daymarkers. They are **both** triangular in shape!

LIGHTS AND AIDS ASHORE

All lights ashore...that is immobile and not floating around, are
designated on a chart by a teardrop.

We are referring now to marine oriented lights, not those atop huge TV
transmitting antennas or aero beacons. If you examine a chart carefully
you will notice that these types of lights use different symbols.

Some lights ashore are **major lights** showing not only the light's
characteristic flash but also the color, how high the light is from the
water **at mean high tide** and how far the light can be seen with the naked eye
at sea level. Jump off your boat, into water and get your eyes even with
surface. Fl 2sec

Some of these major lights might be equipped with a Radio Beacon. The
symbol looks like this:

Fl R 5sec
R Bn 302 ... _...

Basically that's two concentric circles. Note the dot representing the
position of the light is **exactly** in the center of the inner circle. Compare
symbol to this one:

Fl G 10sec
R Bn 285 ... _

In the case above the dot representing the position of the light is not
precisely inside the inner circle. Sounds like we're splitting hairs, but
that's the difference between a major light equipped with a radio beacon and
one which is **NOT**. In your Local Knowledge exam you might be asked to name
several major lights in your area equipped with radio beacons. If the dot
is a little off center from the inner circle it means the small house or
shack which houses the radio beacon is different from the position of the
light itself.

Time to take out the charts for your area and look over the lights, buoys and navigational aids. Learn them and their characteristics. Don't try to memorize the light characteristics of all the buoys in your area...just the major ones and those marking port or harbor entrances. Also check your local area in the government publication called "The Light List". In foreign waters it's called "The List of Lights". Some REC's let you use this when taking your Local Knowledge part of the exam. If so, it would help to know these things in advance. Also, learn to use the index in the Light List, otherwise you could be in that office all day thumbing through pages.

Then go to your latest edition of the **Coast Pilot** and read over your area of operation. CG takes a lot of questions out of that volume. Take some notes.

THE UNIFORM STATE BUOYAGE SYSTEM

Last of all is the "Uniform State Buoyage System". The states are responsible for the upkeep of the buoys and all states are now using the same system. These are found on rivers, lakes and recreation areas. Not in the ocean. They are rather simple and how extensively they show up in your test should be proportionate to the number of such water bodies of this type there are to be found in your section or district. Briefly:

1) Obstruction buoy. Red and white with vertical bands. Away from shore, that is, the obstruction would be between this buoy and land.

2) South and West. White buoy with red top. Pass this buoy on the south or west side.

3) North or East. White buoy with black top. Pass this buoy on the north or east side.

4) Red or Black. If buoy is all red or all black, use the same method you would use in the U.S. System. Keep black ones to port and the red ones to starboard as you work **upstream.**

5) White buoy with blue band is a mooring area. Watch out for mooring lines dangling loose in the water and/or "spreader" lines between the mooring buoys which are often partially submerged and hard to see...also hard on the prop.

～～～～～～～

THE I.A.L.A. SYSTEM

This is the new system which is to be completed by 1989. The changes are not confusing if you look at the three types. Again, before you go to all this trouble, consider contacting your local REC to find out if they're examining on the new system, the old one or both.

1) **The Lateral Aids**

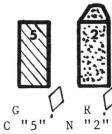

G
C "5"   N "2"

a) Nuns and cans will still be used on their respective sides of the channel and the numbering is still the same. They are still "lateral" aids, marking the sides of the channels. Red right- returning from sea. Progressively numbered moving away from the sea. The nuns are red, but the cans are **green** still maintaining the odd numbers and relative positions in the channel. The **chart symbols** are supposed to be even more complete, but this could take time. The diamond shape denoting the nun buoy will be red and the can symbol will be green. Quotation marks still indicate what is written on the buoy.

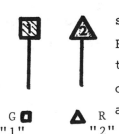

G ▪
"1"   ▲ R
         "2"

b) The daymarks -replacing nuns and cans upstream in shallower water- are almost the same as the "old" ones. Red triangles on the right, even numbered but with a red triangle for a chart symbol. Green squares on the left, odd numbered and a green square for chart symbol. How about the new buoys when they're lighted?

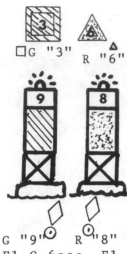

□ G "3"   R "6"

G "9" ⊙   R "8"
Fl G 6sec   Fl R
              5sec

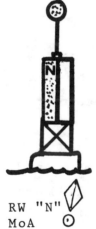

RW   SP "G"

RW "N"
MoA ⊙

GR   RG
C "D"   N "J"

c) Again, pretty much the same. The lighted "sea buoys" on the right will be red, but flash only red and have a red diamond for a chart symbol. The dot beneath the diamond – showing the buoys position– will still be circled with a magenta color. The counterparts on the left will be green and flash only green with a green diamond for a chart symbol and a magenta circle around the diamond's dot. The lighted aids will retain the standard numbering system shown in quotation marks.

d) Remember the black and white vertically striped buoy marking a mid channel? Now they will be **spherical** in shape and have vertical stripes of red and white. The chart symbol will have a vertical stripe running down the diamond and the letters SP by it. These new mid-channel buoys will also have **letters** printed on them. The corresponding daymark, upstream, will be an octagonally shaped sign. The left side will be white, the right side red. Chart symbols will be a square with the letters 'RW' beside it. They will have letters, so look for whatever is in the quotation marks. The lighted mid-channel buoy will also be red-white vertically striped and retain that special flashing light of MoA –morse code "A"–. The chart symbol will be a white diamond with a vertical line down the center. As always, they will have a letter printed on them.

e) The "preferred channel" buoys –or if you're technical type– the bifurcation buoys, are pretty much the same in that nuns and cans are still used. They still denote channel junctions and foul ground areas. Now, the buoys will have letters on them.

The nuns will have a top band –horizontal– of red, with a green band beneath the top red one. The can, on the other side, will have a top band of green with a red band directly beneath the green one. The chart symbol is indicated to the left. Note the 'RG' means 'red-green' on

the nun and 'GR' on the can for 'green-red'. At this
writing the NOS is rumored to be changing the chart symbol
from that which was first agreed upon. At first, the
nun's diamond on the chart symbol would be red on top and
green on the bottom. The opposite was to be the case for
the can. However, the Great Lakes, shared with Canada,
has encouraged a change in the chart symbol. Now, the
buoys **might** maintain the black fill in the diamond for the
cans and a magenta fill for the nuns. If your REC center
is going to use the new system on their exam, you should
check this out.

RG
"B"

GR
"A"

f) The upstream daymarks for these preferred channel
buoys will be triangles -with red borders- on the right
replacing the nuns. This triangle will have a letter and
be red on the top, green on the bottom. The chart symbol
will be a **white triangle** with the term 'RG' beside it with
the **letter** of the daymark -as usual- in quotation marks.
The can daymark replacement will still be square, but with
a green border. The interior of the daymark will be green
over red. This is obviously opposite of the triangles on
the right. The chart symbol will be a **white square** with
the term 'GR' and the letter of the daymark in quotation
marks. How about the lighted aid?

GR "C"   RG "B"
Fl G   Fl R
(2+1)   (2+1)

g) The lighted aid for the preferred channel used to be
Int. Qk. Fl. No more. Now its a composite group flash
called 2 + 1. This means it will flash twice, pause, then
flash once. The color banding will be the same as for the
nuns and cans.

h) Back to the new lighted lateral aids and the types of
flashing lights you will see on these buoys. And
remember, red buoys flash **only** red, green buoys flash **only**
green. Examine the small chart below. These are the
flashes the regular lateral aids -marking the sides of the
navigable channel- will show.

They will flash one of four light signals...or rhythms. The black line indicates the lighted phase.

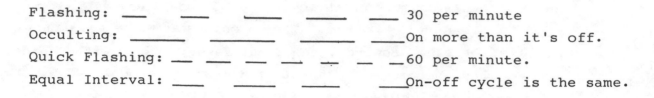

Flashing: ___   ___   ____   ____   ___ 30 per minute

Occulting: _____   _____   _____   ____On more than it's off.

Quick Flashing: __ __ __ __ _ _ _60 per minute.

Equal Interval: ___   ____   ____   ___On-off cycle is the same.

There are two other **types** of buoys involved in the new system. One is called "Special Aids To Navigation" while the other is "Regulatory" or "Information" type. Both are installed by cities or port commissions; not by the Coast Guard.

2) **The Special Aids**

T h e first type in this category is the yellow **unlighted** cans and nuns. They are positioned in the navigable waterway in the usual fashion for cans and nuns. The **lighted** equivalent will show **only** a yellow light. The gimmick is the light flashes these buoys **cannot** show is rather extensive. At this point we are not sure how specific the CG wants to be on this subject. They **could** get real nit-picky and if so, here's some more loaded lumber when the new system is fully operative.

These buoys **cannot show** Morse Codes "A" and "U". ("U" is dit-dit-dah.) Also prohibited is group flashing (2), isophase, (equally on and off), occulting, long flash, quick flashing, very quick flashing, group quick flashing, group very quick flashing, group quick flashing plus long flash, group very quick flashing plus long flash.

3) **The Regulatory and Information Marks**

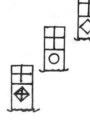

These are white and orange banded with symbols printed right on the buoys. The symbol will be a diamond for a danger area, a circle for a controlled area, and a cross-hatched diamond (lines running diagonally from corner to

corner) for exclusion areas. If lighted, they too must
show only a yellow light.

Would you like a color brochure on the new buoys?

Write: U.S. Department of Transportation, United States Coast Guard, 2100
Second St. S.W., Washington, D.C. 20593. Ask them for their pamphlet on,
"Modifications For A New Look In U.S. Aids to Navigation." If you are concerned
that the pamphlet isn't giving you everything, write:
Commandant (G-NSR-1/14), U.S. Coast Guard, Washington,D.C. 20593.

Also be advised that there is a very excellent laminated 8 1/2" X 11" card on
the market with the buoys, rules and whistle signals. It's called "Quick
Reference Navigation Rules" and sells for about $6.95. If not available,
contact Davis Instruments, San Leandro, CA 94578

- - - - -

Marina del Rey is where the big boats live in California when they can't find
room in Newport Beach. It's a very sterile environment where condos surround
pristine boats, sparkling docks and the crafts are mainly for cocktail parties
and sea stories. I know a charter skipper down there with the ultimate in
working convenience. He monitors the local classified and the L.A. Times.

When someone has a beautiful vessel for sale that doesn't seem to be moving
Archie -not his real name- invites the eager seller out to lunch. Archie
flashes his license and says, "Let me charter that boat for you." Oblivious to
the owner's disappointment in not have a hot buyer in hand, Archie continues.

"If you let me try it maybe we can cut a deal. You've got $50,000 tied up there
and the money's not working for you." This is a terrible sin in the rarified air
of stratified society. "Try depreciating that over five years and tell me how
much income tax you're not going to pay. You'll have a cottage industry that
won't quit and I'll be doing all the work. All you have to do is buy a wheel
barrow to cart if off to the bank. Ask your tax man about this kind of a deal and
watch him smile."

"Keep talking," says the mark, sitting back down and ordering another martini.

Archie continues. "You go get a dba -doing business as- from the county. Call
it something cute, like Pau Hana Charters. You plunk the money in for
advertising, fuel, upkeep, etc. and I'll run the boat for half. Now explain to
me how you're going to lose."

The last time I saw Arch, he had a real class act. Three sailboats ranging in
length from 25 feet to 72 feet and four power boats. He seldom goes out himself.
He goes windsurfing or lies on the beach with those sandy bottomed beach bunnies
while making marks in the sand to keep track of his skippers coming and going.
His skippers go fishing with the big boys from Tokyo, Munich, Rio and New York.

Arch has never owned a boat.

Why bother?

COMPASS ERROR

Compass error comes in two distinct types. Variation and deviation. The object is to compensate for these disturbing factors. Courses on charts are always plotted "true" from one point to the next. Straight up on a chart is always north...or more appropriately, $000°$ which is the same thing as $360°$. South is $180°$...down. West is $270°$, to the left. East is to the right, or $090°$.

The problem arises when we plot a course "true" on the chart and draw lines to where we want to go. Anyone with experience around boats will tell you that it's impossible to plot the course on the chart then expect the compass to take you directly there without a few simple arithmetic adaptations.

The adjustments are on paper. The object is to adjust the compass course to match the true course you have plotted on the chart.

Compasses are strange instruments...sometimes. They need two types of adjustment. Again; for variation and deviation.

VARIATION

Some compass error can't be helped. The earth's magnetic pull forces the compass card the wrong way. The compass card has small magnets mounted beneath it. This pull from the earth is called variation. Variation differs in different parts of the world. You have to look at the chart to determine what variation in that particular area is disturbing your compass.

Along the coast of California it varies from about 14 degrees down near San Diego to 18 degrees off San Francisco. On the west coast variation is always "east" meaning the magnetic attraction pulls the compass needle too far to the east. Too far from what? Too far from true...you know, straight up towards the north pole; the direction we call "true north". The ideal situation would be for you to live in an area which had no variation whatsoever. Unfortunately, those places are rare.

Charts are made with true north at the top. If we didn't want to do the paper work we would have to buy a new chart every time variation changed and that could get expensive. So we make all charts the same way and learn to compensate.

The local variation is printed in the centers of the compass roses which appear on every chart. This variation will affect your compass the same no matter which way your vessel is pointing. On the west coast the variation is always east so the correction is made in predetermined steps.

1) Plot your course "true" on the chart. Look at the next page and follow along. Say from Stud Island to Bunny Isle is true north or 000º.

2) Write down the true course on a scrap of paper. Since the compass needle is pulled 14º degrees east, too far to the right, simply subtract the variation from the true course.

3) 000º (or 360º) minus 014º variation = 346º.

4) Steer 346º by **compass** to travel 000º **true** to Bunny Isle.

Another one. What's the magnetic course to Spa Rock?

What's the magnetic course to Hot Tub Island?

Answers: Spa Rock = 003º, and Hot Tub = 331º.

DEVIATION

Things would be fine now if it weren't for another compass error. This other one is called deviation. Deviation is caused by various ferrous metals aboard a vessel and **generally** located less than three feet from the compass. They make a compass do strange things so you call in an expert to correct the compass as much as possible. To do this he will swing the ship completely around and check various course to see if they are correct. It's called "Swinging Ship" to correct for the deviation. If you want a compass adjustor, look in the yellow pages under "swinging deviate".

Unlike variation, deviation can change by the heading of the vessel. Different heading...different deviation.

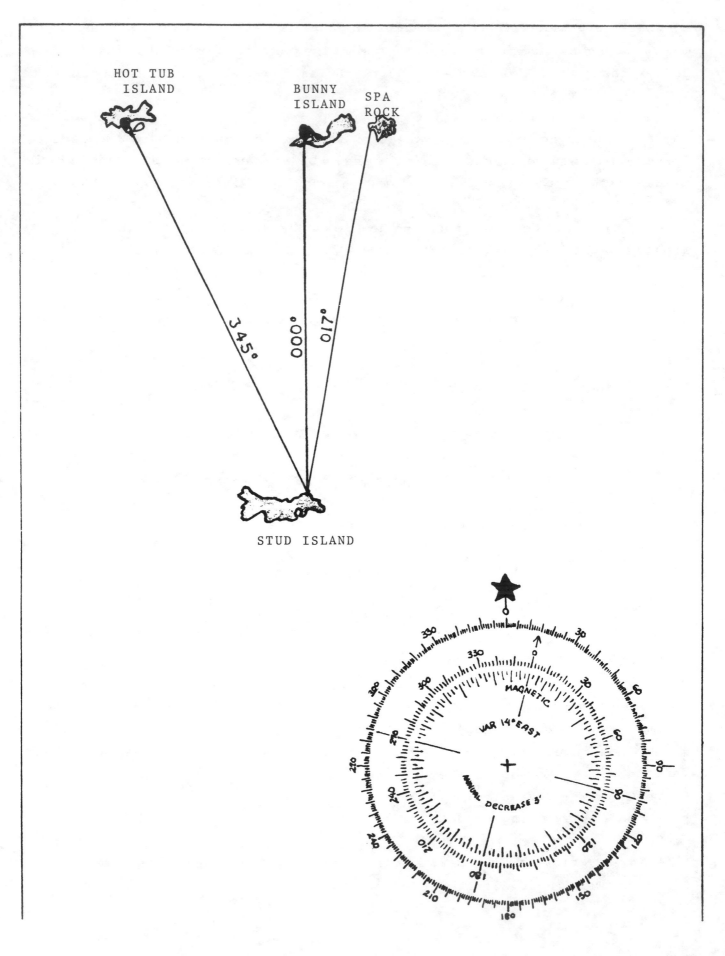

HOT TUB
ISLAND

BUNNY
ISLAND

SPA
ROCK

345°

000°

017°

STUD ISLAND

MAGNETIC

VAR 14° EAST

DECREASE 3'

Sometimes only limited correction is possible so the expert makes what is called a "deviation table". This table shows how far the compass is being pulled off from the magnetic reading on various courses. Most deviation tables worth their salt are calibrated for **at least** each 15 degrees of the compass. The table also indicates in which direction the needle is being pulled. You can then compensate (add or subtract) to get the reading on your compass to take you whichever direction you wish to go.

Let's assume you plot a course on a chart and find your destination is 175° true from your departure point. Also assume the local variation is 15° east. That means 175° – 15° = magnetic course 160°. Let's also assume the deviation table indicates the deviation on magnetic course 160° is 5° west. Thus, 160° + 5° = 165° to be steered on your compass. This course of 165°, then, really is the direction originally worked out on your chart. Make sure you express ALL courses with three digits, even if you only need one or two. Variation and deviation are expressed in only one or two digits.

```
True.....175°
Variation 15° E. (so subtract 15)
Mag.       160°
Dev.         5° W. (so add 5)
Compass   165°  (Compass course to steer in order
                 to make good 175° true.
```

In plotting, everything begins when you plot your course TRUE on the chart. With the subsequent arithmetic you eventually arrive at the course you are to steer by compass. The secret is in when you subtract and when you add. When working for compass course from TRUE TO COMPASS, westerly error is added to the course line and any easterly is subtracted.

Another example: Assume true course to be 285°. Variation (always east on the West Coast and west on the East Coast) is 15° E. Deviation for the magnetic course is 10° W. What compass course would you steer? (Incidentally, compass course is often referred to as PSC – per standard compass).

```
T 285⁰
V 015⁰ E (−)
M 270⁰
D 010⁰ W (+)
C 280⁰
```

On this course the westerly deviation almost made up for the easterly variation. And that's notable. When working DOWN from TRUE to COM-PASS always add west and subtract east. Or, as the old sea adage has it, so you don't forget the proper arrangement of letters:

```
T rue
V irgins
M ake
D ull
C ompany
```

So: **ADD WHISKEY**. "W-hiskey" or "W-est"... get it? Add.

Now if you "add" west that only means that if either error was east you would have to take the alternative...subtraction for east.

Could you reverse the method? That is, could you start with a compass and work your way back up to true? Try it, and this isn't just for fun. You need this. Starting at "C" or compass and moving "up" the TVMDC lineup, things would change a bit. You would have to **subtract** the **west**erly deviations and variations then **add** the **east**erly errors.

Back to T V M D C. Let's try a few practice problems. See if you can fill in the blanks. Please note: Calling for some westerly variation wasn't a mistake. The CG will throw both kinds at you no matter where you live. Good exercise for self-teaching...which indicates that if you have gotten this far, you're a prime candidate for the license. You've got tenacity and this thing must mean a great deal to you. Hang in and plow on.

The exercises following have blanks in various spots. The second section has the answers, so cover them up for now. Try to fill them in **before** looking up the answers.

T	015°	___	___	049°	137°	295°
V	15° E	14° W	1° E	15° W	7°W	___
M	___	___	015°	___	___	298°
D	___	6° W	3° W	10° E	5° E	5° E
C	345°	241°	___	___	___	___

- -

ANSWERS

T		221°	016°			
V						3° W
M	000°	235°		064°	144°	
D	15° E					
C			018°	054°	139°	293°

- -

TRY A FEW MORE

T	000°	010°	___	200°	___	___	265
V	___	___	15° W	___	014° E	10° W	8° W
M	345°	355°	200°	185°	036°	___	___
D	___	___	___	___	3° W	13° E	12° W
C	000°	000°	192°	172°	___	165°	___

- -

ANSWERS

T			185°		050°	168°	
V	15° E	15° E		15° E			
M						178°	273°
D	15° W	5° W	8° E	13° E			
C					039°		285°

General knowledge assumes you know how to check your compass using ranges. For example, if there were two buoys in your area also appearing on your chart you could find the course from one to the other using a course plotter on the chart.   You could then line up your boat, as indicated in the diagrams below, and check the accuracy of your compass.

Assume the two buoys line up on the chart 065° true.   Positioning your boat in line with the two buoys you glance at your compass.   Compass reads 055° and the local variation is 15° east.   Question: What's your deviation **on that particular course**?   This is little more than a T V M D C exercise.

T 065   The T V M D C lineup on your left indicates a blank
V 015   between Magnetic and compass. To get from magnetic of
M 050   050 to compass of 055, obviously you are going to add.
D ?   Add how much? Five degrees, right? Thus, five degrees
C 055   west is the deviation on **that** magnetic course.

Now turn your boat around putting the stern facing the same two buoys. Glancing at your compass it reads 225°.   Since you reversed the boat's heading it is 180° from the previous heading.   And here we have another T V M D C operation.

T 245   To get from the magnetic reading of 230° to the compass
V 15 E   heading of 225°, you must **substract** five degrees.
M 230   Answer: Five degrees east.
D ?
C 225

The object of this exercise is to determine how far offshore your vessel is, or how far off any given object you are such as a lighthouse or prominent landmark. The assumption is based on three things: 1) You can take two relative bearings on the object with the second bearing exactly twice the first; 2) you can compute your distance run between the two and 3) and you can keep the course and speed steady between the first and second sightings.

The term "relative bearing" has nothing to do with your compass heading. The direction of the object sighted might be 20° off your starboard bow, or 90° off your starboard beam. Relative bearings start at the bow working clockwise for 360° when you arrive back at the bow again. That's like holding your arm out pointing at the bow then turning clockwise -keep your arm out- until you're pointing at the bow again. Really doesn't make any difference which way the vessel is facing. Off the starboard beam it's always 90° relative. Astern is 180° relative. Off the port beam is 270° relative and 000° -or 360° - is dead ahead.

One at a time, examine the diagrams on the next page. Notice on #1 when the vessel was at point "A", the relative bearing off the object -"C"- ashore was 45° at 0900. The speed was 12 knots. At 0915, the object was 90° off your bow. Since two times the first bearing (45°) = 90° -which is also the second bearing- the angle was doubled. Here's the important point: The distance run between the bearings is your distance off the object at the second sighting. In this case, 3 miles. This always works out as long as you remember the second bearing must always be twice the first bearing.

Diagram #2 indicates the first bearing on the object ashore at 0330 was 40°. Speed was again 12 knots. The second bearing was doubled (2 x 40°= 80°)...thus the distance run between bearings matches the distance off the object on the **second** sighting taken at 0400. Six miles.

Diagram #3 shows the first bearing at 1345 to be 30° making 8.5 knots. The second bearing, made at 1405, was 60°. Was the second bearing twice the first? Can you compute the distance run? Answer to the first question is "yes". The distance run is S x T divided by 60. That's 8.5 x 20 (minutes) divided by 60. Ans. 2.8 miles.

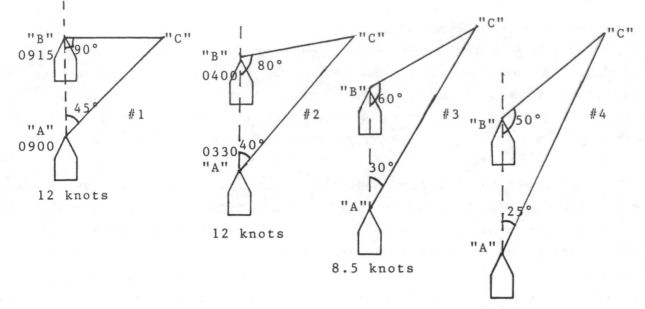

1) Diagram #4 is a vessel making 9.4 knots taking a 25° bearing at 1740.   At 1805 his bearing is 50°.   How far off the object is the vessel?

2) Now for one with no diagram.   A vessel approaches a lighthouse ashore bearing relative 35° at 1145.   Making 10.2 knots a second bearing is taken on the same lighthouse as it bears 070° at 1210.   How far off the lighthouse is your vessel at the time of the second bearing?

3) At 1640 you take a 40° relative bearing on a prominent cliff overhang. Your boat speed is 14.6 knots.   At 1655 the same cliff bears 080°.   How far off the cliff are you at the second bearing?

4) At 0815 you take a 315° relative bearing on a building ashore as you are making 12.6 knots up the channel.   At 0830 the same building bears 270°. How far off the building was your boat at the time of the second bearing?

   Wrong side of the boat, huh?   Not at all.   Subtract each bearing from 360° and examine the answers very carefully before you do anything else. Is the second answer twice the first?   Yes?   Then you doubled the angle and the theory should work.   Compute the distance travelled and you have the answer.

5) Your first relative bearing on an object ashore is 340° at 2005 while making 14.7 knots.   Taking a second bearing at 2030 proves to be 320°. How far off the object is your vessel?

1) 3.9 Mi; 2) 4.3 Mi; 3) 3.7 Mi; 4) 3.2 Mi; 5) 6.1 Mi

ANSWERS

____1) △ △

____2) Fl G "5"

____3) Int Qk Fl "L"

____4) Fl R "4"

____5) Fl "5"

____6) R Bn

____7)

____8)

____9) △ RB "J"

____10) ■

____11) +

____12) C Y

____13)

____14)

____15) C "3"

____16) BW N "D"

____17) ----

____13) BW

____19) N "4" Ra Ref

____20) GW C

____21) C "7" Ref

____22) BW "Q" Mo(A)

____23) F

____24) R Bn

____25)

GENERAL KNOWLEDGE – CHART SYMBOLS

Place the letter from column "B" to the left of the correct chart symbol listed in column "A". Some may be used several times...some not at all.

"B"

a) Light ashore.

b) Light ashore. Not flashing.

c) Range markers.

d) Day beacon. Pass to starboard entering from sea.

e) Offshore mooring buoy.

f) Fish net.

g) Black buoy-flashing green.

h) Sunken rock not dangerous to navigation.

i) Masts exposed at datum level-dangerous to navigation.

j) Oil platform.

k) Radio beacon.

l) Red buoy flashing red.

"B"

m) Major light ashore equipped with radio beacon.

n) Sunken rock dangerous to navigation.

o) 20 fathom line.

p) Quarantine buoy.

q) Lighted mid-channel buoy.

r) Junction buoy.

s) Dredging buoy.

t) Can buoy.

u) Black buoy w/ reflector.

v) Black buoy-flashing white.

w) Six fathom line.

x) Red buoy w/ radar reflector.

y) Mid-channel buoy.

26) All courses plotted on charts are plotted:

   a) Magnetic, b) True, c) Compass, d) Any of these.

27) All lights ashore, or fixed on a jetty or breakwater and not afloat are indicated on a chart by a magenta colored:

   a) Circle, b) Triangle, c) Teardrop, d) Dot.

28) If the true course is 219º, the variation is 15º west and the deviation is 6º east, the compass course is:

   a) 228º, b) 213º, c) 211º, d) None of these.

29) The magnetic course is 357º, variation is 12º east and deviation is 4º west, the true and compass courses respectively are:

   a) 369º and 361º, b) 357º and 001º, c) 009º and 357º, d) 009º and 001º.

30) On a chart, two buoys line up 269º true where the local variation is 13º east. Lined up parallel with these buoys your compass reads 267º. Your deviation on that course is:

   a) 11º east, b) 6º west, c) 11º west, d) 6º east.

31) Regarding #30 above. You then turn your boat around so it is facing the reciprocal direction. Your compass now reads 075º. Your deviation on that course:

   a) 1º east, b) 13º east, c) 1º west, d) 27º west.

32) A nun buoy with red and black bands means:

   a) Stay close to the buoy, b) the marking for a preferred channel, c) Could be safely passed to port, d) All of these.

33) The heights of lights ashore are calculated based on:

   a) Mean high water, b) Mean lower low water, c) Low water, d) From sub-datum levels.

34) The heights of lights ashore determine how far a light can be seen. This distance is calculated assuming the viewer's eye is:

   a) At sea level, b) On board a ship, c) At 15 feet above sea level, d) Your freeboard is less than 8 ft.

 35) Entering a harbor these markers are seen. It means you should:

   a) Turn right, b) Turn left, c) Maintain your present course, d) Wait for the harbor pilot's radio instructions.

36) The symbols cited above in #35 are called:

a) Day beacons, b) Obstructions, c) Range markers, d) Posted lights ashore.

37) Depths of water on a chart are calculations based on:

a) Mean low water, b) Mean high water, c) The average of the high tides, d) The datum level.

38) The description of the basis for determining water depths is found in:

a) The chart's margin, b) The Coast Pilot, c) The Title Block, d) The Local Notice to Mariners.

39) Charts are published by:

a) The Coast Guard, b) National Ocean Survey, c) The U.S. Goverment Printing Office, d) Federal Tidelands Commission.

40) The Local Notice to Mariners is published by:

a) National Ocean Survey, b) U.S. Coast Guard, c) Geodetic Survey, d) None of these.

41) The chart symbol for daybeacons is:

a) D Bn, b) Black circles, c) Triangles, d) Squares.

42) Range markers on a chart are symbolized by:

a) Circles, b) R Mk, c) D Mk, d) Squares.

43) The letter "F" next to a teardrop marks a:

a) Flashing light, b) Fair weather light, c) Occulting light, d) Continuously lighted light.

44) This symbol indicates:

a) Wind direction and speed, b) Tidal range, c) Current speed, d) Set and drift.

45) This symbol on a chart indicates:

a) A wreck dangerous to navigation, b) A sunken ship, c) A wreck not dangerous to navigation, d) Masts.

46) On which type of chart will you find more references to symbols adjacent to a coast?

a) Small scale chart, b) Large scale chart, c) Pilot chart, d) Sailing directions.

47) Entering a strange harbor at night you notice two white range lights ashore which are also indicated on your chart. Looking at the lights, the lower one is to the left of the higher one. You should:

a) Wait for the top one to turn green, b) Come left, c) Come right, d) Consult your latest Notice to Mariners.

48) The Local Notice to Mariners would tell you which of the following?

a) Recent shoalings, b) Recently extinguished lights, c) Relocation of buoys, d) All of these.

49) A black and white vertically striped buoy would be found:

a) Always lighted, b) Marking a channel junction, c) In mid-channel, d) All of these.

50) Which is correct?

a) Nun buoys are always banded and cans are always black, b) Cans are always banded and nuns are always red, c) Nuns and cans can be black or red in color, d) The top band on a nun is always red.

51) A buoy symbol on a chart indicates the letter 'S'. This is a:

a) Signal buoy, b) Of doubtful situation, c) A spar buoy, d) To be passed to starboard.

52) Which buoy is posted on your starboard hand entering from seaward?

a) "R", b) BW, c) N, d) "N"

53) A white and green buoy designates:

a) A dredging buoy, b) Mooring buoy, c) Quarantine buoy, d) Special purpose buoy.

54) Variation in your local area is found:

a) In the Title Block, b) Coast Pilot, c) Compass rose, d) Chart #1.

55) Damage to aids to Navigation can be found by:

a) Listening to 2182 Kc/s or channel 16, b) Reading Local Notice to Mariners, c) Listening to CG broadcasts, d) All of these.

56) The official Tide Tables are published by:

a) NOS, b) USCG, c) DMAHC, d) Government Printing Office.

57) Current tables are published by:

a) NOS, b) USCG, c) U.S. Government Printing Office, d) DMAHC.

58) The Coast Pilot is published by:

a) NOS, b) DMAHC, c) USCG, d) U.S. Government Printing Office.

59) The National Notice to Mariners is published by:

a) NOS, b) USCG, c) DMAHC, d) Coast & Geodetic Survey.

60) The Sailing Directions are published by:

a) DMAHC, b) USCG, c) U.S.C.G.S., d) NOS.

61) A "flashing buoy" flashes:

a) 30 times per minute, b) 60 times per minute, c) Unpredictably, d) As indicated on chart.

62) A quick flashing buoy flashes:

a) 30 times per minute, b) 60 times per minute, c) So that it is on more than it is off, d) As indicated on chart.

63) An occulting light is:

a) On more than it is off, b) Off more than it is on, c) As indicated on chart, d) With the period and cycle the same.

64) An interrupted quick flashing light would be found:

a) At a harbor entrance, b) In the middle of a channel, c) At an intersection of two fairways, d) At a sharp bend.

65) A horizontally banded black and white buoy marks:

a) Mid-Channel, b) Channel junction, c) Harbor entrance, d) Fish net.

66) Which is correct?

a) Nun buoys have red lights, b) Can buoys have green lights, c) Black and white vertically striped buoys flash MoA, d) All of these.

67) A white buoy with a black top would be:

a) At a harbor entrance, b) A sea buoy, c) Marking a wreck exposed at low tide, d) An inland waterway buoy.

68) Which two terms mean the same thing?

a) Datum level and charted depth, b) Datum level and range of tide, c) Spring tides and high tides, d) Neap tides and low tides.

69) The inner circle on a compass rose is for plotting:

a) True courses, b) Magnetic courses, c) Compass courses, d) Azimuths.

70) The Datum Level is established by:

a) Measuring the water depths electronically at mid-tide, b) Averaging the lowest tides, c) Averaging the tidal ranges, d) Use of a lead line.

71) The charted depth on a chart is established by:

a) Averaging the lowest tides, b) Averaging the mean tides, c) Averaging the range of tides, d) All of these.

72) Spring tides:

a) Have higher highs and lower low tides, b) Have a minimum range, c) Have lower highs and higher lows, d) Come in March, April and May.

73) Neap tides:

a) Occur during full moons, b) Have higher highs and lower lows, c) Have lower highs and higher lows, d) Occur in early morning hours.

74) Reference station "A", found in the tide table, shows a high tide of 3.2 feet at a given time. Harbor "B" shows a correction factor of 0.9. The height of the tide at harbor "B" would be:

a) -4.1, b) -2.3, c) +4.1, d) +2.3.

75) Reference station "A" shows a tide of -2.9, with harbor "B" indicating a -0.8. The tide at harbor "B" would be:

a) +3.7, b) -2.9, c) -2.1, d) -3.7.

76) The range of a tide means:

a) From high tide to the next high tide, b) From high tide one day to the same high tide the next day, c) The difference from one day to the next of the low tide, d) From one high tide to the next low tide.

77) A slack tide:

a) Has no movement, b) Is going out, c) Is coming in, d) Is the peak of flow in either direction.

78) An ebb tide:

a) Has no movement, b) Is going out, c) Is coming in, d) Is the peak of flow in either direction.

79) A flood tide is:

a) Incoming, b) Outgoing, c) Still, d) Very rapid.

80) Variation is 14° east, deviation is 16° west, magnetic course is 345°. The true and compass courses respectively are:

a) 001° and 359°, b) 331° and 329°, c) 359° and 001°, d) 359° and 004°.

81) Your speed is 10 knots. The river current is 3 knots. You run up the river for 2 miles turn around and run back to your starting point. Allowing no time for turn-around, the trip should take:

a) About 20 minutes, b) A little over 30 minutes, c) Closer to 40 minutes, d) 26 minutes.

82) Your speed is 12.2 knots, the distance is 40.7 miles. Time to travel:

a) 2 hrs. 20 min., b) 2 hrs. 50 min., c) 3 hrs. 20 min., d) 3 hrs. 40 min.

83) Speed - 9.8 knots. Time - 1 hr., 16 min. Distance=:

a) 11.4 miles, b) 12.4 min., c) 8.6 miles, d) 12.4 miles.

84) Distance - 20.5 miles. Time - 47 minutes. Speed=:

a) 22.6 knots, b) 26.2 miles, c) 26.2 knots, d) 27 knots.

85) Where would you find the deepest water in this river?

a) A, b) B, c) D, d) C.

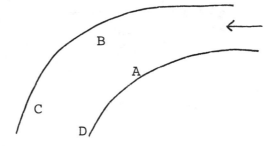

86) Underway at a speed of 12 knots. At 0930, a lighthouse bears relative one quarter off your starboard bow. At 1015 at the same course and speed the same light bears abeam. Distance off the light is:

a) 6.5 miles, b) 9 miles, c) 5.5 miles, d) 8 miles.

87) You are on a steady course making 14.2 knots at 2140 when an offshore rock bears 22 1/2° relative. At 2225 the same rock bears 045° relative. Distance off the rock is:

a) 10.7 miles, b) 10.6 miles, c) 11 miles, d) Inadequate information to make computation.

88) Underway at 1205 as a Radio beacon ashore indicates a relative bearing of 030°. At 1255 the same RBn bears 060° relative. At the same course and speed as the first bearing, how far off the RBn are you?

a) 18 miles, b) 8 miles, c) 1.8 miles, d) Inadequate information.

89) From your port bow a lighthouse bears 315° relative at 1145 at a speed of 9.8 knots. At 1225 the bearing is 270° relative. Distance off the light is:

a) 7.1 miles, b) 6.3 miles, c) 6.5 miles, d) Inadequate information given.

90) At a relative bearing of 325° a prominent landmark appears at 1732. After running 8 miles and on the same course 1 hour and fifteen minutes later the bearing on the same landmark is 290°. Distance off the landmark is:

a) 6.8 miles, b) 7.0 miles, c) 8 miles, d) Inadequate information given.

91) Object off port bow bears 320° relative at 0930. Boat speed of 16.3 knots. At 0955 same object bears 290°. Distance off is:

a) 8.6 miles, b) 6.8 miles, c) 6.5 miles, d) Inadequate information given.

92) Deviation on a compass can be determined by:

a) Ranges ashore, b) Charted ranges, c) Sun azimuths, d) All of these.

93) If your compass course is the same as your magnetic course, there is:

a) No variation, b) No deviation, c) No declination, d) None of these.

94) The compass heading of a vessel differs from true heading by:

a) Compass error, b) Magnetic heading, c) Variation, d) Deviation.

95) If a buoy ashore bears 195° from the boat, the bearing from the buoy to the boat is:

a) 020°, b) 195°, c) 015°, d) 000°.

96) This symbol ⟨RED on a chart indicates a region of:

a) Radius of the limit of the light, b) Visible portion of the light as seen from seaward, c) Danger sector, d) A range daybeacon ashore.

97) The angular difference between the direction of geographic and magnetic meridians is called:

a) Variation, b) Deviation, c) Compass error, d) Magnetic reading.

98) How is a diaphone activated?

a) Compressed air, b) Electricity, c) CO_2, d) None of these.

99) The government agency which maintains a radio beacon is:

a) The FCC, b) U.S.C.G., c) FBI, d) Coast and Geodetic Survey.

100) This symbol represents a: △ BW "R"

a) Day beacon, b) Channel marker, c) Unlighted bell or whistle buoy, d) Mid-channel marker.

101) Which symbol indicates a lighted aid?

a)   b)   c)   d)

102) Where would you find information on radio beacons?

a) Notice to Mariners, b) Light list, c) Buoy and Beacon Notices, d) Coast Pilot.

103) The "set" of a current means:

a) The direction from which it is coming, b) The direction it is going, c) The speed of the current, d) None of these.

104) You have a draft of 3.5' in 6 fathoms of water. The depth beneath your keel is:

a) 22.5', b) 32', c) 38.5' d) 32.5'

105) You make a run against a 3 knot current turning rpm that would ordinarily produce 10 knots. Running for 45 minutes you have travelled:

a) 5.3 miles, b) 5 miles, c) 5.2 miles, d) 5.1 miles.

106) Heading due west for 30 miles, you stop to fish and are set 135° true at 3 knots for 2 hours. Heading back to port, the true course you steer is approximately:

a) 010°, b) 080°, c) 090°, d) 100°.

107) As the tint on your chart becomes a lighter blue, the water is becoming:

a) Calmer, b) More shallow, c) Deeper, d) Colder.

108) You depart for your fishing grounds with two one hundred gallon tanks of fuel. Vessel uses 17 gallons per hour (gph). Cruising for four hours and using an additional 28 gallons for idling and fishing at the grounds, what is your maximum running time remaining?

a) 3 hours, b) 4 hours, c) 6 hours, d) 9 hours.

109) Running from point "A" to point "B" for 2.5 hours at a speed of 15 knots, you cover thirty miles. You are running:

a) Against a 2.5 knot current, b) With a 5 knot current, c) With a 2.5 knot current, d) Against a 3 knot current.

110) The best way to locate your position in a fog is by taking:

a) Radar bearings on two distant objects at sea, b) Radar bearings on two or more aids to navigation, c) Compass bearings, d) Radar bearings on two or more distant mountain peaks.

111) When taking bearings with an RDF:

a) Do not take them on an AM radio station, b) Keep RDF in same position while taking bearings, c) Use only radio marine beacons ashore, d) Keep RDF away from other radios on board.

112) The proper radio procedure on 2182 Kc/s is:

a) Use only for calling, then shift to another channel, b) Use for official business only, c) Not to be used except for conversing with shore stations, d) Use only when conversing with Coast Guard.

113) The term "securite" means:

a) MAYDAY call to follow, b) PAN call to follow, c) Meterological information follows, d) Secure all radio transmissions on this frequency until further notice.

114) When taking a three bearing fix, what is the best angle to have between the objects?

a) 15o. b) 25o, c) 45o, d) 90o.

115) A buoy in shallow water will tend to:

a) Lie down, b) Spin in a wide circle, c) Be off station, d) All of these.

116) The number of slack tides on the west coast in one day is:

a) 1, b) 2, c) 3, d) 4.

117) Reference station "X" indicates a low tide of -2.4. Inlet "Y" has a correction factor of 0.5. The lowest tide at "Y" would be:

a) -0.9, b) -1.9, c) 1.9, d) -2.9

QUIZ QUESTIONS ON NEW I.A.L.A. BUOYAGE SYSTEM

118) The chart symbol for port hand daymarks working upstream is a:

a) Circle, b) Square, c) Triangle, d) None of these.

119) Port hand buoys entering from sea are:

a) Green, b) Odd numbered, c) Cans, d) All of these.

120) Lighted lateral aids are:

a) Numbered, b) Lettered, c) Both, d) Neither.

121) An even numbered lighted aid will not show which flash?

a) Morse code "A", b) White, c) 2 + 1, d) None of these will be evidenced.

122) Which identification below will be found on bifurcation buoys?

a) Lettered, b) Flashing red, c) Flashing green, d) All of these.

123) Which lighted buoy has a spherical topmark?

a) Nuns, b) All banded buoys, c) Mid-channel, d) All sea buoys.

124) A banded unlighted buoy, top band red, would:

a) Mark a potential hazard to navigation, b) Be lettered, c) Be passed on the port hand, d) All of these.

125) Spherical buoys:

a) Are black and white, b) Mark a mid-channel, c) Are numbered, d) All of these.

126) A special lateral aids, installed by a governmental body other than the Coast Guard, would not flash which characteristic below?

a) Morse Code "A". b) Group flash (2), c) Isophase, d) None of these should be used.

127) Special lateral aids have the distinct characteristics of:

a) If lighted-always yellow, b) Black and white, c) Marked with squares and/or letters, d) All of these.

128) White and orange regulatory marks and buoys are installed by any governmental body other than the Coast Guard and mark:

a) Danger areas, b) Controlled areas, c) Exclusion areas, d) All of these.

129) Which statement below is true regarding symbols found on white and orange regulatory marks and buoys?

a) Squares mark danger areas, b) Circles indicate controlled areas, c) Cross-hatched diamonds mark exclusion areas, d) All of these are true.

GENERAL KNOWLEDGE QUIZ KEY

Multiple Choice

Matching

1) C

2) G	26) B	51) C	76) D	101) D	126) D
3) R	27) C	52) C	77) A	102) B	127) A
4) L	28) A	53) A	78) B	103) B	128) D
5) V	29) D	54) C	79) A	104) D	129) D
6) K	30) C	55) D	80) C	105) A	
7) A	31) A	56) A	81) D	106) B	
8) N	32) D	57) A	82) C	107) B	
9) D	33) A	58) A	83) D	108) C	
10) J	34) A	59) C	84) C	109) D	
11) H	35) B	60) A	85) B	110) D	
12) P	36) C	61) A	86) B	111) D	
13) I	37) D	62) B	87) A	112) A	
14) O	38) C	63) A	88) D	113) C	
15) T	39) B	64) C	89) C	114) D	
16) Y	40) B	65) D	90) C	115) B	
17) W	41) C	66) C	91) D	116) D	
18) F	42) A	67) D	92) D	117) B	
19) X	43) D	68) A	93) B	118) B	
20) S	44) C	69) B	94) A	119) D	
21) U	45) C	70) B	95) C	120) C	
22) Q	46) B	71) A	96) C	121) D	
23) B	47) B	72) A	97) A	122) D	
24) M	48) D	73) C	98) A	123) C	
25) E	49) C	74) C	99) B	124) D	
	50) D	75) D	100) D	125) B	

Common sense, experience and a little reading helps.   But, who could pretend
to give a concise seamanship lesson in a few pages?   Thus, a few high points
some REC's love to throw at prospective candidates are in order.   Then you can
take the test to find what they are currently emphasizing along the common sense
line.   Remember, a lot of the test is plain vocabulary, much of which went out
with WW II.   If in doubt, see the glossary at the end of this volume.

Some offices have no concern for the practicality of the questions on their
seamanship tests. However, in the entire CG test, this is a close as you'll get
to anything practical.   For example: There are still several REC's with tests
that make no mention of the Heimlich method for extracting something from a
choking person's throat.

Some offices have a bevy of questions regarding **river navigation.**   For an
area with navigable rivers this is great, but they show up in areas which have no
navigable rivers...so don't be lulled.

Some things you could never get from a glossary.   To wit: Pile Dikes are
pilings driven into the river bottom generally extending in a right angle of a
curve from the river bank.   They stop erosion of the river bank.   Thus, a good
anchorage would be on the down-stream side "behind" these pile dikes.   The
force of the river is abated somewhat by the dikes thus lessening the pull on
your anchor.

Bank Cushion refers to the increased water pressure **built up** between the bow
and the bank nearest you (to starboard if you are on the right side of the river).
Stern Suction refers to the decreased water pressure between the stern and the
nearest bank.   The combination of the two can cause a vessel to be thrown off
course to port.   Hence, you must "oversteer" to maintain the given course.
Both effects increase in intensity when the draft of the vessel is nearly the
same as the depth of the water.

Here's another one hardly applicable to anyone striving for a license to
operate small boats on lakes **or** offshore.

On extremely **large tankers,** the lifelines are wire cables. These are
"wormed, parcelled and served" **to protect your hands.** If you want an excellent
.s

picture of the process see the "Bos'n Locker" section under 'Seamanship' in Chapmans, **Piloting, Seamanship and Small Boat Handling.**

The point is, you would have to possess some rather technical knowledge of the physics of river navigation and big tankers to score well on this test. Thus, you must ask yourself, what kind of weird question will I get on **my** exam? If you are on the Great Lakes, will they ask you questions regarding the validity of Mexican navigation aids?

What's the point here? Why the stories? Do they apply to your case if you live in, say, Florida?

Maybe. Consider: Each REC makes up its own exams. Again, they don't come from Washington. Fortunately, the so-called "Seamanship" part of the test requires only a seventy percent grade for passing. As mentioned, a great deal of it is common sense. Our introduction to the test will emphasize some highlights to watch for, while the test itself will teach you a lot more. This approach is different from the rest of the text, but you'll catch on as we breeze through the quiz.

Marlinspike Seamanship

Most of the time the CG doesn't have time to stand around and watch you tie knots. They do incorporate questions into their quizzes they believe are designed to test your knowledge as to what purposes the various knots serve. In other words:

1) A knot that doesn't slip is a bowline..
2) To join two lines of **similar size** try a square knot.
3) Joining two **dissimilar** lines requires a Sheet Bend.
4) Tieing up to a bollard or to tie a **knot on a spar** use a Clove Hitch.
5) To strengthen a clove hitch...add a half hitch.
6) A sheepshank serves to shorten a line. Can also be used to temporarily circumvent a break or worn spot in the line.
7) A long splice is used when it is necessary to maintain the original diameter of the line, e.g., when the line must be passed through a small metal eye. A short splice or knot would enlarge the line.

FORTY KNOTS

Don't assume you are supposed to know them all. They are here for identification purposes only. The ones with which you should be familiar are indicated in the Seamanship section.

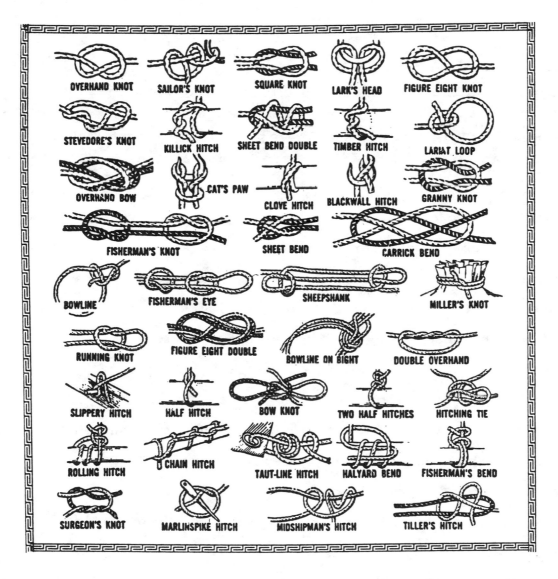

8) Nylon line is tough stuff! However, one recent question on the Long Beach Office test derived from the "shock" load or "snap" strength of nylon. Chapman states the factor is about "4" meaning the line will snap at about twenty-five percent of its stated normal load strength. The CG suggests, that a 20,000 lb. line will snap at 4,000 lbs. That's about twenty percent! Conservative? Well, maybe, but maybe you had better pursue Chapman's section on lines under Marlinspike Seamanship on this subject. Don't be foolish and try to memorize everything.

9) When you coil line it is coiled clockwise. When removing line from a new packaged coil the line is removed from the **center** of the coil. If it doesn't seem to be coming out smoothly-kinking-then turn the entire coil over and remove from center of the opposite side.

10) **Please Note:** All of this sounds crazy and minute...granted. But also remember...there is **NOTHING** in this book that you can glaze over. If you didn't **need** it to pass the exam...it wouldn't be here. We're not loading this book just to impress people. To ignore or pass off lightly any facet herein would be like purchasing an overseas airline ticket on Kamikaze Airlines.

I. Seamanship

1) To tie together two similar sized lines, use a:

a) Bowline, b) Sheet bend, c) Square knot, d) Clove hitch.

2) To tie together two dissimilar size lines, use a:

a) Bowline, b) Sheet bend, c) Square knot, d) Clove hitch.

3) To tie a knot which will not slip, tie a:

a) Bowline, b) Clove hitch, c) Fisherman's knot, d) Half-hitch.

4) To stop a clove hitch from slipping what other knot should be added?

a) Bowline, b) Sheet bend, c) Figure eight, d) Half-hitch.

5) The best compound to use to stem a leak is:

a) Thin waxed marlin, b) Hemp, c) Caulking, d) Hogging line.

6) A lead line:

a) Is a hogging line, b) Measures depth, c) Secures the anchor from running out, d) Is used as a weight on a fishing line.

7) Broad on the beam means:

a) 45° off of your starboard bow, b) 45° forward of your stern, c) At a right angle to the bow, d) 6 points aft of the bow.

8) There are how many points in a compass?

a) 32, b) 24, c) 16, d) 8.

9) When "yawing":

a) The stern swings about, b) The bow submerges in a wave. c) The bow crests a wave, d) You are in a trough and in danger of capsizing.

10) When "yawing":

a) You are in danger of losing steerage way, b) The bow is high in the water, c) The stern is low, d) The boat is in a trough.

11) Broaching is when:

a) The boat is broad to the wind, b) The boat fills with water but remains upright, c) You have gone aground, d) The boat is capsized.

12) When the stern is clear of the water in a heavy following sea you are in danger of:

a) Pitching, b) Yawing, c) Broaching, d) Pitchpoling.

13) A drogue is used to:

a) Keep the bow into the sea, b) Keep the vessel in a trough, c) Keep the stern into the oncoming sea, d) Aid as a flotation device.

14) A nautical mile measures approximately:

a) 5280 ft., b) 5820 ft., c) 6706 ft., d) 6076 ft.

15) Before stowing manilla line you should:

a) Let it dry, b) Rinse with salt water and let dry, c) Subject it to a thorough inspection for fraying, d) Rinse in fresh water and let dry.

16) The best holding ground for anchoring is:

a) Soft sand, b) Soft mud, c) Sandy mud, d) Rocky sand.

17) When a vessel is laboring into the sea you should:

a) Abandon this course and seek shelter, b) Quarter off, c) Slow to minimum speed to maintain steerage, d) Bring the vessel to a plane.

18) A ratio of depth to anchor scope under "storm conditions" is:

a) 5:1, b) 7:1 c) 10:1, d) 12:1.

19) A trip line is used for:

   a) Freeing a mooring line from a buoy, b) Retrieving a sea anchor, c) Departing a dock using spring lines, d) A downhaul backup.

20) A drogue is in the shape of a:

   a) Cylinder, b) Prism, c) Sea anchor, d) Sphere.

21) Which would make the best jury-rigged sea anchor?

   a) Oars and canvas, b) Life jackets and anchor, c) A very heavy hawser run aft, d) A large empty sealed drum.

22) Man overboard. First:

   a) Post a lookout to keep him in view, b) Send someone in after him, c) Stop the boat, but keep way on for maneuverability, d) Come about.

23) The basic difference between nylon and manilla line is:

   a) Nylon will stretch more, but is stronger, b) Manilla stretches more but is stronger, c) Nylon is stronger but manilla will stretch more, d) They are about equal.

24) A nylon line with a test of 20,000 lbs., will snap at:

   a) 3,000 lbs., b) 4,000 lbs., c) 5,000 lbs., d) 6,000 lbs.

25) Worming, parcelling and serving a lifeline is intended to:

   a) Protect the cables, b) Stiffen the cable, c) Protect the hands, d) Prevent cable wear on stanchions.

26) Which item(s) should not be placed near a compass?

   a) Aluminum tools, b) Steel nuts and bolts, c) Fish hooks, d) Lead line and sinkers.

27) A light weight type of anchor gets its holding power from:

   I. Stock, II. Flukes

   a) I, b) II, c) I & II, d) Neither I nor II.

28) Choose the most accurate statement:

   a) Wire rope and rope are measured by radius, b) Both are measured by circumference, c) Wire rope by diameter, rope by circumference, d) Wire rope by circumference and rope by radius.

29) In determining the length of rode, which of the following must be considered:

   a) Depth, b) Freeboard, c) Weather, d) All of these.

30) When wind "veers", relative to your position, it is:

   a) Decreasing in intensity, b) Hauling, c) Increasing in intensity, d) Moving clockwise.

31) When wind "hauls", relative to your position, it is:

   a) Moving clockwise, b) Moving counter-clockwise, c) Decreasing in intensity, d) Veering.

32) A Yellow smoke bomb would indicate:

   a) A submarine in distress, b) A surfacing sub, c) SCUBA divers in the area, d) Underwater construction area-keep clear.

33) A hogging line:

   a) Is stretched beneath a boat, b) Is attached to a spar, c) Attaches to a lead line, d) Is a stern tie-down.

34) The pivot point of most power vessels is:

   a) Midships, b) 1/3 aft of the bow, c) The stern, d) The bow.

35) Around a spar you tie a:

   a) Timber hitch, b) Clove hitch, c) Square knot, d) Bowline.

36) A water light is found on:

   a) A sea anchor, b) The stern of a disabled craft, c) On liferings, d) On signal lamps.

> Under an unwritten law of the sea, all ships were created equal. With apologies to George Orwell – Now some are more equal than others.

WEATHER

There are several things you will have to familiarize yourself with in your local area before going near any CG weather quiz. For those candidates striving to challenge the test in any district, the tips below will give you an idea of what they want.

1) Learn the **usual** weather patterns in your area.

2) Learn the **unusual** weather patterns in your area. If the predominant winds change at a certain time of the year...know them and the dates. Also learn the nick names of any local weather phenomenon.

3) This next one takes a little imagination. Every area has a "freak" weather happening which occurs during any given time of the year. Unusual, but it happens and when it does, it's significant for anyone afloat. For example: big rains, massive storm fronts coming from a certain direction, tornadoes, squalls or hurricanes. Every area has it freaks. Know them and when they're due. Then, one more thing.

4) If you're at sea when one of these freaks hits...where do you go for shelter? Fast shelter. The quickest shelter. This may not involve heading for home.

5) Now some generalities:

   a) A cold front overtaking a warm front produces rain.

   b) A rapidly falling barometer means high winds and soon.

   c) A slow steady decline in the barometer generally means rain. The term "precipitation" is often used.

   d) Become familiar with the vertical arrangement of cloud layers. For example; on top is cirrostratus. On a lower level would be altocumulus and closest to earth would be stratus. Naturally, there are many sub-categories of the above, but those three seem to fascinate test makers.

   e) High and low pressure areas are bound to crop up. A "high" dumps wind into an adjacent "low". Thus, a low pressure area is windy. How the wind

gets there is the important thing. Wind moves in a **cyclonic** pattern.
That means as it travels it does so in a huge circle.   The "circle" can be
500 to 1,000 miles in diameter.   Note the backward "S" below on the left.
Now look at the one to the right of it wherein the beginning and ending
lines of the "S" have been extended inwards.

That's the part to watch.   Notice the little arrowheads?   Hence, a
conclusion: A "high" moves clockwise and "out".   A "low" moves counter-
clockwise and "in".   (At least this is true north of the equator and the
down-under side is out-of-bounds.)

Now comes the neat part.

If you were **facing into the wind** in a "high" area, where would the center
of the "high" be located? Ans: To your left and a little bit forward.

If you were **facing into the wind** in a low pressure area, where would the
center of the "low" be located? Ans: To your right and a bit behind you.
Or, if you like, behind your right ear.

If your mind goes blank in the exam room...draw a backwards "S" and
reconstruct the entire scenario.

f) Aneroid barometers are used aboard ships.

g) American barometers are calibrated in inches of mercury...or, "to an
   equivalent column of mercury". Never mind what that means...just
   remember it.

h) Standard barometers and/or barometric pressures can be expressed as:

   1) Inches- e.g., 29.92.

2) Millibars- e.g., 1013.25 millibars.

3) psi- pounds per square inch.

4) mm- millimeters, as in 760.1 mm.

i) Fog over the ocean is an "advection" fog. You need to know what causes fog.

Warm air masses over land contain moisture. You cannot see the moisture until it is condensed into a small volume, that is, squeezed together. When a warm body of air moves out over the ocean it loses some of its heat. The heat is "drawn off" by the cooler air upwelling from a cold sea. When the volume of onshore air loses heat, the moisture particles condense. The result is a cloud which cannot rise because it is too heavy. Fog.

Dewpoint temperature, or just **dewpoint**, is the term applied to the **temperature** of the warm air moving from onshore to offshore. When the dewpoint reaches (or comes close to) the temperature of the surrounding offshore air, we get fog.

Fog can also be caused by warm tropical air moving into a colder region. In other words, the warm air might be coming from a tropical area farther south.

k) Occluded front. This is one they throw in to confuse the masses. Visualize a mass of cold air moving down from the north. The cold air moving along overtakes a warm front. Warm air rises, so the oncoming cold front "lifts" the warm air up off the ground and into the high sky which causes the rain. There are various kinds of "occluded fronts", but one main example to remember is the cold front overtaking the warm front produces rain.

l) Currents. Know your local currents, their direction and force. If they change during the year, know when this occurs. In the northern hemisphere, currents revolve in a clock-wise motion. Careful. Check the Coast Pilot for the names of these currents. The names may not match names bestowed upon them by the locals.

Quiz time.

II. **Weather**

1) A slow steady decline in the barometer indicates:

   a) Onset of strong winds, b) Approaching storm, c) Rough weather within 24 hours, d) Precipitation coming.

2) A rapidly dropping barometer indicates:

   a) Thunder showers due, b) 24 hours of bad weather, c) Strong winds soon, d) Precipitation.

3) Wind in a low pressure area moves:

   a) Clockwise and offshore, b) Counter-clockwise and in, c) Clockwise and onshore, d) Counter-clockwise and offshore.

4) Wind in a high pressure area moves:

   a) Clockwise and outwards, b) Counter-clockwise and in, c) Offshore and south, d) Counter-clockwise and out.

5) The best way to check the accuracy of your barometer is:

   a) To call the local weather bureau, b) Call the CG, c) Check with other boats nearby, d) Call the Harbor Master.

6) The significant thing to watch on a barometer is:

   a) The direction of change, b) The rate of change, c) The time of day change is taking place, d) All of these.

7) In order of mounting intensity which is the proper arrangement?

   a) Small craft, storm, gale, hurricane, b) Small craft, gale, storm, hurricane, c) Gale, small craft, storm, hurricane, d) Small craft, storm, hurricane, gale.

8) 2670 K/cs is:

   a) A weather station, b) A Notice to Mariners Stations, c) Coast Guard announcements frequency, d) All of these.

9) Channel 16 is:

   a) A distress frequency, b) A calling station, c) Standby station for ships underway, d) All of these.

10) Information on currents within harbors are:

   a) Unimportant, b) Found in the Tide Tables, c) Found in the Current Tables, d) Impossible to predict.

11) The set of the water along the Southern California coast is:

   a) Parallel to the coast, b) Easterly along south facing coasts, c) Southerly along west facing coasts, d) All of these.

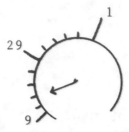

12) The picture of this barometer reads:

   a) 29.90, b) 28.94, c) 28.90, d) 29.94.

13) The California Current is sometimes called:

   a) The Davidson Current, b) The Alaskan Current, c) The Baja Current, d) All of these.

14) Cold air flowing over warm water will cause:

   a) Advection fog, b) Steam fog, c) Radiation fog, d) Tooly fog.

15) What is the best use for an uncalibrated compass in fog?

   a) Running reciprocal courses, b) Courses most often run, c) Magnetic charting, d) No safe use possible.

16) A "low" produces:

   a) Fog and mist, b) Strong winds and rough seas, c) A warm front, d) Cold front overtaking a warm front.

17) A "high" indicates the possibility of:
   a) Precipitation, b) Fog, c) Thunderheads over the mountains, d) Rough seas.

18) A light and high cloud formation along the west coast generally indicates:

   a) Fair weather, b) Approaching storm a day off, c) Rain soon, d) Strong winds soon.

19) The type of fog found offshore on the west coast is termed:

   a) Advection, b) Radiation, c) Tropic, d) All of these.

20) Offshore fog is formed by:

   a) Warm air onshore moving offshore, b) Tropic air moving north to encounter colder air from the sea, d) The dewpoint reaching the same temperature as the sea air, d) All of these.

21) An occluded front occurs when:

   a) Thunderheads well up over coastal mountains, b) A clearing can be seen directly overhead, c) Fog occurs, d) A cold front overtakes a warm front.

22) An occluded front, as in a cold front overtaking a warm front produces:

   a) Strong winds, b) Clear skies, c) Rain, d) Dewpoint.

23) Horizontally and from highest to lowest in altitude, in what order will these clouds be formed.

   a) Cirrostratus, altocumulus, stratus, b) Altocumulus, cirrostratus, stratus, c) Stratus, altocumulus, cirrostratus, d) Altocumulus, stratus, cirrostratus.

24) When rain showers occur with strong shifting winds, the rain is caused by:

    a) A warm front, b) A cold front, c) An occluded front, d) A precipitation front.

25) A front is defined as:

    a) Dissimilar air masses, b) Dissimilar cloud formations, c) A cold front overtaking a colder front, d) A cold front overtaking a warm front.

26) When the barometer drops rapidly, the weather is:

    a) Cool and clear, b) Very cloudy, c) Warm, d) Raining.

SMALL BOAT HANDLING

No way is the Coast Guard going to ask you to demonstrate your boat handling ability.   Like everything else...only on paper.   However, there are some basic theories the CG has on boat handling.

When docking or departing a pier, dock, slip or wharf there are two things to remember.   When departing, the stern goes out first.   When docking the stern comes in last.   Maneuver your craft's clutches and wheel accordingly.

Just for a moment, assume you're in the water astern of a twin screw craft. Stick your head under the water and watch her take off.   The screw on the right will turn clockwise.   The left one will go counter-clock-wise.   When backing down, the opposite occurs.

Spring lines are important, but not many know their technical names.   Study the pictures and descriptions below.

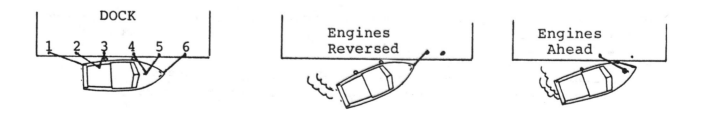

Now compare the numbers on each of the lines with these definitions. Try to remember that the **direction** the line is tending is called out first.

1) Stern line. However, led forward and secured to a cleat on the dock it becomes a "quarter spring line".

2) An after spring line.

3) A forward spring line again. Called "forward" because it's tending forward.

4) An after (the way it's tending) forward spring line.

5) A forward spring line.

6) Bow line. Tended aft it would become an after bow spring line.

7) A line tending directly out from amidships is called a breast line.

Now learn some more from the following quiz. If some of the vocabulary stops you check the glossary.

III. Boat Handling

1) Rode is:

   a) A bow chock, b) Mooring line c) Anchor line, d) A stern cleat.

2) A heavy following sea tends to make a vessel:

   a) Pound, b) Pitch, c) Yaw, d) Roll.

3) Man overboard: The first thing to do is:

   a) Send someone in after him, b) Throw a lifering to him, c) Stop the vessel, d) Come about.

4) You are moored port side to with a twin screw vessel utilizing a forward bow springline with the helm amidship. Departing this dock with wind hard on your starboard side, you would use:

   a) Forward thrust on port screw, b) Foreward thrust on starboard screw, c) After thrust on port screw, d) After thrust on starboard screw.

5) You are moored starboard side to with a twin screw craft. Utilizing an after bow springline with wind on the port beam, to depart you would use:

a) Forward thrust on port screw, b) After thrust on starboard screw, c) Forward thrust on starboard screw, d) After thrust on port screw.

6) Where is the best place to stow life preservers when underway?

a) Loose and on deck, b) Out of the weather in a plainly marked box, c) Secured but readily available, d) On the passengers.

7) The pivot point of most power vessels is:

a) Midships, b) 1/3 aft of the bow, c) The stern, d) 1/3 forward of the beam.

8) If your steering gear goes out on a twin screw vessel the best method for maintaining steerage way is:

a) Using both throttles alternately, b) A bucket over the stern, c) Using gear levers alternately, d) One engine in gear at half-speed using the other to steer.

9) At anchor in a river, a vessel's anchor is "veered" in order to:

a) Allow for reserve of chain, b) Force the vessel to swing, c) Allow for flukes to bite, d) Prevent drifting.

10) A spring line is used for:

a) Backing away from a dock, b) Securing the boat to the dock, c) Pulling away from the dock in a forward motion, d) None of these.

11) A single screw vessel with a right hand screw, when backing down with helm amidship, will tend to veer in which direction?

a) Right, b) left.

12) When using oil to calm a rough sea in which direction do you dump the oil?

a) To the windward, b) To the lee, c) Bow to stern, d) Completely encircling the vessel.

13) When approaching a vessel on fire you should approach:

a) From upwind, b) From downwind, c) Bow on, d) From the stern.

14) What happens to a high speed vessel when approaching and/or operating in shallow water?

a) Planes higher, b) Entire boat planes lower, c) Bow tends to lower, d) Stern tends to lower.

15) Navigating in ice is dangerous to what part of a ship's propulsion mechanism?

a) Scuppers, b) Engine discharge, c) Propeller, d) Cooling water intake.

16) Man overboard. First:

   a) Post a lookout to keep him in view, b) Send someone in after him, c) Stop the boat, but keep way on for maneuverability, d) Come about.

17) When viewing a twin screw vessel from the stern, in which direction does the starboard screw turn when in forward propulsion?

   a) Clockwise, b) Counter-clockwise, c) Same as the port screw, d) Both "a" & "c" are correct.

18) The line tending from a vessel to the dock in a right angle to the boat is called a:

   a) Beam spring line, b) Tie-down, c) Spring line, d) Breastline.

19) To turn a twin screw vessel completely about clockwise within its own length you must:

   a) Put the helm hard left with the port clutch forward and the starboard clutch in reverse, b) Helm amidship with starboard clutch forward, port clutch reverse, c) Helm full right with port clutch forward, starboard clutch in reverse, d) Helm hard left with port clutch reverse, starboard clutch forward.

20) Anchoring for the night on a river you should anchor:

   a) Midstream to allow passage of other vessels on either side, b) Tie up to a tree or rock just offshore, c) Tie off to a navigation buoy, d) Anchor downstream from a pile dike.

21) When backing down, the pivot point of a vessel is:

   a) One-third aft of the bow, b) Midships, c) The stern, d) About one-third forward of the stern.

22) Someone yells, "Man overboard, port side". You should:

   a) Turn right, b) Back down, c) Make a wide circle, d) Turn left.

23) When a man is overboard you approach him from:

   a) Upwind, b) Downwind, c) Starboard side to the lee, d) Bow on.

24) To keep a vessel from yawing:

   a) Shift weight to midships, b) Keep tiller amidships, c) Shift weight aft, d) Wiggle tiller vigorously.

25) A vessel which rolls sluggishly and is in tender condition is:

   a) Weighted so the center of gravity is too low, b) Top heavy, c) Has too much freeboard, d) Has too heavy a load aboard.

26) Broad on the starboard quarter is how many degrees relative from the bow?

a) 90°, b) 45°, c) 135 °, d) 225°.

27) Entering a harbor over a bar, which is the best way to enter?

a) Faster than the waves at flood, b) Same speed as the waves at flood, c) Slower than the waves at ebb, d) Same speed as the waves at ebb.

28) The important thing to remember when using a RDF for positioning purposes is:

a) Not to use an AM radio station, b) Keep RDF in same position when taking bearings, c) Use only radio marine beacons ashore, d) Keep RDF away from other radios on board.

29) Your vessel is suffering from unwarranted vibrations in a calm sea. You suspect:

a) Water in the gas, b) Engine out of timing, c) Bent shaft or prop, d) Steering linkage out of alignment.

30) The best way to enter a confined harbor is:

a) Against the wind, b) With the wind aft, c) With wind and current aft, d) During a windward tide.

31) You are sailing on a course of 270° true with a strong southerly current. To compensate for the current, steer more:

a) Easterly, b) Southerly, c) Northerly, d) To the left.

32) Displacing gasoline with saltwater in the midship tanks will:

a) Increase stability of the craft, b) Lower the center of gravity, c) Stem the pitch and roll, d) All of these.

33) To determine if your anchor is holding fast, you should:

a) Check ranges ashore, b) Feel the line for tremble, c) Watch for stirred up or cloudy water, d) Test it by pulling on the anchor line to see if it holds fast.

34) When anchoring from the bow:

a) Keep your boat motionless, b) Maintain slight forward motion, c) Maintain slight reverse motion, d) Stay at right angles to any apparent wind.

35) A safe ratio of rode to depth in heavy weather is:

a) 5:1, b) 6:1, c) 7:1, d) 10:1

150

36) As the depth of keel and depth of water tend to equal on a river, the pressure increase resulting will force a pilot to:

a) Decrease speed, b) Increase speed, c) Seek deeper water, d) Oversteer.

37) Which instrument is most helpful near land in a heavy fog?

a) Pelorus, b) Compass, c) Lead line, d) Dividers.

38) The fathometer is giving double readings. You suspect the bottom is:

a) Rocky, b) Clay, c) Mud, D) Sand.

FIRST AID

There always seems to be a narrow range of first aid questions on CG exams, but it's the stone age in action. Most of the CG's first aid concepts bring gales of laughter from paramedics and doctors taking my course on the west coast and the three day seminars presented around the country. It's interesting. At this writing, if you plan on sitting for a 300 ton license, or higher, you must hold a valid Red Cross First Aid Certificate and a CPR card. Yet, the questions utilized by so many CG offices ignore modern first aid concepts entirely. For example, many REC's have little if anything on such current items as pressure points of the body and the Heimlich method for ejecting foreign matter from the throat of a choking victim.

Some points are well made within the body of test. Others you probably wouldn't touch with a twenty foot boathook. Consequently, the CG directions of "choose the best answer" should be emphasized. The directions, information and answers to the following questions do not reflect the opinion or advice of the author.

Here's a current list of items high on the CG list.

1) Heat exhaustion: Body temp normal or sub-normal. Perspiration profuse. Get patient out of sun. Cool him off before he loses all body moisture. Bathe with cool cloths. Rest. Immobilize.

2) Heat stroke: Body temp high and skin dry and hot to the touch.   Get him out of sun and/or heat.   Call doctor immediately.

3) Burns:

   a) 1st degree; reddening of skin.   2/3 of body is serious.

   b) 2nd degree; blistering.   1/3 of body is serious.

   c) 3rd degree; loss of skin in burned area.   1/10 of body is serious.

   Burn treatment: Cold water quickly.   No grease or butter.   Wrap in sterile gauze to prevent infection.   Do not bind tightly.

4) Blood loss: Body has five qts.   Loss of one pint not serious.   Two pints can cause shock.   Capillary blood is brick red and oozes slowly.   Venous blood is dark and escapes in steady even flow.   Arterial blood is bright red and if near surface, spurts.   If deep, blood comes in a steady stream.

   For heavy bleeding, apply direct pressure to wound.   No tourniquets.

5) Broken bones: With "simple fracture" bone does not penetrate skin. Compound fracture ruptures skin.   Do not attempt to set.   Immobilize-prevent movement.   Call doctor.

6) Do not attempt to treat or administer first aid to unknown injury.

7) Never try to give liquids to unconscious person.

8) When choking, do not slap on back, especially between shoulder blades. Might force object into lungs.

9) Heart failure: Symptoms-pain on left side below breastbone, numbing of left arm or fingers.   Pain down left arm.   Cold sweat and pale.   Lips blue, pulse weak.   Treatment: Immobilize patient.   Keep him from any exertion.   If heart stops, go to CPR.

10) Drowning: Artificial respiration. Clear mouth of any foreign objects. Administer for minimum of four hours OR until relieved by a doctor. If patient regains consciousness, starting to breathe, **don't stop artificial respiration**. Regulate your timing to his or her breathing. Rate of administration of either Shaeffer-Prone method or Pressure-Arm Lift method is 15-20 per minute.

11) Shock: Symptoms-Shallow breath, low blood pressure, ashen face. Immobilize, raise feet, lower head and make comfortable.

Here's some test questions from Coast Guard tests.

IV. First Aid

1) An unknown type of injury occurs on board. You witness slurred speech, pupils differentially dilated, right side in paralysis. You suspect:

a) Heart attack, b) Epilepsy, c) Stroke, d) Shock.

2) A passenger suffers what appears to be a heart attack then stops breathing. First:

a) Apply artificial respiration, b) Apply mild electric shock, c) Call doctor and head for port, d) Keep patient on his feet.

3) What is the first treatment for a burn victim?

a) Apply butter or salad oil, b) Wrap burned area to keep sterile, c) Apply sterile bandage with cool water, d) Treat for shock.

4) How do you treat severe lacerations with blood spurting at regular intervals?

a) Apply tourniquet, b) Bandage, c) Apply direct pressure, a) All of these.

5) Assume a passenger is suffering from frost bite of the toes.   You should not:

a) Rub them gently to restore circulation, b) Elevate the patient's head, c) Wrap them in warm blankets, d) Give aspirin.

6) When applying artifical respiration how many breaths per minute should be induced?

a) 8, b) 18, c) 12, d) 24.

7) With a choking person you should:

a) Let him cough it up, b) Slap him on the back between his shoulder blades, c) Make him lie on his stomach, d) Try to extract the object from his throat.

8) What do you do first with a drowning victim?

a) Call a doctor for advice, b) Place him on his stomach and clear mouth of obstructions, c) Place him so as to drain excess water from lungs, d) Begin artificial respiration immediately.

9) How long do you administer artificial respiration?

a) One hour, b) Until relieved by a doctor, c) two hours, d) Until the patient has obviously expired.

10) How long do you administer artificial repiration?

a) One hour, b) Two hours, c) Three hours, d) Four hours.

11) Which of these symptoms indicate heart attack?

a) Blue lips, b) Pain, c) Numbness on left side, d) All of these.

12) With a broken bone temporary action is:

a) Make a temporary set, b) Administer inhalants, c) Make comfortable by moving to bunk or chair, d) Immobilize.

13) More than anything else a heart attack victim should be:

a) Immobilized, b) Kept awake, c) Kept with head down and feet up, d) Treated immediately for shock.

14) An unknown injury occurs. First you should:

a) Administer first aid, b) Treat for shock, c) Call a doctor, d) Head for the nearest port.

15) Which is a symptom of heat stroke?

a) Body temperature is high, b) Skin is dry, c) Skin is hot, d) All of these.

16) Which is the symptom of heat exhaustion?

a) Sub-normal body temperature, b) Normal body temperature, c) Perspiration, d) All of these.

17) Which is a symptom of shock?

a) Difficult or shallow breathing, b) Low blood pressure, c) Pale or ashen face, d) All of these.

18) A passenger on board becomes ill. He is moist and clammy to the touch and cold. You suspect:

a) Coronary, b) Shock, c) Respiratory infection, d) Acute halitosis.

19) A temporary treatment for a shock victim is to:

a) Keep patient conscious, b) Keep him ambulatory, c) Head down and raise his feet, d) Apply CPR.

FIRE FIGHTING

The Coast Guard will expect you to know some specifics on fire fighting. Here's a primary list of things you should know. The rest should become obvious by taking the test and scoring it.

I) To create a decent respectable fire you must have three elements:

Fuel---Oxygen---Heat

This is often called the "fire triangle" because if any of these elements are removed, the fire dies.

II) There are three **types** of fire. Each has a capital letter to identify it. You're supposed to know these.

Type A: Wood, paper, and trash in general.

Type B: Petroleum-Such as gas, alcohol*, diesel, paint, thinner, kerosene.

Type C: Electrical.

III) There are four basic types of fire extinguishers:

a) **Water.** This stuff isn't good on just **any** kind of fire. Only on Type "A" fire. For example, don't throw it on an electrical fire and never use water on petroleum fires. Water will spread the burning fuel around.

b) **Carbon Dioxide.** Better known as CO_2. Great stuff on petroleum fires, (Type "B") and even on Type "A". Not to be used on electrical. It evaporates quickly and the theory is the fire will restart. However, CO_2 is recognized as the one extinguisher capable of taking heat out of a fire very quickly. CO_2 extinguishers are measured by weight. When they get below 90% capacity, they are supposed to be recharged by a reputable fire extinguisher company.

*While water can be used to douse an alcohol fire, the NFPA insists the substance is a class I flammable liquid.

    c) **Dry Chemical**.   This is a capacity extinguisher measured by weight as in a can of coffee.   Good on any fire.   Particularly on petroleum fires.   Sometimes mistaken for the old "soda-acid" extinguisher which had to be turned upside down to activate.   Most dry chemical extinguishers have gauges on them indicating current reliability status.   Should be shaken up once a week as contents tend to solidify over a period of time.

    d) **Foam**.   Not generally found on small boats.   Takes a special "mixing" nozzle.   This is the stuff they "foam" down airport runways with when a crippled plane is coming in.   Great on petroleum fires, but should be bounced off a bulkhead so it will spread out over the fire.

All of the above provides us with a jungle of possibilities regarding which extinguisher should be used on what fire.   Here's some statements the CG utilizes to construct their fire quiz.

1) Type "A" fires are fought with water.

2) Type "B" need CO_2 or foam.   Dry chemical will do it, but the former two are preferred.

3) Do not use CO_2 on electrical fires.   Evaporation problem.

4) Never use water on petroleum fires.

5) Never use water on electrical fires.

6) Thus, dry chemical can be used on petroleum "B" fires, or electrical "C" fires.

7) Foam can be used on electrical or petroleum fires.

8) When there is an electrical fire, **first** secure the power source.

9) When there is a petroleum fire, **first** secure the source of the fuel supply.

10) Combustible liquids have a flashpoint above 100° F.   Flammable liquids have a flash point below 100° F with a vapor pressure below 40 psi.   In other words, flammable liquids give off explosive vapors.

V. **Fire**

1) There is a fire on the bow. You should first:

   a) Remove combustibles from bow area, b) Pull into the wind, c) Head downwind, d) Make lifejackets available.

2) What is the first thing to consider in the event of an electrical fire?

   a) Use CO_2, b) Possible shock, c) Never use water, d) Turn off power.

3) How are CO_2 fire extinguishers measured?

   a) Weight, b) Volume, c) Capacity, d) Operable time.

4) Which of the following is most likely to ignite fuel vapors?

   a) Static, b) Hot oil, c) Engine running hot, d) Loose wire.

5) Which of these types of fire extinguishers best removes heat from fire?

   a) Foam, b) Water, c) Dry chemicals, d) CO_2.

6) When fire extinguishers have branch lines, the branch lines should be:

   a) Closed when re-charging, b) Closed at all times, c) Closed when not in use, d) Open at all times.

7) An electrical fire should be treated with:

   a) Water, b) Foam, c) CO_2, d) Any of these.

8) What type of fire extinguisher is not normally serviced aboard ship?

   a) Carbon dioxide, b) Foam, c) Dry chemical, d) a & c.

9) Which of the following should not be used on Class "C" fires?

   a) CO_2, b) Water, c) Carbon-tet, d) All of these.

10) Which of the following could be absent in a fire?

   a) Flame, b) Oxygen, c) Smoke, d) Heat.

11) Which of the passenger carrying vessels need have no fire extinguisher aboard?

   a) Outboards, b) Operating inland only, c) Excursions within the confines of a harbor, d) None of these.

12) Class "A" fire can be economically fought with:

   a) Water, b) CO_2, c) Foam only, d) Dry chemical.

13) Which of the following cannot be used on a Class "A" fire?

   a) Water, b) Dry chemicals, c) CO_2, d) Any can be used.

14) The best way to use foam on a petroleum fire is to apply it:

   a) Directly to the base of the fire, b) By bouncing the foam off a bulkhead, c) Under high pressure, d) Under very low pressure.

15) The fixed CO_2 system in the engine room accidentally discharges. You should:

   a) Call the Coast Guard, b) Notify the Coast Guard immediately upon return to port, c) Vacate and ventilate, d) Head into the wind.

16) The most important consideration in an electrical fire is:

   a) Is it in the passenger space? b) Is it in the engine room? c) Is it on deck exposed to the wind? d) Will it spread to the paint locker?

17) Fire in the engine room. You should:

   a) Activate the fixed CO_2 system in the engine room, b) If a fuel fed fire, secure the fuel lines, c) Secure all engine room hatches and ports, d) All of these.

18) "Non-reigniting fires" are:

   a) Everything except electrical fires, b) Those deemed to be totally extinguished, c) Electrical fires, d) Type "C" fires.

ENGINES

In some offices, this topic will come under "Boat Handling". Again; many REC's mix the entire mish-mash into one test with the seven basic topics spread throughout the test. The concept of engine maintenance is more common sense than any other quiz. Those defying common sense or are ambiguous are something we have to live with. Those below will show need for a vocabulary the way the CG wants it with the few variations they have in mind. Try the test and you'll see. And don't laugh. These have appeared on tests.

VI. **Engine Maintenance and Mechanics.**

1) When a fuel line leak is discovered what do you do first?

   a) Shut off fuel supply at engine, b) Shut off fuel supply at fuel tank, c) Stop all engines and standby with CO_2, d) Head into the wind.

2) How do you stop a small diesel engine in an emergency?

   a) Turn off key, b) Crimp jet lines, c) Ground out engine, d) Cover air intake.

3) A gasoline engine becomes hard to start when cold. You suspect:

   a) Fuel, b) Ignition, c) Low batteries, d) Low oil pressure.

4) At the point the shaft enters the hull is found:

   a) The stuffing box, b) Shaft mold, c) Gear box, d) All of these.

5) When fueling a vessel:

   a) Leave tank room for expansion, b) Have 10% reserve for emergency, c) Keep the nozzle touching the fill pipe, d) All of these.

6) When fueling a vessel:

   a) Close up all hatches and ports, b) Ventilate the engine space when finished fueling, c) If portable tanks, place on dock to fuel, d) All of these.

7) A fuel tank intake pipe should extend:

   a) Almost to the bottom of the tank, b) To the top of the tank, c) Half-way to the bottom of the tank, d) Any of these.

8) Drain plugs on gasoline fuel tanks:

   a) May be used only on the top of the tank, b) May be used on the bottom but must be checked periodically for rust or leaks, c) May be used on the sides of any tank, d) Must be threaded.

9) All carburetors must have:

   a) Vibration free connectors, b) Drip pans, c) Backfire arrestors, d) All of these.

10) Drip pans are necessary on:

   a) Up draft carburetors, b) Down draft carburetors, c) Any batteries containing liquid, d) None of these.

11) A battery compartment should be ventilated because:

   a) Fresh air will inhibit corrosion on cable connectors, b) A dangerous and explosive gas mixture can result without ventilation, c) Batteries accumulate moisture which must be given an escape route to evaporation. d) An electrolytic spontaneous combustion can occur without daily ventilation.

12) Drip pans on gasoline engines are located:

a) Beneath down-draft carburetors, b) Beneath up-draft carburetors, c) Beneath fuel filters, d) All of these.

13) A diesel engine emitting black smoke is running:

a) With contaminated fuel, b) Too lean, c) Too rich, d) Any of these.

14) A gasoline engine misses underway due to faulty ignition. First:

a) Install a new fuel filter, b) Inspect the ignition system, c) Check the alternator connections, d) File the points.

15) Fuses are installed on a vessel:

a) As electrical gate valves, b) To prevent overload, c) To enhance the flow of energy, d) As connectors to the batteries.

16) Fuel tanks should be filled:

a) To allow for expansion, b) 10% more than would be used on the expected trip, c) To capacity, d) To allow for ample spillage and/or evaporation.

17) Which is the safest metal for fuel fill pipes?
a) Iron or steel, b) Aluminum, c) Stainless steel, d) Brass.

18) Gas vents should lead:

a) To open air, b) Into the engine room, c) Aft, d) Forward.

19) If the engine refuses to start what do you check first?

a) Spark plugs, b) Fuel, c) Ignition, d) Points.

Up early and feeling bored on Sunday morning? Tune in to the greatest comedy in town. Go watch 'em down at the launching ramp. It's a gas.

RULES AND REGULATIONS

The following questions were derived by the Coast Guard from several of their publications. A substantial portion comes from one of their booklets entitled, at this writing, "Rules and Regulations for Small Passenger Vessels (under 100 gross tons). It is sometimes referred to simply as Subchapter "T". The CG publication number is "CG-323". There is a separate test for Ocean Operator candidates on section Subchapter "T". Most districts make it an open book exam, but Ocean Operators would do well to check their local district's policy on this exam. A word of advice to Ocean Operator candidates. If they give you the Subchapter "T" pamphlet with an open book test, be sure to use the index which starts on page 103.

The questions below are for both Six Pac and Ocean Operator candidates because both are required to take the test. Many offices make this an open book for Six Packers. Be sure to ask.

VII. Rules and Regulations.

1) Upon death of a passenger the CG should be notified within:

   a) 1 hour after docking, b) 24 hours, c) After next of kin is notified, d) Within 12 hours.

2) The color of CG approved life jackets is:

   a) There is no requirement for color, b) Always orange, c) International orange, d) Buff colored.

3) The proper radio procedure on 2182 K/cs is:

   a) Use for calling then shift to another channel, b) Use for official communications only, c) Do not use except for conversing with a station ashore, d) Use only when conversing with the Coast Guard.

4) Which passenger carrying vessel needs no license to carry for hire?

   a) Inland only, b) Less than 12 meters, c) Auxiliary sailboats operating under sail, d) A sailboat less than 100 gross tons with no engine aboard.

5) All gasoline engine equipped vessels, whether carrying passengers for hire or not, shall be equipped with:

   a) Fire extinguishers, b) Backfire arrestors, c) A lifejacket for each person aboard, d) All of these.

6) Which of the following is not required on a six passenger uninspected vessel carrying passengers for hire?

a) Compass, b) Fire extinguisher, c) Bell, d) Whistle in clear weather.

7) Auxiliary air cooled engines shall be installed:

a) As far aft as possible, b) Securely on deck, c) Away from all exhausts, d) Below decks.

8) LPG fuels may be used on which passenger carrying craft?

a) Propelled solely by outboard with no decking, b) On auxiliary sailing craft, c) Vessels over 50 meters, d) None of these.

9) If your vessel spills oil at sea you should:

a) Inform the local Pollution Control monitor, b) Determine your position and fill out & file special "spill" forms upon return to port, c) Clean it up to the best of your ability, d) Make your position known to the CG immediately.

10) A fire axe is required of which type of charter vessel?

a) "S" vessel, b) Six passenger vessel, c) "L" vessel, d) All passenger carrying vessels.

11) Anyone found guilty of negligence or failing to conform to the Bridge to Bridge Radiotelephone Regulations can be fined not more than:

a) $500, b) $1,000, c) $1500, d) $2,000

12) The River and Harbor Act of 1899 imposed a maximum fine of how much for dumping refuse into harbors and rivers?

a) $500, b) $1,000, c) $1500, d) $2,500

13) The fine for dumping pollutants in the ocean is now:

a) $5,000, b) $10,000, c) $20,000, d) $50,000

14) The fine for not informing the CG you have caused an oil spill is:

a) $10,000, b) $15,000, c) $20,000, d) $25,000

15) The term "Pan" as used on a radiotelephone channel 16, means:

a) Standby for possible emergency, b) Another term for Mayday, c) Missile firing schedule to follow, d) The Russians are coming.

16) "Plead control" is:

a) A term used by the FCC to clear the airways, b) The Coast Guard's motto, c) The Navy radio at Pt. Mugu, d) A request for assistance not of a major nature.

SEAMANSHIP KEY

I. SEAMANSHIP

1) C	28) C			
2) B	29) D			
3) A	30) D			
4) D	31) B			
5) C	32) B			
6) B	33) A			
7) C	34) B			
8) A	35) B			
9) A	36) C			
10) A				
11) A				
12) B				
13) C				
14) D				
15) D				
16) C				
17) B				
18) D				
19) B				
20) C				
21) A				
22) A				
23) A				
24) B				
25) C				
26) C				
27) B				

II. WEATHER

1) D
2) C
3) B
4) D
5) C
6) B
7) B
8) D
9) D
10) C
11) A
12) B
13) D
14) B
15) B
16) B
17) B
18) A
19) A
20) D
21) D
22) C
23) A
24) C
25) A
26) A

III. BOATS

1) C
2) C
3) B
4) C
5) A
6) C
7) B
8) D
9) B
10) B
11) B
12) A
13) A
14) D
15) C
16) A
17) A
18) D
19) C
20) D
21) D
22) D
23) B
24) C
25) B
26) C
27) B
28) B
29) C
30) A
31) C
32) D
33) A
34) C
35) C
36) D
37) D
38) C

IV. FIRST AID

1) C
2) A
3) C
4) C
5) D
6) B
7) A
8) B
9) B
10) D
11) D
12) A

V. FIRE

1) C
2) D
3) A
4) D
5) D
6) D
7) B
8) C
9) D
10) C
11) D
12) B
13) A
14) C
15) D
16) D
17) D
18) B
19) C

VII. ENGINES

1) B	6) A
2) D	7) B
3) B	8) D
4) A	9) D
5) D	10) C
6) D	11) A
7) A	12) D
8) D	13) A
9) C	14) A
10) A	15) A
11) B	16) C
12) B	
13) C	
14) D	
15) B	
16) A	
17) D	
18) A	
19) C	

VII. RULES

1) B
2) C
3) A
4) D
5) D

OIL POLLUTION

This is a sore subject on the west coast. Perhaps it was the environmentalists who lobbied this into the test. However, since the Coast Guard is the oil pollution watchdog these days, maybe it was a combination of both. There is a manual on this subject entitled: "Oil Pollution Control For Tankermen". It was first published sometime in 1973 and the CG has been using it for their ten question **open book** test for licenses. It's not a difficult book to read, but hard to look anything up because the CG does not list their questions in the order you would find the answers in the book. Here are the most commonly asked questions. The answers are at the end of the test. Read them. They **could** show up in another quiz.

1) The minimum pressure allowed for hose assemblies is:

   a) 2000 lbs., b) 400 lbs., c) 500 lbs., d) 600 lbs or more

2) The emergency shut-down mechanism required on a tank vessel carrying oil and having a capacity for 250 or more barrels must be operable from:

   a) The bridge, b) The Control Room, c) The Cargo Deck, d) b & c

3) The operator of each vessel required to have oil transfer procedures shall maintain said procedures then current and the procedures must contain all of the following **EXCEPT:**

   a) A copy of the vessel's certificate of inspection.
   b) Procedures for reporting oil discharges into the water.
   c) A line diagram of the vessel's oil transfer piping.
   d) The number of persons required to be on duty during oil transfer operations.

4) The Oil Pollution Act of 1961 prohibits the discharge of oil or oily mixtures within the prohibited zones. Prohibited zones are generally areas with the following limits:

   a) The three mile shore limit which may be extended to six miles.
   b) " 12 " " " " " " " 24 " .
   c) " 50 " " " " " " " 100 " .
   d) " 100 " " " " " " " 200 " .

5) The Federal Water Pollution Control Act requires the person in charge of a vessel to immediately notify the CG as soon as he knows of any oil discharge. Failure to notify the CG can, upon conviction, lead to a fine of:

   a) $500 or 30 days in jail or both.
   b) $1,000 or 60 day or both.
   c) $10,000 or one year or both.
   d) $50,000 of five years or both.

6) Each hose must be marked (or recorded elsewhere) with all of the following information **EXCEPT:**

   a) Date of manufacture.
   b) Name of Manufacturer.
   c) Burst pressure.
   d) Recommended working pressure

7) The minimum bursting pressure for each hose assembly must be:

a) 600 lbs. per sq. in. or more.
b) At least 4 times the pressure of the relief valve setting plus the static head pressure of the oil transfer system.
c) a & b.
d) Neither.

8) For you to serve as a person in charge of oil transfer operations on more than one vessel at a time, one of the conditions is that:

a) There is a ready means of access between vessels.
b) It must be stated on the certificate of Inspection.
c) It must be included and posted with the oil transfer procedures.
d) The Captain of the port must authorize such procedures.

9) Which of the following is **NOT** considered "Oil" as defined in the pollution regulations:

a) Petrolem and fuel oil.
b) Oil mixed with dredged spoil.
c) Sludge.
d) Oil refuse and oil mixed with wastes.

10) Oil spills...

a) Usually disappear quickly.
b) Cause serious pollution as the effect tends to be cumulative.
c) Either a or b.
d) Neither

11) If your vessel spills oil at sea, you should:

a) Report it to the Coast Guard at the next port of call, b) Fill out and file a special "spill" form, c) Clean it up to the best of your ability, d) Inform the Coast Guard immediately making your position known.

12) Which of the following substances is it not forbidden to dump overboard:

a) Oil, b) Oily sludge, c) Kerosene, d) Gasoline.

13) Which of these substances is it acceptable to dump to inhibit rough seas?

a) Kerosene, b) Crude oil, c) Diesel, d) Vegetable oil.

ANSWERS

1) d, 2) d, 3) a, 4) c, 5) c, 6) b, 7) d, 8) a, 9) b, 10) c, 11) d, 12) b, 13) d.

LOCAL KNOWLEDGE

For some, this is a tricky subject. **Some** offices administer this test as an open book exam. The open book theory is; while you might not know every nook and cranny of your area, you should know how to look up the information. One assumes, therefore, that the closed book theory states you should know **everything** about your area of operation. To this writer's knowledge, there is no directive from Great White Father stating all REC's are to administer the test either using open **or** closed book.

What are your options? Be prepared to do either, but checking can't hurt. However, REC's have been known to change their minds overnight. REC's have been known to lean heavily on official publications, the leading one of which is the Coast Pilot. Read through your area in the Pilot then learn how to use the index. Use of the index in official publications is a must. Without it you will wallow in the printed pages for countless hours. Many offices will also let you use the Light List. **ASK.** Ask **before** you go into the exam room for the local knowledge quiz. They get busy and frequently forget to tell you if it's open book!!!

West coast candidates will notice there are several questions for which no answer will be found in the Coast Pilot. There is no reason to assume the same will not happen in other districts. You should know your charts well, especially **local hazards** and **unusual weather conditions.** The Coast Guard seems to assume that you have been rolling and patrolling out there for so long that the charts are an integral part of your being and all candidates are possessed of a photographic memory.

There is one bright star on the horizon. When the new license changes are inaugurated, the Local Knowledge test **could be** eliminated entirely since the licenses **might** then be valid in "navagable waters of the United States." This is a big maybe.

What kind of questions should you expect? Here are some samples from past tests in Long Beach, (including the popular Mexican Baja California waters which Long Beach endorses on licenses). The answers are at the end of this test for the Southern California area.

If you work another coastline, run through these anyway. They will give you an idea of how to prepare for your own area. For the San Francisco area, you have some research to do. In both areas, the questions weren't invented. They came from friendly readers who went before you.

SOUTHERN CALIFORNIA - ELEVENTH CG DISTRICT

1) Name five radio beacons equipped with major lights from Pt. Conception to the Mexican Border.

2) Name five small boat harbors from San Diego to Los Angeles.

3) Name five small boat harbors from Los Angeles to Santa Barbara.

4) Name five places where a small craft and/or storm warnings would be posted during the day and night.

5) Name three national monuments along the coast.

6) Where is Table Mountain?

7) How many islands are there in the Coronado Group and how far off shore are they?

8) Name five coastal light houses.

9) What is the magnetic bearing on Shelter Island Light when entering San Diego Harbor?

10) Where is Ballast Point?

11) What is the light characteristic of the Shelter Island Light?

12) What is the light characteristic of the Ballast Point Light?

13) What is the light chartacteristic of the Pt. Loma Light?

14) What is the light characteristic of the Los Angeles Light?

15) Name two harbors of refuge on each of the channel islands.

16) If en route to Catalina Island from Anacapa Island and a sudden SE'er came up, to what harbor would you run?

17) Name one harbor of refuge on each of the channel islands in the event of southeaster.

18) Describe the so-called "Santana" winds indicating the time of year most likely for them to occur.

19) What is the depth of the channel entering San Diego Harbor?

20) What is the depth of the channel entering L.A. Harbor?

21) Name five prominent land marks entering L.A. Harbor.

22) Where is Santiago Park?

23) What is a fish haven?

24) What special precautions would be taken while navigating near San Clemente Island and the Sixty Mile Bank?

25) Where is Anchorage A-2?

26) What is the name given to the large fissure near the west end of Catalina Island?

27) Describe the Point Conception Light characteristic.

28) Describe the Point Dume buoy.

29) What is a particular hazard offshore from Rincon Pt. to Summerland?

30) Where is the Redondo Beach King Harbor Radio Beacon located?

31) What area in the L.A. outer harbor is not navigable by small craft?

32) Describe the Coast between Dana Point and Laguna Beach.

33) Describe the coast on the NW area of Descanso Bay.

34) Name a prominent navigational hazard in Descanso Bay.

35) What is the only discernible landmark from Pt. Descanso to Salsipuedes Point?

36) Describe the bottom at Santo Tomas.

37) Name some of the offshore hazards between Punta Banda and Cape Colnett.

38) Describe the coast from Punta Miguel to Ensenda.

39) Where on the island is the Santa Barbara Island Light located?

40) Where is Begg Rock?

41) Where is Bishop Rock?

42) Where is the Osborn Bank?

43) What is the prominent hazard just outside Oceanside Harbor?

44) Describe Alamitos Bay.

45) Describe Zuniga Jetty.

46) Where is "Angel's Gate"?

47) The California Current runs:

a) East in the Santa Barbara Channel, b) South in the Gulf of Santa Catalina, c) Neither of these, d) Both of these.

48) The entrance buoy to the Ventura Marina is:

a) A large nun buoy numbered "2", b) A large can buoy numbered "1", c) A bell buoy, d) A whistle buoy.

49) From San Diego, Bishop Rock is:

a) 100 miles bearing 260°, b) 100 miles bearing 270°, c) 96 miles bearing 270°, d) 96 miles bearing 260°.

50) Cojo is a good anchorage during:

a) SW wind, b) SE wind, c) NW wind, d) Fair weather only.

51) A hazard to navigation peculiar to Santa Barbara Island is:

a) Backwash from the island, b) Numerous rocks which are covered at high tide, c) A kelp line extending out from the island in 10 fathoms, d) The complete absence of navigational aids.

52) An obstruction situated off Huntington Beach is:

a) An obsolete privately maintained buoy, b) A fish haven, c) A large rock in shallow water, d) A pipeline protruding almost to the surface.

53) The light characteristics of the oil platforms between Carpinteria and Point Conception are:

a) Flashing white, b) Flashing green, c) One fixed white light on each corner of the platforms, d) A red aero beacon on each one.

54) A characteristic of the shoreline from Gaviota to Point Conception is:

a) Many inlets, b) Low sandy beaches, c) Large homes situated on the cliffs, d) A kelp line extending out about a mile from shore.

55) San Nicolas Island has which combination of navigational aides?

a) Lights on the NE, SE, E, and an aero beacon near the east end, b) Lights on the NE, SE, E, and an aero beacon near the west end, c) An aero beacon south side, plus three lights close to the western tip of the island, d) Two lights ashore, an aero beacon and a buoy offshore.

56) Many CG offices are giving the Local Knowledge test allowing candidates to use the Coast Pilot and Sailing Directions. To prepare for this you should:

a) Become familiar with these publications, b) Realize this "open book" policy could change at any time, c) Learn to use the **index** in these publications, d) All of the above.

57) Which is not a landmark entering Angel's Gate?

a) The Kaiser Gypsum plant, b) The Vincent Thomas Bridge, c) The Palos Verdes Peninsula, d) Oil Islands off Long Beach.

58) What part of the L.A. harbor is not navigable at low tide?

    a) Immediately east of the breakwater opening, b) Near the CG buoy docks, c) The west end which supports a reef, c) Off the customs docks.

59) What hazard is there entering L.A. Harbor?

    a) A rusty pipe protruding from the breakwater, b) Heavy shoaling near each end of the breakwater, c) Heavy small boat traffic, d) Unlighted mooring buoys.

60) Where is the only radio beacon between Pt. Dume and Point Vincente?

    a) The Santa Monica Pier, b) The Manhattan Beach Pier, c) The Hermosa Beach landing, d) Redondo Beach's King Harbor.

61) What is the danger entering Alamitos Bay in restricted visibility?

    a) Mistakenly sailing up the San Gabriel, b) The oil islands, c) Shoaling alongside the pier, d) Small boat traffic.

62) What is the chief navigational danger in the Santa Barbara Channel?

    a) Abandoned well heads, b) The Channel Islands, c) A thick kelp line, d) Offshore oil platforms.

And Some More From Mexican Waters.

63) How many lights are there on the Coronados and where are they?

64) What are the inland boundary lines to:

    Todos Santos, San Miguel and Punta Bonda?

65) What is the approximate height of the bluff at Cape Colnett?

66) Approaching San Quintin from the south, describe the appearance.

67) What is the appearance of Geronimo Island-approaching from the South?

68) Where is the best anchorage around San Martin Island and how would you anchor there?

69) How far offshore and how shallow can the Sacramento Reef become?

70) Cite five hazards to navigation between San Martin and Cedros Islands.

71) Can the "entrance" to San Quintin be navigated or must a vessel anchor outside?

72) How many islands are there in the Bonitos Group?

73) How many lights are there on Cedros Island and where are they?

74) Describe the entrance and buoys entering Scammons Lagoon.

75) Would you say Turtle Bay is well stocked and supplies available?

76) Does Cape Colnett show up well on a radar scope?

77) Describe the current at Abreojos and Magdalena Bay.

78) Is Cape San Lucas an all weather anchorage?

79) Describe Punta Tosca in terms of an anchorage.

80) Describe the entrance to Magdalena Bay, Punta Entrada and Punta Redondo.

81) Should Mexican navigation aids be considered undependable?

SAN FRANCISCO

1) Where is Pt. Conception?

2) What is the distance between Pt. Conception and Pt. Arguello?

3) Which areas are considered to be the most dangerous between Pt. Sal and Pt. Arguello?

4) Name the types of buoys, plus the sound and light characteristics for the respective buoys located at the following places:

   a) Souza Rock

   b) Westdahl Rock

   c) Pt. Buchon

   d) Von Helm Rock

5) Following the ten fathom curve south in a fog you hear a horn and see a large white rock. Where are you?

6) In what direction do you enter Morro Bay Harbor?

7) What type of buoy marks San Simeon Bay?

8) Name two conspicuous landmarks between Ragged Point and Cape Martin.

9) South of what point would you expect to see a white barn in the midst of a group of buildings?

10) Give the light characteristics of Cape San Martin light.

11) Between Pt. Pinos and Pt. Sur there are hazards which make it unsafe to navigate inside of a certain fathom line. Which fathom line is it?

12) What is the direction of the prevailing winds south of San Francisco?

13) 0.7 of a mile off Pt. Pinos there is a buoy. What type is it?

14) What are the characteristics of the Pt. Pinos Light?

15) Sharp turns should _____ when leaving Morro Bay Harbor in heavy weather.

16) A pier with a group of warehouses and buildings south of Piedras Blancas would indicate what landing?

17) A prominent landmark of a square black rock would put you between what two well known points?

18) Montara Mountain is a prominant feature from the north or south of what area?

19) There is a restricted area in the SE part of Monterey Bay. What is it?

20) There is an aid to navigation about one mile SE of Pt. Santa Cruz. What is it?

San Francisco facts to be committed to memory.

A few of these will answer some of the questions above.

20) The Gulf of the Farallones extends from Point Reyes on the north to the Farallon Islands on the west and to Point San Pedro on the south.

21) Mile Rocks Light is off **Lands End on the north face of Pt. Lobos.**

22) From the north and south, Pt. Sur looks like an **island.**

23) At night, the **mission** at Carmel is conspicuous from Carmel Bay.

24) Atop **Pt. San Pedro,** there is a large triple headed rock about 100 feet high and white on its south face.

25) The light marking the south boundary of Monterey Bay is on **Pt. Pinos.**

26) A building and two white radar antennas are conspicuous at **Pillar Point.**

27) The precautionary area off the entrance to San Francisco Bay is marked by a **lighted horn buoy.**

28) The Farallon Light is on **SE Farallon Island.**

29) Boats can anchor in eight fathoms in **Fisherman Bay** on SE Farallon Island.

30) There are numerous radio towers at Bolinas Point.

31) South of Pt. Sur, vessels should stay in depths greater than **thirty fathoms** due to rocks and breakers which are marked by kelp.

32) The 5,000 yard short firing range used by Fort Ord is in the SE part of Monterey Bay and is restricted as follows: a) Dawn to midnight - Monday through Friday; b) Dawn to dusk - Saturday and Sunday.

33) A naval area of operations is in the **NE part** of Monterey Bay.

34) There is foul ground to the **NE and SE** of Ano Nuevo.

35) The depths at Pillar Point Harbor are **2 to 20** feet.

36) The main danger when entering Pillar Point is the **reef to the SE.**

37) The San Francisco Approach Light, which replaced the Light Ship in 1971, is 11 miles from the Golden Gate Bridge. (Ed note: The Coast Pilot states that it is 9 miles WSW of San Francisco Bay Entrance.)   The answer to the CG seems to remain 11 miles!!

38) The Point Sur Light is on a **gray stone tower.**

39) There is a **lighted whistle 0.7 miles** off Pt. Pinos.

40) The Santa Cruz Light is a **lantern house on a square building.**

41) South of Anna Nuevo is a **lighted whistle.**

42) Pigeon Point Light and the Montara Point Light are on **white conical towers.**

43) The Farallon Light is on a **conical tower,** on the **SE Farrallon Island.**

44) On Noonday Rock, there is a **lighted whistle buoy.**

45) Both the Point Bonita Light and the Mile Rocks Light are on **white towers.**

46) The Point Reyes Light is on a **steel pole** on a square building.

47) The demarcation line for the San Francisco Bay entrance is a line between **Pt. Bonita** and the **Mile Rocks Light.**

48) There is a **lighted whistle buoy** two miles south of Duxbury Point.

The two happiest days of a man's life are when he buys his boat...and when he sells it.

LOCAL KNOWLEDGE KEY

Southern California

1) Ventura-Channel Islands-Marina del Rey-King Harbor-L.A. Light-San Pedro Bay Light-Corona del Mar-(Newport, Balboa)-Dana Point-Oceanside-Mission Bay-Pt. Loma. Ed. note: Use extreme caution. These positions change frequently. Consult your chart or a current Coast Pilot.

2) Mission Bay-Oceanside-Del Mar (Camp Pendleton) -Dana Point-Corona del Mar-Huntington Harbor-Seal Beach.

3) King Harbor-Santa Monica-(open but limited shelter) Marina del Rey-Paradise Cove-just inside Pt. Dume)-Port Hueneme-Channel Islands-Ventura Marina-Santa Barbara.

4) In San Diego-Municipal Pier #2 and Shelter Island Yacht Club. Harbor Master's Office in Ventura-Harbor Master's Office Channel Islands-Harbor Office Santa Barbara-Avalon's Pleasure Pier, L.A. Light. Ed. note: These also change. Check.

5) U.S. Mexico Boundary-Channel Islands Nat'l Monument at Anacapa Island, Cabrillo Nat'l Monument at Pt. Loma.

6) A flat topped mountain about 25 miles SE of Pt. Loma. Inland.

7) Four islands about 7 miles offshore.

8) Los Angeles-Pt. Vicente-Port Hueneme-Pt. Loma-Santa Barbara and Pt. Conception.

9) 339°

10) In San Diego Harbor on left before Shelter Island when entering.

11) White- 2 1/2 second.

12) White- 5 second.

13) Flashing white- 15 second.

14) Flashing green- 15 second.

15) San Miguel Island: Tyler's and Cuyler's.
    Santa Rosa Island: Johnson's Lee and Becher's Bay.
    Santa Cruz Island: Pelican and Fry's.
    Anacapa Island: Frenchy's and Fisherman's.
    San Nicolas and Santa Barbara Islands: Indicate the lee side in rough weather.
    Santa Catalina: Isthmus and Avalon.
    San Clemente: Wilson's Cove and Northwest Anchorage.

16) Chinese Harbor-Santa Cruz Island.

17) San Miguel Island: Simonton Cove.
    Santa Rosa Island: SE Anchorage or Becher's Bay.
    Santa Cruz Island: Chinese Harbor.
    Santa Catalina Island: Goat Harbor.

San Clemente Island: Northwest Anchorage.

18) Offshore from desert. From 50 to 60 knots. Sudden and hot. October to April.

19) 42 feet.

20) 47 feet.

21) Vincent Thomas Bridge, L.A. Light, Palos Verdes Peninsula, Breakwater, Oil Islands in San Pedro Bay.

22) 17.5 miles NE of Dana Point. Famous as inland "bearing point".

23) Artificial reef to attract fish. Old autos, tires, etc.

24) Sudden and unexplainable excess magnetic variation.

25) This is the commercial anchorage in L.A. Harbor.

26) Isthmus.

27) Fl white 30 sec.

28) Fl white 4 sec.

29) Mooring buoys.

30) On extreme end of King Harbor breakwater.

31) West Basin off south shore of Terminal Island. Stay out of traffic pattern for commercial vessels frequenting berths 45-50.

32) Bold rocky cliffs, to 100 feet high separated by deep valleys.

33) Marked by 400 foot cliff.

34) Sugarloaf Rock.

35) Concrete tower.

36) Rocky.

37) Oil rigs, detached rocks half-mile offshore and piers.

38) Rocks and kelp.

39) On extreme NE point

40) NW of San Nicolas Island.

41) Cortes Bank. Due west of San Diego and south of Tanner Bank.

42) South of Santa Barbara Island.

43) A fish haven.

44) A shallow water yacht basin and marine stadium off Belmont Shores and just

45) A mile long jetty extending southward from Coronado Island in the San Diego Harbor area. Mounts five lights.

46) Nickname for the entrance to L.A. Harbor.

47) D

48) D

49) A

50) C

51) C

52) B

53) C

54) D

55) D

56) D

57) A

58) C

59) A

60) D

61) A

62) D

MEXICO ANSWERS

63) Two on the south island (Coronado del Sur)-one on the NE section and one on the south end.

64) From Punta San Miguel on a line to the Todos Santos north island light thence roughly to the lighted buoy NW'ly off Punta Banda.

65) High bluffs-300' to 400' high.

66) Low lying and sandy.

67) Small, low and sandy. Located just north of the Sacramento Reef. Has a light.

68) SE anchorage and has a rocky bottom with sandy spots. Give southern end of island a wide birth. Submerged rocks.

69) The reef is about 5 miles offshore awash at low water. Rocks & kelp beds. Geronimo Island Light has a danger sector bearing on this reef.

Geronimo Island Light has a danger sector bearing on this reef.

70) Roca Ben Shoals south of San Martin Island. Sacramento Reef. Shoal areas south of Punta Baja which is north of Germonimo & the reef. Shoal area off Punta Rosarito. A shallow pinnacle rock about 700 yards south of Punta Canoas.

71) Shallow entrance. Big vessels outside. Call for guide if low water. With small craft use caution as shifting sands at entrance make markers there often in error.

72) Three.

73) Two. One on NE tip and one on SE tip.

74) Entrance buoy with red and white bands. Very narrow sandy entrance.

75) Yes. Food, supplies and fuel.

76) Yes. Excellent bearings.

77) Current moves south and "out" to sea.

78) No. From May to November SE storms enter here.

79) Strength of tidal flows through Rehusa Channel make it dangerous. Anchor about one-half mile east of Cabo Tosco in 7-9 fathoms.

80) Magdalena: Well marked with light on southern tip. Fifteen fathoms. Enter from SW. Entrada: Low, sandy and very narrow. Redondo: GP FL (3) light 62' high, visible 13 miles. Main entrance to Mag Bay.

81) Any and all Mexican navigation aids should always be considered undependable.

Only the most depraved with nothing to do would hang around a boat yard...and watch others suffer.

The following eight pages of diagrams and instructions are devoted to teaching you to use the course plotter. If you have completed a basic boating class with the U.S. Power Squadron or the Coast Guard Auxiliary you already know how to use it. If you hold a rank of AP in the Power Squadron, you're wasting your time. And forget about parallel rules. This will work faster and better and more accurate. Honest.

The top of a chart represents north; true north. The bottom is south, to the right is east and to the left is west. These terms are seldom used when plotting. North is 000⁰ or 360⁰. East is 090⁰ and west is 270⁰. Everything in between also has a **three digit** number.

Look at the circles on the next page. They're numbered -in the center- #1 through #8. Examine the direction of the arrows. The direction of the first arrow falls between 000⁰ and 090⁰. If you were moving across a chart, your direction would be indicated by a more exact number. Maybe something like 040⁰ or 045⁰. Exactness at this point isn't necessary. We're merely looking for rough estimates. Glancing at #2, estimate the direction. 185⁰ or even 190⁰? Write down your estimations for 3 through 6.

Number 3 would be someone on a course of around 280⁰ Number 4 would be close to 140⁰. Number 5 is a course line of around 080⁰ and #6 about 240⁰. Don't go any further until you've established why the above answers are within rough approximations.

The following page contains nine more of like kind except the circles and numbers are missing. Pretend this page is a chart -north at the top- and see how close you can come by **estimating** these course lines. Looking at the first one it appears to be on a heading of less than north or 360⁰. Maybe 350⁰ or 340⁰? Close enough for now.

Can you see that #2 is to the right of straight up or 000⁰? Maybe 010⁰? And doesn't #3 appear to be slightly greater than 090⁰? Perhaps 100⁰ or 110⁰? Try to **estimate** the remaining six within 25⁰ of the answers below. The object is merely to be within the correct quadrant.

ANSWERS

4) 245⁰, 5) 190⁰, 6) 155⁰, 7) 050⁰, 8) 290⁰, 9) 080⁰.

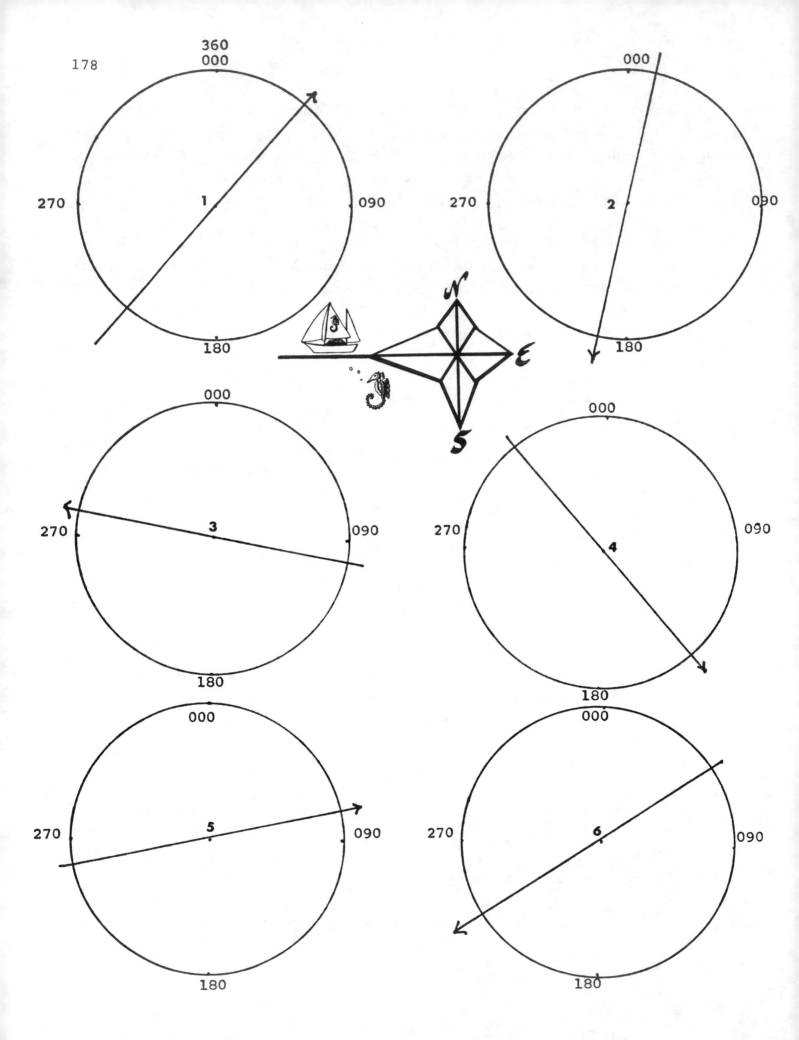

178

360
000

270   1   090

180

000

270   2   090

180

000

270   3   090

180

000

270   4   090

180

000

270   5   090

180

000

270   6   090

180

N
E
S

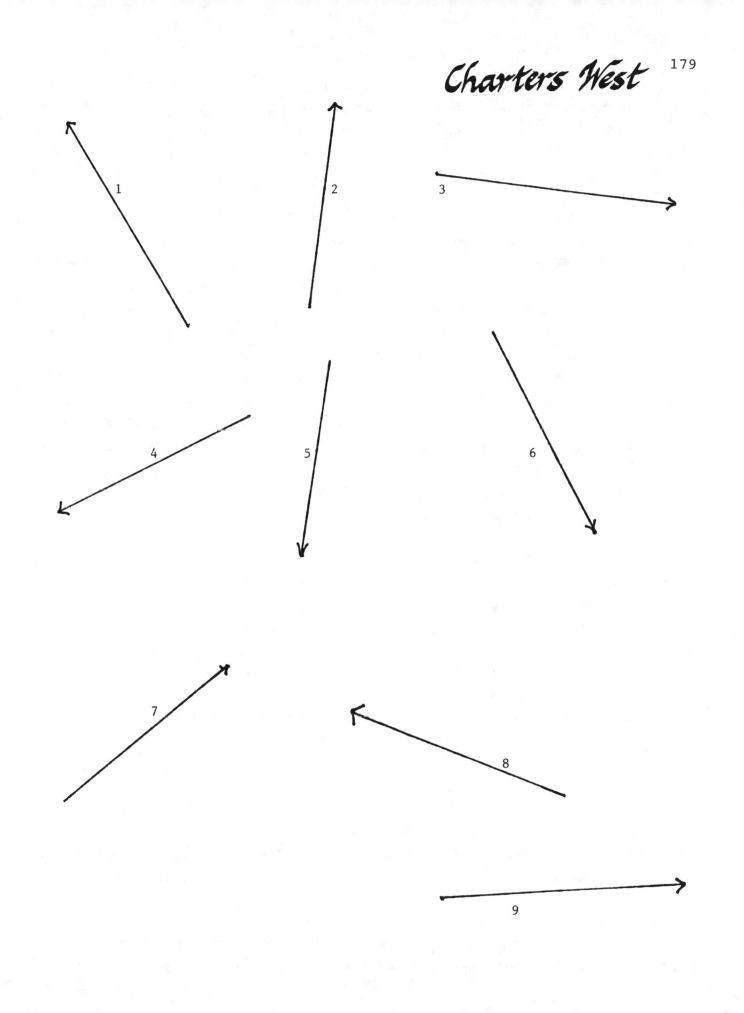

Now for the good part. You'll need our big book chart. Flatten it out and grab your course plotter. **Don't put the course plotter on the chart** yet. You need to make an estimate. Estimate the course if you were travelling from the West Point Light to the Bunny Isle Light. Someplace between 000° and 090°, right? **Remember that estimate.** If you don't understand the estimate, go back until you **do** get it.

Now look at the next page which has part of the course plotter smeared all over it. 1) Notice that the first **line** of the plotter leads from West Point Light to Bunny Isle Light. 2) Find that little circle near the bottom center of the course plotter. Line it up on any longitude line that's handy. Careful. Keep the top line of the plotter lined up on the two lights. 3) Since the plotter is plastic, you can see through it. Notice the longitude line over which you have centered the little circle (target). Follow that longitude line "up" to the top of the **outer** scale. The longitude line intersects two numbers on the outer scale. O.K., what's the course? You have two choices. 252° or 072°. **Wait!** What was that **estimate** you made a minute ago? Someplace between 000° and 090°. H-m-m-m. Must be 072° from the West Point Light to Bunny Isle Light. Now, I ask you. Ain't that cute? Let's go to the next course plotter smeared page and try another one.

This time we're heading from Spa Rock Light to the West End Light. Take the bottom **line** of your course plotter and arrange it so it cuts through Spa Rock Light and West Point Light. Now jiggle the plotter around until it intersects that longitude line running down the middle of the page. Again, this diagram is laid out for you on the page following our last attempt. With the bottom line intersecting the two lights and the target over the...**OH GOD!** We forgot to estimate the course first. Without an estimate, we might read the wrong number on the outer scale of the course plotter. Estimate, estimate, quick. Ah, greater than 090° and less than 180°. O.K., where were we?

Let's see. Bottom **line** of course plotter intersecting both lights. Target over the handiest longitude line. Look at longitude line and follow it **straight up** to the top of the course plotter. What'll you have? 148° or 328°? So, going **from** Spa Rock Light **to** West Point Light makes a true course of 148°. **Don't move the course plotter.** We're not finished with this one yet.

What if you wanted to travel in the opposite direction? You know, from West Point Light to Spa Rock Light? **DON'T TOUCH THAT COURSE PLOTTER.** Make an estimate. A course greater than 270° and less than 360°, you say? Right.

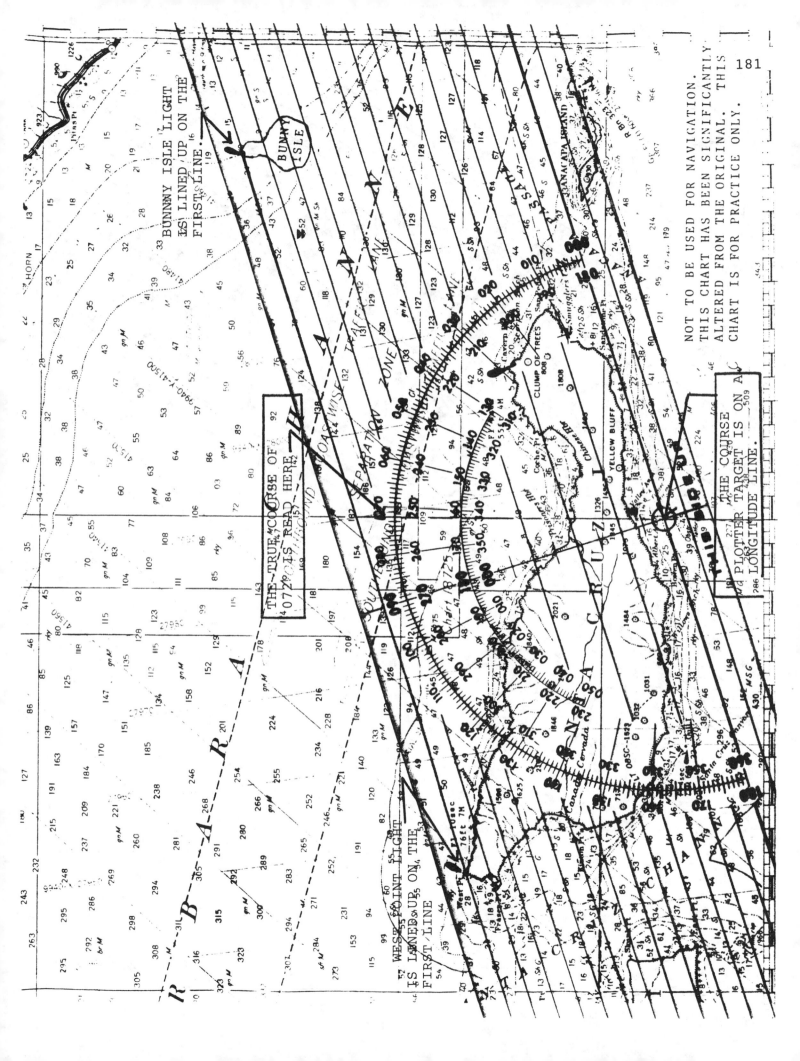

181

NOT TO BE USED FOR NAVIGATION. THIS CHART HAS BEEN SIGNIFICANTLY ALTERED FROM THE ORIGINAL. THIS CHART IS FOR PRACTICE ONLY.

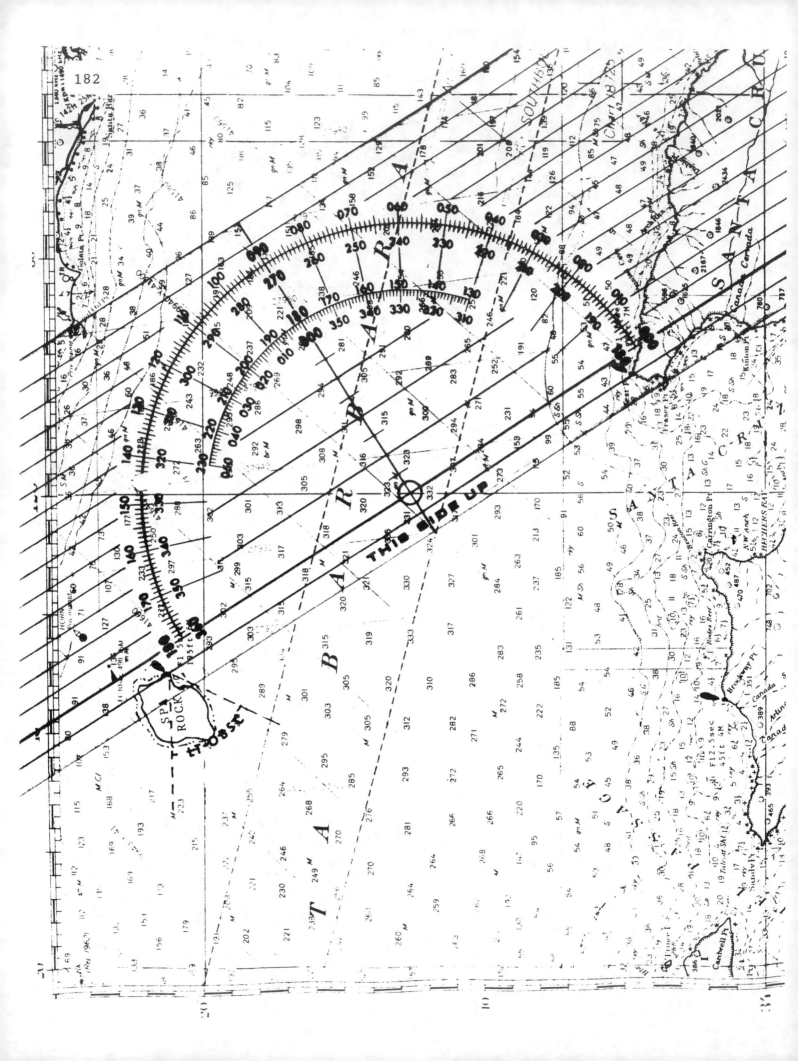

Look at your course plotter which is still lined up on both lights. Now it's not 148° but one hundred eighty degrees in the opposite direction...328°. That's the reading right under the 148° on the same outer scale. Thus, on a course plotter, you get two for the price of one. Reciprocals are built right in. Get that straight before you go on.

Time to turn to the third course plotter smeared page. Looks like someone's trying to get either from the Anacapa Light to the Bunny Isle Light, or vice versa. Throwing temptations to the winds, we elect to go **towards** Bunny Isle from Anacapa Light if for no other reason than to check and see if what they say about that island is true.

The top line of the course plotter, (or **any of the lines** on the course plotter that are handy) now intersects both lights. However, it would be difficult to place the target over a longitude line. So place it over a **latitude** line. Follow the latitude line into the **bottom scale** on the course plotter. That's the shorter scale of the two. Take a reading. You can have 168° or 348°. (Ah ha! Forgot to make your estimate first, eh?) I think I'll take 348° and you can go find your own island.

Try these for practice. Remember to estimate your course lines first, then go for the plotter.

1) Indicate the course from Bunny Isle Light to Cavern Point Light.

2) Find the course from Cavern Point Light to West Point Light.

3) What's the course from Brockway Point Light to the Santa Barbara Fl G Bell Buoy?

4) Try going from Spa Rock Light to West Point Light.

5) How about Bunny Isle Light to the Santa Barbara Bell Buoy?

6) How about a true course from Spa Rock Light to Cavern Point Light?

ANSWERS

1) 217°, 2) 275°, 3) 046°, 4) 148°, 5) 310°, 6) 122°

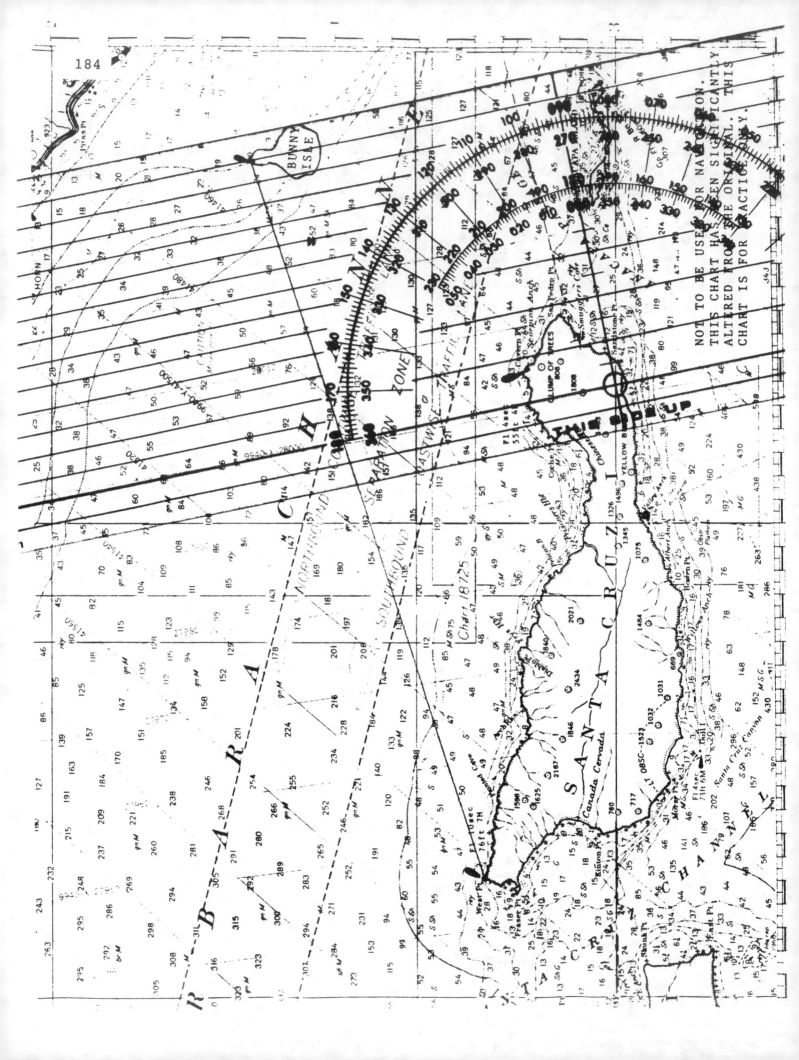

NOT TO BE USED FOR NAVIGATION.
THIS CHART HAS BEEN SIGNIFICANTLY
ALTERED FROM THE ORIGINAL. THIS
CHART IS FOR PRACTICE ONLY.

LATITUDE AND LONGITUDE

We save the most simple for last. This is not to say that "positioning" is unimportant. If you have been bobbing around out there for the minimum required year then you've been exposed to charts and should be aware we are located in latitude north and longitude west. Use the abbreviated Mercator world map on the next page. In doing so, take note that "lat is flat". Those are the lines running horizontally across the page. The longitude lines are the ones running up and down converging on the north and south poles.

Latitude is always listed first in calling out a position. Latitude numbering starts from the equator and goes "up" and "down" numerically. In other words, it you come north from the equator for one degree, you are in latitude 1 north. If you go south of the equator for one degree, then you're 1 south. Santa Barbara, California is about 34° north. Ka Lae (South Point) on the big island of Hawaii, is a slight bit less than 19° north latitude ranking as the southern most point in the U.S. Point Barrow, Alaska is a shade less than 72°) north, making it the northern most point in the U.S. If it helps, Sydney is about 34°) **south** of the equator.

I'll never know how they worked it out, but even the Russians agree that longitude counting starts at Greenwich, England. (The "w" is silent). From Greenwich, which is 0° longitude, the counting goes east and west, but remember the **lines** are running north and south.

Starting from Greenwich working west, the numbers increase and are called "longitude west". Eventually, you get across the Atlantic and hit New York. New York is about 74° west longitude. Coming across the U.S., you hit Santa Barbara which is about 120° west longitude. Catch a plane heading across the Pacific to Hawaii and you land in Honolulu which is about 158° west longitude.

You can't travel much farther in west longitude. It stops at 180° which is neither east nor west. The 180° line is the half-way point. Cross that line and you are in **east** longitude. From this point, you have to count backwards, (179° east, 178° east, 177° east, etc.) until you reach Greenwich again. On the way, you will hit an island in the Alaskan Aleutian Island chain called Attu. Attu is about 176° east longitude which means Alaska is the easterly most state in the U.S! Well, that's more easterly than Maine. This next one comes free of charge.   Technically, Alaska is the northern most, western most and eastern most state in the U.S.

Yards are broken down in feet.   Feet break into inches.   Degrees of latitude and longitude break down into "minutes".   Not minutes in time, but minutes of arc.   A closer fix on Santa Barbara Harbor would read latitude 34o 24.2' north, longitude 119o 41.6' west.   That reads: Thirty four degrees twenty-four and two tenths minutes north and one hundred nineteen degrees forty-one and six tenths minutes west.

An arc is part of a circle, so in measuring this circle we call earth, it fits. The Coast Guard will want you to call out latitude and longitude to the nearest **tenth** of a minute of arc.   There are sixty minutes to a degree, whether it's latitude or longitude.   After looking over the world map below, try calling out the positions labeled "A" through "H" on the next page.   The answers are on the following page.   When you have the understanding worked out, then try the positions labeled 1 through 10 and check the rest of the answers.

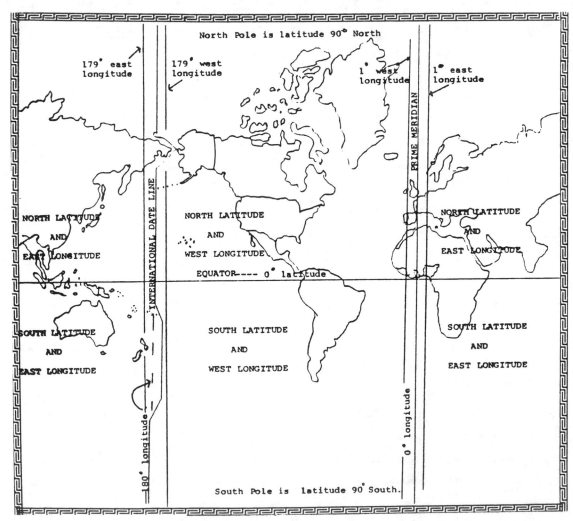

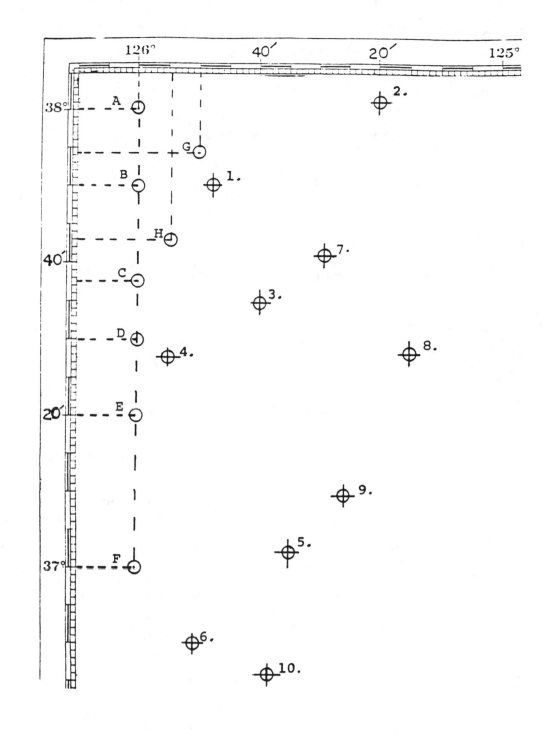

	North Latitude	West Longitude
A)	38° 00.0'	126° 00.0'
B)	37° 50.0'	126° 00.0'
C)	37° 37.5'	126° 00.0'
D)	37° 30.0'	126° 00.0'
E)	37° 20.0'	126° 00.0'
F)	37° 00.0'	126° 00.0'
G)	37° 54.2'	125° 50.0'
H)	37° 43.0'	125° 54.8'

Wondering why all the zeros? Use 'em. Remember that's how the CG officer learned to do it and when he sees YOU use the same system...well, ahem, he might even think you know what's you're doing.

Now go for the numbers 1-10.

Notice how the answers below are recorded.

Latitude is listed first. The "N" for north always follows latitude and the "W" for west after the longitude. Format can become very important when you're trying to impress someone. Develop the habit now. And don't become discouraged if you're off a tenth or two at first. To answer a position question THAT close with the spaces so small is an almost impossible task. However, you will get lots of practice if you follow the lesson schemes from start to finish in this volume. Surprising how adept you can become.

1)	Lat 37° 50.0'N	Long 125° 47.9'W
2)	Lat 38° 01.0'N	Long 125° 20.0'W
3)	Lat 37° 34.7'N	Long 125° 40.0'W
4)	Lat 37° 27.6'N	Long 125° 55.0'W
5)	Lat 37° 01.9'N	Long 125° 35.0'W
6)	Lat 36° 50.0'N	Long 125° 51.0'W
7)	Lat 37° 40.8'N	Long 125° 29.2'W
8)	Lat 37° 27.8'N	Long 125° 15.2'W
9)	Lat 37° 09.1'N	Long 125° 26.0'W
10)	Lat 36° 45.8'N	Long 125° 38.5'W

The following page is nothing more than one-half of the book chart you will be using in the charting section. The page demonstrates the conventional use of a pair of dividers to find latitude and longitude on a chart. In the first exercise, we'll go for the Spa Rock Light.

Latitude always comes first so spread the dividers so one tip touches the dot representing the light's exact location while the other stretches out to meet the nearest latitude line. In this example, this would be the silhouette showing the narrowest opening on the two sets of dividers. Once you have determined the distance of the light from that latitude line, carefully move the dividers over to the **left** side of the chart, (or the right side if it were closer). The reading indicated is 32° 21.1' north.

Next, go for the longitude by spreading the dividers to reach the light and the nearest longitude line. Then, without closing or opening the dividers, go to the top of the page, (or the bottom if it were closer) and take your reading. How about 120° 07.5' west?

There's more practice coming up.

> **If you bob around out there long enough, you're going to get into big trouble someplace along the line. Better be prepared.   Take plenty of olives...and some gin and vermouth.**

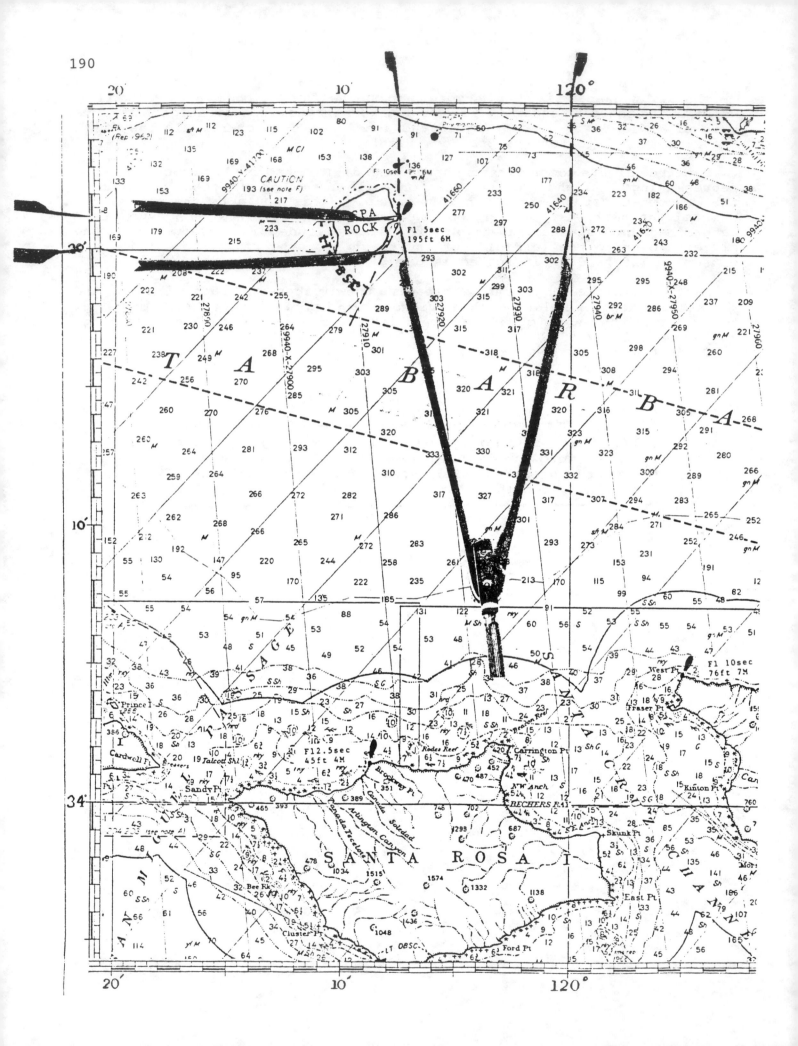

The real workout comes next. Take the textbook chart which was located inside the back cover. Try measuring for latitude and longitude of the following places. No fair peeking until you have finished all five. By the way, have you had that chart copied yet? Don't mess it up if you haven't. About 14,000 copies should do it and all of them will be in rags when you're finished.

1) The Bunny Isle Light.

2) Anacapa Island Light.

3) Cavern Point Light.

4) West Point Light.

5) Brockway Point Light.

ANSWERS

1) Bunny Isle Light: Latitude 34° 12.8' N.
Longitude 119° 24.6' W.

2) Anacapa Island Light: Latitude 34° 01.0' N.
Longitude 119° 21.6' W.

3) Cavern Point Light: Latitude 34° 03.4' N.
Longitude 119° 36.4' W.

4) West Point Light: Latitude 34° 04.7' N.
Longitude 119° 55.0' W.

5) Brockway Point Light: Latitude 34° 01.5' N.
Longitude 120° 08.8' W.

CHARTING I

The next ten problems were measured for an easy start to charting. Your real efforts should be aimed at getting to be a fast expert with the course plotter. An excellent second aim would be to get in the habit of keeping concise and methodical notes as you work. If you attain the habit of keeping them organized, looking back to check for errors will become much easier. Don't become discouraged at first with the amount of time spent solving any given problem. It's like typing. Practice will automatically produce speed and accuracy. The solutions and helpful hints are on the next page following #10.

Time to turn some of the chart copies into rags. You **DID** get copies? On all problems, assume 15° east variation.

1) How long would it take to sail from the Santa Barbara Fl G Bell buoy to the West Point Light assuming you were making 15.8 knots? What will be your compass course if your deviation is 4° east on this course?

2) If you left the Santa Barbara Fl G Bell buoy at 0800 making 12.3 knots, what would be your ETA (estimated time of arrival) at the Cavern Point Light? What will be your compass course if the deviation is 3° west?

3) Friends are waiting on Bunny Isle. They're leaving at noon and taking the dancing girls with them. Thus, what is the latest time you can leave the West Point Light making 14.6 knots and drop anchor by Bunny Isle Light by 1200? What will be your compass course with deviation at 1° east?

4) Sail from Spa Rock Light at 1415 to Bunny Isle Light making 6.2 knots with deviation on this course at 3° west. What is the compass course to Bunny Isle Light and what time will you arrive?

5) From Spa Rock Light to Brockway Point Light your deviation is 7° east making 16.8 knots. On the trip back to Spa Rock Light, the deviation will be 7° west. If the speed of your craft is the same in both directions, how long will the round trip take? What are the compass courses each way?

6) Departing Bunny Isle Light at 1015 on a true course of 280° making 13.5 knots, what will be your position at 1235? (Latitude and longitude to the nearest tenth of a minute). Can you see the Spa Rock Light?

7) Departing Brockway Point Light at 1345 on a true course of 052° you take a loran reading at 1713 fixing your position at latitude 34° 20.0' N. and longitude 119° 40.0' W. Are you on course? What was your speed made good?

8) A gusty southeaster is blowing as you depart Cavern Point Light at 2230 en route to Santa Barbara's Fl G Bell Buoy. You are making what you assume to be 11.6 knots. At 2342 your loran indicates a position of latitude 34° 20.0' N and longitude 119° 50.0' W. What was your true course made good and speed made good to 2342 hours? If the wind dies off, what time will you reach the buoy? What will be your compass course if the deviation is 3° west?

9) Departing Cavern Point Light at 1335 for some channel fishing you take off on a compass course of 287° with deviation of 4° west making 11.3 knots. At 1440 you stop and fish for 30 minutes before deciding to head for a night's refuge in the harbor by Spa Rock Light. What was your true course to the fishing grounds? What was the position you stopped to fish? What were you doing wrong? If the deviation was the same as the former course, what is the compass course to Spa Rock Light? What's your ETA at Spa Rock Light?

10) You are enroute from the Bunny Isle Light to Spa Rock Light departing at 0855 making 13.4 knots. Assume deviation 3° west. One hour and forty-five minutes later you encounter a disabled craft desiring a tow to Santa Barbara. Since you are a licensed skipper you can charge them for this service and spend twenty minutes negotiating and taking their vessel in tow **after** collecting in advance. Your speed is now reduced to 9.9 knots. At the Santa Barbara Bell Buoy, the harbor master takes your tow which takes another fifteen minutes off your schedule. From there you proceed at your former speed for Spa Rock.

    a) What was your compass course from Bunny Isle to Spa Rock?
    b) At what time **and** position did you encounter the disabled craft?
    c) What was the true course from the disabled craft's position to the Santa Barbara Bell Buoy?
    d) How long did it take to tow the craft to Santa Barbara?
    e) What was your new ETA at the Spa Rock Light after leaving the tow with the harbor master and resuming your former speed?

AID AND ANSWERS

Anytime a charting problem arises requiring the plotting of courses write down T V M D C only do it vertically. Anytime speed-distanc-time calculations are required write down S-D-T and number the problem and page.

```
1) T 212          S 15.8
   V  15 E        D 22.8
   M 197          *T 87 minutes or 1h 27m.
   D   4 E
  *C 193
- - - - - - - - - - - - - - - - - - - - - - - - - - - - - - - -
2) T 164          S 12.3
   V  15 E        D 21.9
   M 149          *T 107 minutes or 1h 47m
   D   3 W           Add 1h 47m to departure time of 0800
  *C 152             which makes for an ETA of *0947.
- - - - - - - - - - - - - - - - - - - - - - - - - - - - - - - -
3) T 072          S 14.6
   V  15 E        D 26.7
   M 057          *T 110 minutes or 1h 50m
   D   1 E           If it takes 1h 50m to travel to Bunny Isle Light
  *C 056             you should have left W. Pt. Lt. 1h 50m before
                     noon thus, departure would have been at *1010.
- - - - - - - - - - - - - - - - - - - - - - - - - - - - - - - -
4) T 103          S 6.2
   V  15 E        D 36.6
   M 088          *T 354 minutes or 5h 54m.  Add 5h 54m to departure
   D   3 W           time of 1415 to get *2009.
  *C 091
- - - - - - - - - - - - - - - - - - - - - - - - - - - - - - - -
5) From Spa to Brockway T 183     From Brockway to Spa  T 003
        S 16.8              V  15 E                     V  15
        D 19.8              M 168                       M 348
        T 71 minutes        D   7 E                     D   7 W
         or 1h 11m         *C 161                      *C 355
         x 2 for the
         round trip is *2h 22m.
- - - - - - - - - - - - - - - - - - - - - - - - - - - - - - - -
```

6) S 13.5   *Position 34° 18.8' N-120° 02.1' W.
   D 31.5   Since the light is visible for 6 miles
   T 140 minutes or 2h 20m.   and you are only 5.3 miles away, yes
                     the light would be visible.

- -

7) *S 8.7   *Yes! You are right on course.
   D 30.4
   T 208 minutes or 3h 28m.

- -

8) Your speed made good would be found by measuring the distance
   from Cavern Point to the loran position indicated, finding the
   time then solving for speed.   *S 18.0 = speed made good.
   True course made good was   D 21.6
   321°.   T 72 minutes or 1 hr 12m.

   New course to buoy T 062
                  V 15 E   ETA to S.B. Buoy S 11.6
                  M 047   D 8.9
                  D   3 W   *T 45m
                 *C 050   Add 46m to 2341 = *0028.

- -

9) **To the fishing grounds:**
   *T 298   S 11.3   *Fishing position was
    V 15 E   D 12.2   34° 09.0' N & 119° 46.3'
    M 283   T 65 minutes (1h 05m)   W. which makes you fishing
    D   4 W   illegally in a shipping
    C 287   lane. Shame!
     To Spa Rock: T 304   S 11.3
                  V 15 E   D 21.4
                  M 289   T 114 minutes or 1h 54m.
                  D   4 W
                 *C 293
     Accumulated times: Depart Cavern at 1335 + 1h 05m travel time = 1440.
     Add 30m for fishing = 1510.   Add 1h 54m to get to Spa Rock = *ETA 1704.

- -

10a)   T 283   S 13.4   **10b)** Encountered craft at *34°18.3' N &
     V 15 E   *D 23.5   119° 52.3' W.   Encounter = 0855
     M 268   T 105m (1h 45m).   +145
     D   3 W   **10c)** True =*058° to S.B. ------
    *C 271   1040

     10d) From disabled craft to S.B. S 9.9 (new speed)
              1040 + 20m to take in tow.   D 11.2
              Depart for S.B. 1100.   *T 68m (1h 08m)
              Add 1h 08 to S.B. = 1208.

10e) Add 15 minutes to offload tow on harbor master. 1208 + 15, =
     1223. Computations to Spa Rock from S.B.   S 13.4
                                                 D 22.3
     Add 1h 41m to 1223 S.B. departure.   T 100m (1h 40m)
     ETA Spa Rock *1403.

```
Consistently off from 0.2 to 0.3 miles?  Some copying
machines have a "bug-eye" lens thus reducing charts
irregularly.  Try comparing a few distances with the
book's original chart.
```

CHARTING II – BEARINGS AND FIXES

First consider the following. Assume you are sitting offshore gazing at a lighthouse. The lighthouse bears, from your boat, 270°; in other words, west. If someone were sitting up in the lighthouse looking at your boat, what would your boat bear **from** the lighthouse?

The opposite direction, right? More appropriately, 090°. Now change the directions. If the lighthouse was bearing 225° what is the bearing from the light house to your vessel? Again, the opposite direction. Subtract 180° from 225° and you get 045°.

The next question is: How did you figure out the true direction? You only have a compass and chart on board. Simple -you aim the boat at the lighthouse and look at the compass. Assume the compass reads 320°. Now we have a T–V–M–D–C problem in which you **start** with the compass direction.

    T 311
    V 13° W (which says so on your chart).
    M 324
    D   4 E (which is on your ship's deviation card).
    C 320

Now you know the true direction is 311°. Therefore, anyone in the lighthouse would look at your boat and say, "He's bearing 131° **from** the lighthouse." You could even pick up your course plotter and draw a bearing line **from** the lighthouse and know you were on that line someplace. Well, maybe you don't know how **far** you are from the lighthouse, but you have what is called a "line of position", (LOP).

If you had two (or even three) LOP's you would have a fix. So look around and find something else you can see which also shows up on your chart.

In fact, that's what the guy on the next page is doing.

First he found a buoy. Aiming his boat at it got took a bearing per standard compass (psc) of 037°. He worked that up to a true bearing of 050° and plotted it on his chart. He then turned the boat (second panel on the same page) towards a light house for a psc of 302°. That worked up to 319° true. The third panel shows the same boat taking a bearing on a rock using the same technique.

He probably could have got away with only two bearings, but just to make sure, he shot three. If one of the bearings had been off a little bit the three LOP's would not have intersected perfectly at the boat's position. If not, he would have a small triangle. If this happens, pick the middle of the triangle.

The Coast Guard will **generally** only give you two bearings for a fix. They will either tell you the deviation on each bearing or provide you with a deviation table to use on any courses plotted or bearings taken for a fix.

A fix is always better than a DR. A DR is still only an educated guess. A fix is a more reliable thing. Notice also that the DR's are indicated by a half circle. The fixes are shown by a full circle.

There is also a certain way to lable bearing lines. The time of the bearing is written on top of the line. The true bearing is recorded beneath the line.

First bearing by aiming the
bow of your boat at an object
which is also on your chart. <u>Read your compass</u>

Second step is to work "compass"
bearing up to "true" so you
can plot it on your chart.

Bearing is recorded "true" beneath
the bearing line. The time of the
bearing is recorded above the line.

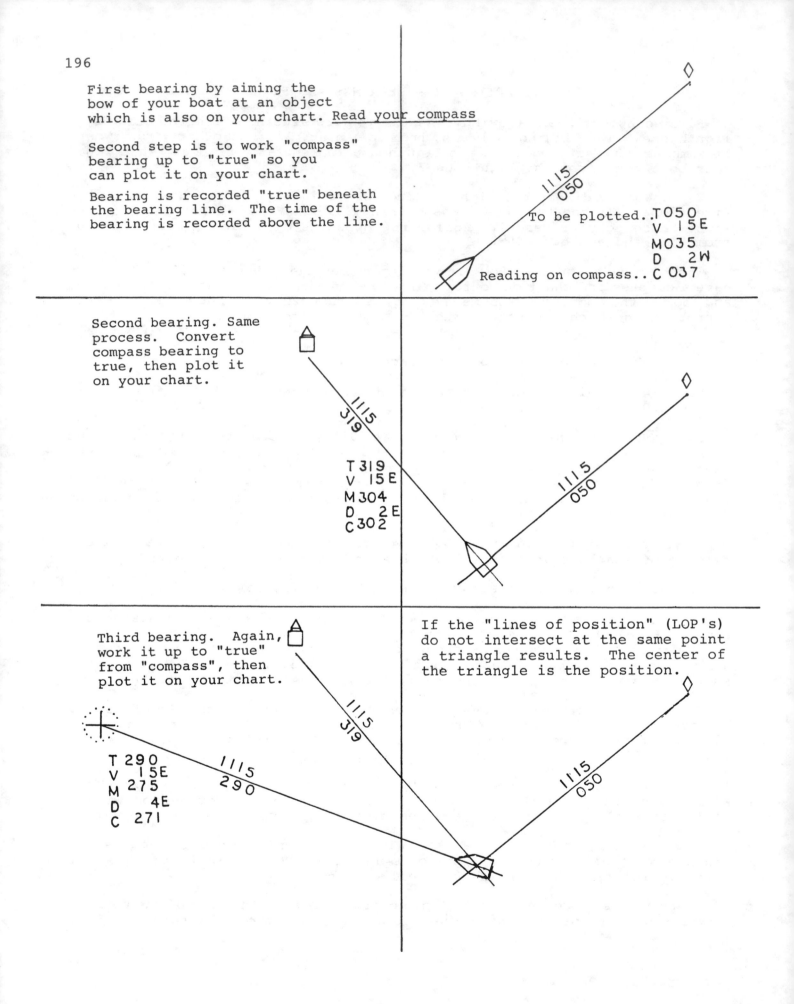

1115
050

To be plotted.. T 050
          V 15 E
          M 035
          D   2 W
Reading on compass.. C 037

Second bearing. Same
process. Convert
compass bearing to
true, then plot it
on your chart.

1115
319

T 319
V 15 E
M 304
D   2 E
C 302

1115
050

Third bearing. Again,
work it up to "true"
from "compass", then
plot it on your chart.

T 290
V   15 E
M 275
D   4 E
C 271

1115
290

1115
319

If the "lines of position" (LOP's)
do not intersect at the same point
a triangle results. The center of
the triangle is the position.

1115
050

This next bit is a variation on the last technique of taking bearings to establish a fix. The CG uses both types in their exams. In this case the boat isn't turned to face the buoy, lighthouse or prominent land mark. Instead, the boat maintains a steady course while the bearings are taken.

Large compasses, as found on military and merchant vessels, come equipped with an object called an azimuth circle. Azimuth means direction. This brass ring fits around the outside of the compass mount and can be revolved back and forth. Two sighting vanes mounted on the detachable ring permit viewing a distant object and checking the bearing simultaneously by glancing down at the compass. On smaller craft, a pelorus is used as indicated in the diagram. The revolving base is set to match the compass course. The vane is then pivoted to line up the bearing object. The bearing number is then read from the base.

All of this means that while underway you can take bearings on objects without turning the vessel to face them. The one thing to remember while converting such sightings to true bearings, **the deviation of the ship's heading must be used each time** when working the sighting "up" the T-V-M-D-C ladder to true so it can be plotted. Since deviation is relative to the direction the vessel is travelling, the mere fact someone takes a bearing on a passing object could hardly affect the magnetic characteristics of the ship.

With this in mind, examine the first two problems on the next page. The third problem is for you to work out. **After** you have digested the sketches and worked out the third problem, come back to this page.

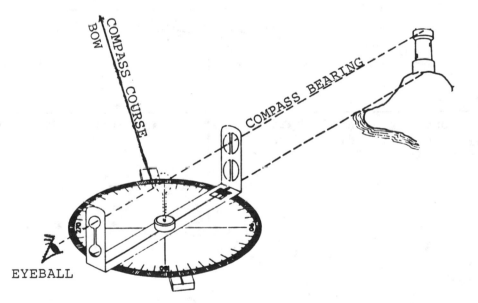

In #1, the vessel is on a course of 095° true. At 1055 she takes three bearings. One is almost astern, on an outcrop, another on a buoy and finally a third on a lighted buoy. Each compass bearing is worked up to true then plotted. Note: each bearing is written below the line and the time above the line.

The second panel is the same type with the vessel on a true course of 232° while shooting three objects which are also depicted on the chart. In both of these panels, practice using the course plotter before you try the third panel yourself. And how do you know you're right on the third one? All bearing lines should intersect at the same point.

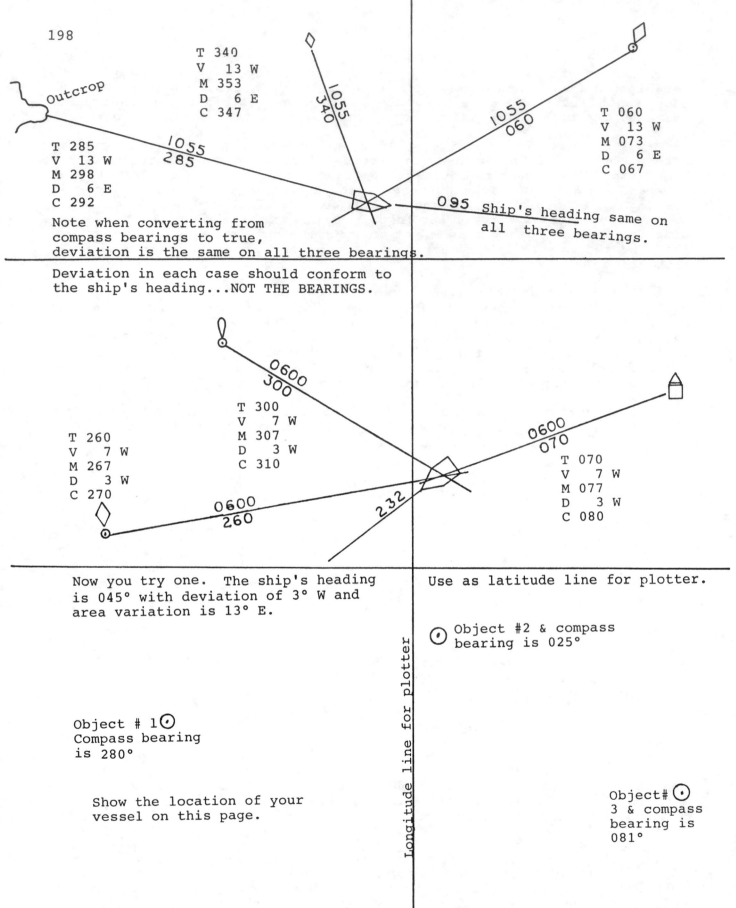

198

Outcrop

T 340
V 13 W
M 353
D 6 E
C 347

1055
340

1055
060

T 285
V 13 W
M 298
D 6 E
C 292

1055
285

T 060
V 13 W
M 073
D 6 E
C 067

095 Ship's heading same on
all three bearings.

Note when converting from
compass bearings to true,
deviation is the same on all three bearings.

Deviation in each case should conform to
the ship's heading...NOT THE BEARINGS.

0600
300

T 300
V 7 W
M 307
D 3 W
C 310

0600
070

T 260
V 7 W
M 267
D 3 W
C 270

0600
260

232

T 070
V 7 W
M 077
D 3 W
C 080

Now you try one. The ship's heading
is 045° with deviation of 3° W and
area variation is 13° E.

Use as latitude line for plotter.

⊙ Object #2 & compass
bearing is 025°

Longitude line for plotter

Object # 1 ⊙
Compass bearing
is 280°

Object# ⊙
3 & compass
bearing is
081°

Show the location of your
vessel on this page.

CHARTING III - THE RUNNING FIX

If you romped through the previous exercises with any degree of accuracy the time has come for the Running Fix. A running fix infers there is only one object from which to take a bearing. On an accuracy scale of one to ten the running fix falls someplace between a six or seven. Actually, the running fix is better than a DR and not quite as good as a two or three body fix.

The next page depicts three **separate** running fixes. In #1 the vessel is on a course of 260° true. At 0205 the light ashore yields a bearing of 330° **true**. At 0225 the same light shows up as 020°. Basically is a speed-distance-time problem. The distance travelled between the two bearings is 4 miles.

Here's the hard part to understand when working with running fixes. **It doesn't matter how far the course line is plotted from the object you are shooting.** You can take the bearing from any distance off.

Notice where the first bearing line intercepts the courseline? From that point measure 4 miles along the course line. Place a small mark on the course line to mark the DR which is twenty minutes (4 miles) from the first bearing.

The next part is tricky. Remember that first bearing line of 330°? You need to "advance" it four miles so it crosses through the 0225 DR. So, take the mark on the course line indicating the 0225 DR and draw a 330° line right through the DR mark. Now both 330° lines are parallel. That is the first one at 0205 and the second one we just put though the 0225 DR are parallel.

Take a close look and see how that "advanced" bearing line intersects the 0225 bearing line of 020°. That's the running fix...or chartwise, it's called the 0225 R Fix.

The second problem is another one of like kind. This time the vessel is on a course of 080°. He takes his first bearing at 2120 and gets 040° true. Thirty minutes later (making 16.2 knots) he takes a second bearing on the same buoy and gets 330°. He marks his 2150 DR which is 8.1 miles (thirty minutes at 16.2 knots) along the course line. Then the 2120 bearing is advanced 8.1 miles **along the course line.** In other words, another 040° line is drawn through the 2150 DR. Where does that advanced bearing intersect the second bearing on the buoy? That's the 2150 R Fix.

The third problem is a repeat exercise. The vessel is on a true course of 060° making 10.6 knots. The first bearing is 110° at 1145. Then, 7.1 miles later the DR is indicated. The second bearing yielded 070° at 1225 and is plotted (true) on the chart. Next, the 1145 bearing of 110° is advanced 7.1 miles which means it will pass right through the 1225 DR. Where this advanced bearing line intersects the second bearing line one finds the 1225 R Fix.

How come all the bearings were given to you true? Well, most likely the CG will give them to you psc requiring you to work them up the T-V-M-D-C ladder to true before they are plotted. Think you can remember that? It's kind of important. If you forget, you will be plotting your bearings by compass producing a triangle the size of the side of an Egyptian pyramid. This will become rather apparent in some later exercises we have planned.

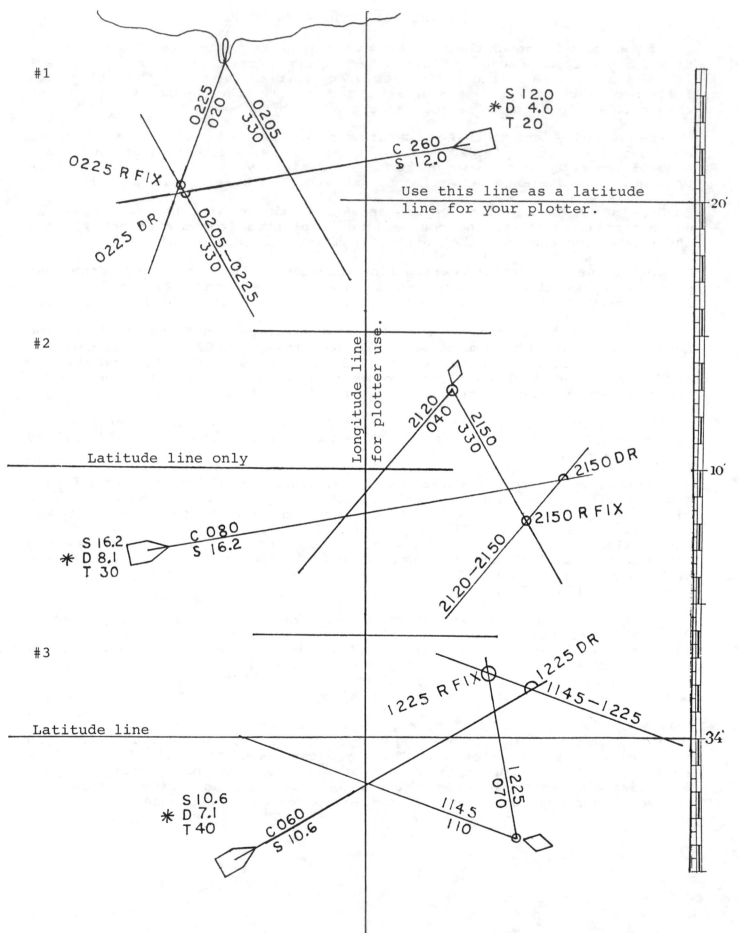

#1

S 12.0
* D 4.0
T 20

0225

020

0205

330

0225 R FIX

C 260
S 12.0

Use this line as a latitude
line for your plotter.

20'

0225 DR

0205-0225

330

#2

Longitude line
for plotter use.

2120

040

2150

330

2150 DR

Latitude line only

10'

S 16.2
* D 8.1
T 30

C 080
S 16.2

2150 R FIX

2120-2150

#3

1225 DR

1225 R FIX

1145-1225

Latitude line

34'

S 10.6
* D 7.1
T 40

C 060
S 10.6

1145

110

1225

070

CHARTING IV – SET AND DRIFT

Anyone with any sea time knows it doesn't work like that. If there's any wind or the sea is rough, the boat bobs around like a soap dish. Any resemblance to course steered and course made good is purely luck. Formal plotting recognizes this and has a method for compensating. It's called Set and Drift. However, in order to compensate, you must first know the set and drift.

Set is the word used to indicate the **direction** of the current. That is, the direction the current is moving...not the direction from which it is coming, like the wind. Drift is the term used to indicate the **speed** the current is moving. Current can best be described as "all slop". Anything contributing to throwing your boat off course is current. That means wind, waves, tides, or errant whales pushing your boat around.

We start by working a simple problem on the next page to get the basics down. We'll procede as though the page was a chart. Notice the latitude scale on the right side for measuring distance; an important factor in set and drift problems. The two perpendicular lines running across the page are to be used as latitude-longitude lines; obviously for your course plotter.

Departure time is from point "A" at 0800. We're making 12 knots on a course of 315° true. The course line has numbers written across the top and bottom. The one on top is the true course, the one on bottom represents the speed of your boat. That is, the speed you **think** your boat is making. The speed you know you ordinarily make at a given rpm in a bath tub sea. These two facts were left out on your original plotting problems, but you had your hands full without having to worry about labeling. Get use to labeling your problems. Should you come **close** to the answer the Coast Guard wants and one small error on the chart is making the difference, labeling could be important. The OinC, on a slow day, may ask to see your chart. If he sees everything labeled the way he was taught at the academy, who knows, he might think you know what you're doing and hand you the benefit of the small doubt. This could be the difference between receiving your license then and there, or returning on another day to start all over again. Think about that.

At 1000 you have presumably arrived at the DR (dead reckoning) point "B" so you check it out with a loran fix or bearings. Egad! You're at point "C", the fix. Draw a line **from** "B" to "C". Using the course plotter, check the direction **from** "B" **to** "C". You should find it's 270°. That's your **set**.

Since **drift** means "speed" of the water's movement, we now have a speed-distance-time problem and you will be solving for speed. This means you need the time and the distance to solve it. The distance is the length of the line from "B" to "C". The time is the length of time your vessel has been underway. Well, isn't that the length of time the current has been affecting your boat ever since you left home at 0800?

By measuring, you should find the BC line is four miles. You've been underway for 2h, or 120m. Thus, drift is 2.0 knots. Yep! Just like computing the speed of your boat; take the answer to the nearest tenth.

Set = 270°. Drift = 2.0 knots. Notice how they're written on the set-drift line.

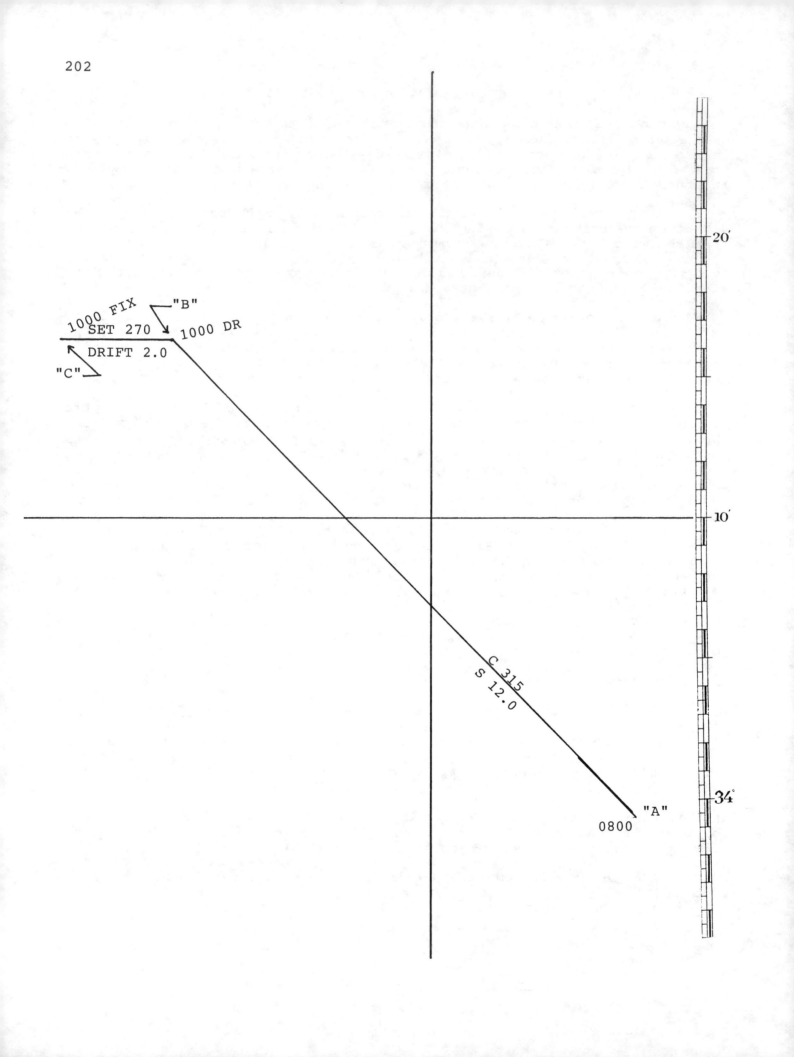

1000 FIX   "B"

SET 270   1000 DR

DRIFT 2.0

"C"

C 315
S 12.0

"A"

0800

20´

10´

34´

Set and Drift Practice.

Time for the real thing on our favorite chart. The following page is a slightly reduced version of the **western half** of the book chart. All of the problems below are worked out on that chart. After the chart is a page explaining the various moves to realize the plotted answers on the next page.

DON'T LOOK NOW

Try these on one of your own copies then make a comparison. If you need help, turn **back** a page and review the principle again. Briefly summarized, there are some outstanding points to watch for when methodically attacking the problems below.

1) Plot your DR first. Find out, using speed-distance-time formulas, where you "thought" you were.

2) Then plot the Fix which will be given to you

3) Use your course plotter to plot the direction of the current (set) **from** the DR **to** the fix.

4) Then do the speed-distance-time bit all over again to find the drift. The **time** will be the same as when you plotted your DR. This is because your vessel was affected by that current during your entire length of time underway. The distance is found by measuring between the DR and the fix. With your time and distance in hand...go for the **speed** because that's the **drift.**

1) Depart Brockway Point Light at 1230, speed 12.5 knots on a true course of 020. At 1400 your position is found to be latitude 34° 16.9' N & longitude 120° 05.0' W. What is your set and drift?

2) You depart Cardwell Point (lower left on chart just above 34°) at 0504 on a course to the West Point Light making 8.9 knots. At 0715 you stop to check your location wherein a loran fix places you at latitude 34° 10.0' N & longitude 120° 00.0' W. What is your set and drift?

3) On a true course of 195° making 9.3 knots you depart Spa Rock Light at 2245. One hour and fifteen minutes later you take a fix to find yourself located at latitude 34° 11.0' N & 120° 11.9' W. What is your set and drift?

4) Leaving Spa Rock Light behind on a true course of 153° at 1324 you make 10.6 knots until 1559 when a fix places you at latitude 34° 00.0' N and longitude 120° 00.0' W. What is your set and drift?

5) Departing Goleta Point (top of chart near the 119° 50.0' mark) you set a course for Cardwell Point at 1836 making 11.6 knots. At 2040 you take a fix placing your craft at 34° 09.5' N and 120° 17.1' W. What is your set and drift?

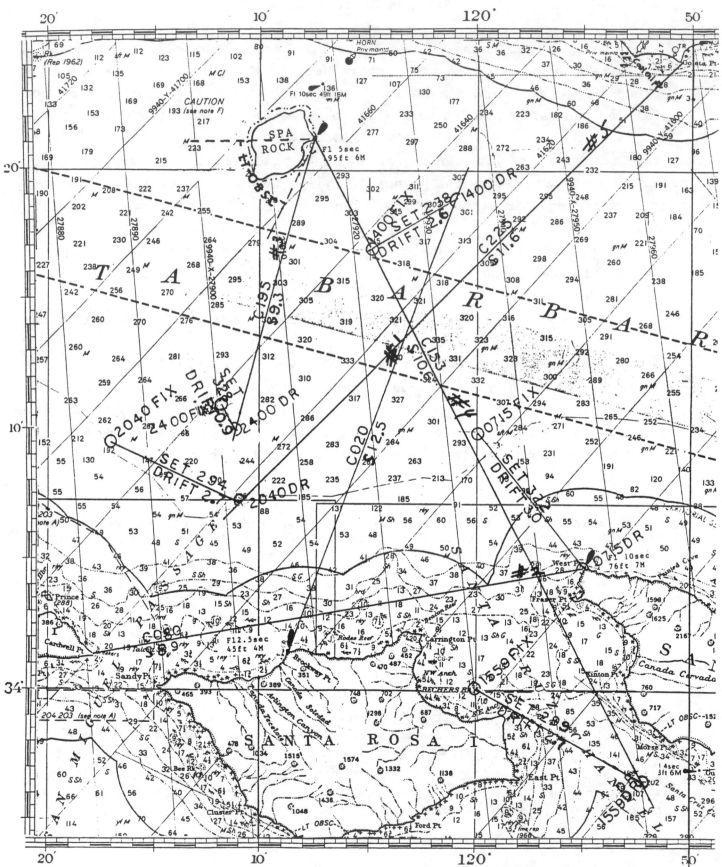

CHARTING V – SET AND DRIFT – TYPE #3

So you can do set and drift problems. Great! Now, what good is it?

Used properly, you can sail to another location with accuracy assuming the set and drift doesn't change during the voyage. In short, you can pick another destination and using the information from your previously calculated set and drift, hit the new destination right on the buoy. The numbered directions below correspond to the large black numbers on the next page. It's a step-by-step procedure. Those of you who remember studying vectors in analytical geometry will be right at home, but for the sake of simplicity, we won't go into theory here. Merely step-by-step solutions. Watch the next page and follow along.

Our departure point is at the bottom of the page showing 0800. We depart on a course of 030° making 13 knots. At 1000 hours we plot our DR then take a fix.

1) The fix (big black "1") is acquired by taking a two body fix from Ooga Island and Booga Rock. At the point of the fix we label it "O". From the DR to the fix we plot the set and drift. Note the drift is 2.0. That means the current is moving two knots. How long is the set-drift line? Go on, measure it. Four miles, right? Divided by two hours, that's a two knot current. That's what made the drift 2.0.

2) Next, we extend the set-drift line for one hour of current movement. One hour would be two knots because that's how fast the current is moving. Thus, from point "O" we measure along a continuation of the 290° set line for two miles. That gives us point "W". In other words, whatever the drift is – written beneath the "set-drift" line– is how far we extend the line. If the drift worked out to be 4.2 miles, that's how far you would extend the line. If it said 3.9 miles, extend it 3.9 miles from "O" to "W".

3) Now that you know your set and drift...where would you like to go? To bed? No, no, not yet. Just a bit farther. Let's assume the captain wants to return to his original departure point. He wants to go home. So, he draws a line from where he is –the fix– to where he wants to go...home. That's the big black "3". If you saw his girl friend you'd know why he wants to go home.

4) How do you get point "P" at big black"4"? Careful here. Spread your dividers apart to equal the speed of your boat. Thirteen knots. Measure out thirteen miles on the side of the page. Steady now. Put one end of the dividers on point "W" letting the other end fall on the course line leading home. Point "P" is thirteen miles from point "W". Draw a line from "W" to "P".

5) Now we have two lines. One is called line "OP". If you measure it with your dividers on the side of the page you will find the new speed you will **make good** heading for home (big black 3). Measuring the OP line carefully, you should get 12.7. Remember, line OP gives you your **new speed**. This means if you turn up the same rpm you usually do to get 13 knots, you will only make good 12.7 knots due to the current offset. At least now you will know what speed you will be making due to the current offsetting your boat.

6) Whip out your course plotter and measure the other line..."WP". Did you get 192°? Good! That's the course to steer to hit home base (big black 3) right on the buoy. If you steer 192° you will offset the current working against you.

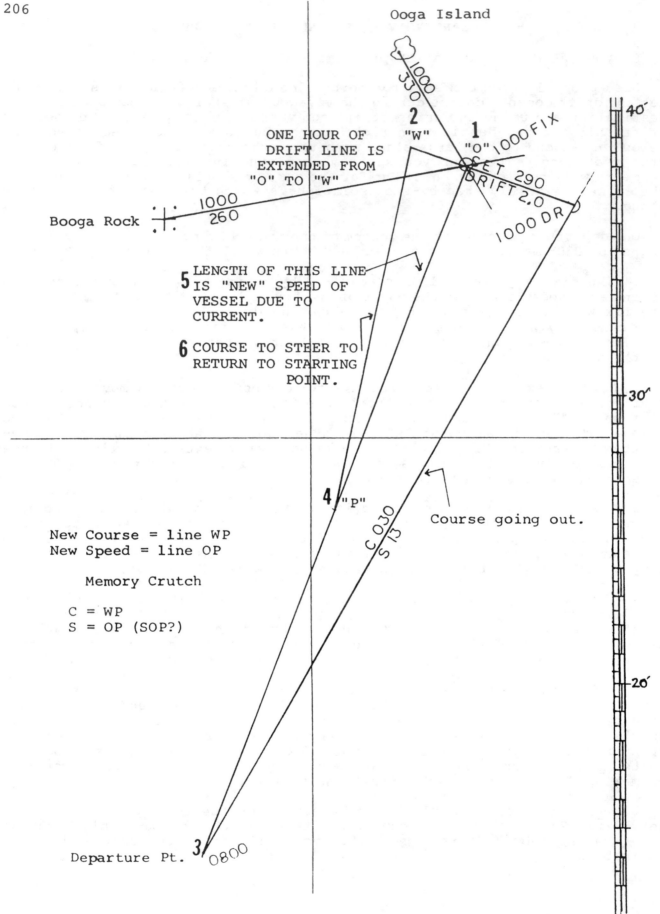

Ooga Island

1 "O" 1000 FIX

1000
330

2 "W"

ONE HOUR OF
DRIFT LINE IS
EXTENDED FROM
"O" TO "W"

SET 290
DRIFT 2.0

1000 DR

Booga Rock
1000
260

5 LENGTH OF THIS LINE
IS "NEW" SPEED OF
VESSEL DUE TO
CURRENT.

6 COURSE TO STEER TO
RETURN TO STARTING
POINT.

40'

30'

4 "P"

C 030
S 13

Course going out.

20'

New Course = line WP
New Speed = line OP

Memory Crutch

C = WP
S = OP (SOP?)

Departure Pt. **3** 0800

TOGETHERNESS IN SET AND DRIFT

This is a co-op problem. We solve it together.

"X" marks the departure point. What is the course?

What time should be inserted in the DR position? What time should be inserted in the fix position?

What is the set and drift?

"Y" marks the new destination. Extend the set drift line for one hour of drift. Where does the letter "O" belong? Where does the letter "W" belong?

Open your dividers to the speed of your craft. Use the distance scale for this. From "W" let the other end of the dividers intersect the course line to the new destination. Mark the intersection point "P".

What will be your new speed over the ground? What will be the new course?

Check the next page against your answers on this page.

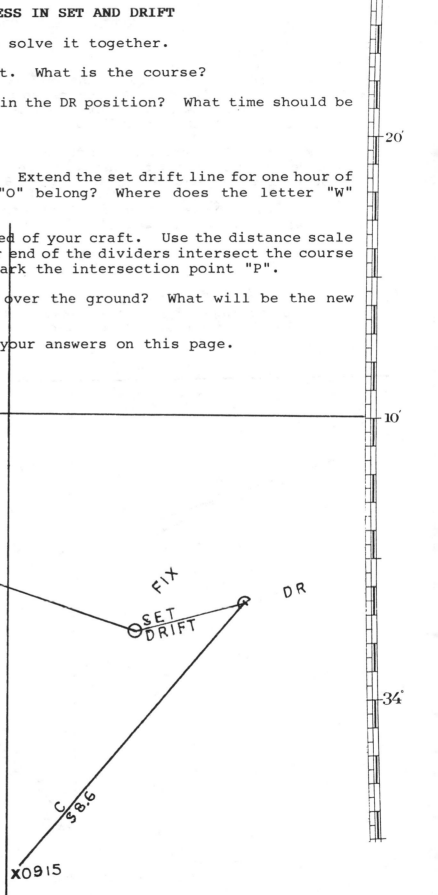

TOGETHERNESS ANSWERS

Step by step.

1) You need the distance from the 0915 departure to the DR.   That's 12.3 miles and while you're at it, the course to fill in is 040°.   If the speed is 8.6 & the distance is 12.3, the time must be 86m or 1h 26m.   This gets added to 0915 for a 1041 DR & a 1041 fix.

2) From the DR to the fix is a distance of 4.0 miles.   That current has been affecting your craft for the 86 minutes you have been underway.   If D=4 & T=86 then the speed (drift) must be 2.8.   The set is 255°.

3) Extending the set-drift line for the drift of 2.8 means drawing a line 2.8 miles long.   At the end of this line is "W".

4) Spread your dividers 8.6 miles.   From "W" mark a point on the new course line.   This is point "P".   This gives you two lines: OP and WP.

5) The length of line OP gives you your new speed: 10.8 knots.   (The current is working with you this time.)   Line WP is your new course, 299° to reach point "Y" (your new destination) despite the current.

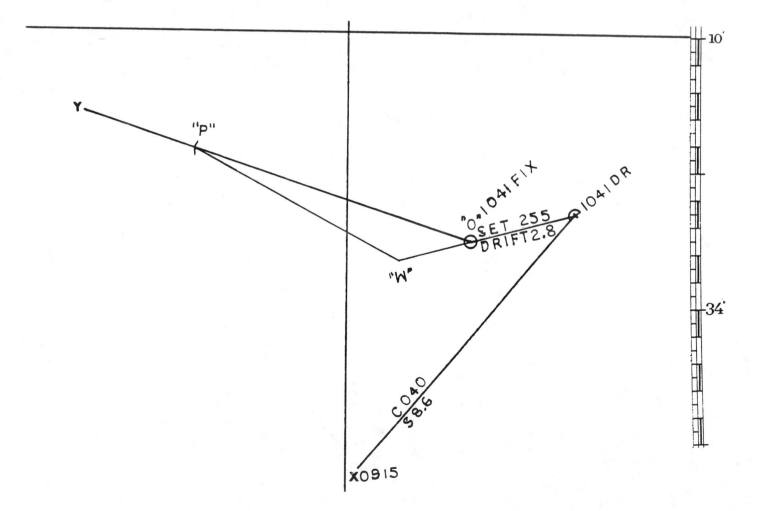

LOGIC IN ACTION

On many problems the CG will give you minimum information, but just enough to solve the problem. Take some time with this one. What you learn on this page could be very helpful and rewarding. Above all, be cool and take your time. There **is** enough information to solve the problem.

1) See if you can determine your course and speed to the DR.

2) Now find your fix by taking bearings on the two buoys. Your **compass** bearing on the lighted buoy is 271° with deviation at 3° E. and variation for the area is 12° W. The unlighted buoy bears psc 057°, deviation 3° W. From this, find your fix.

3) Now determine the set and drift.

4) What will be the course to steer and the speed made good to your final destination?

5) Assuming no time lost in computations, what will be your ETA at the final destination?

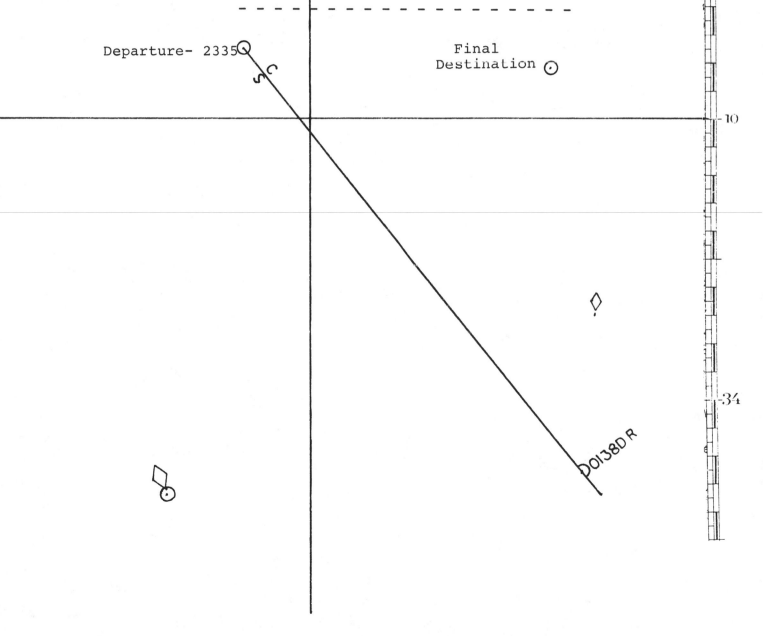

The course is 141°.   Departing at 2335 & arriving at 0138 makes for 2h 03m or 123 minutes. Working a S-D-T problem, that yields 9.4 knots.   The lighted buoy bears 262°, the unlighted buoy 042°.

The set drift line is 4.1 miles long. D=4, T=123m, so S (drift)= 2.0. Now   extend the set-drift line for 2 miles giving you point"W".   Draw your track line from point "O" -also known as the fix- to your new destination. From "W" swing an arc on the new track line 9.4 miles (speed of your boat) up the line.

Line OP measures 9.1 miles which is your **new** speed assuming your craft is still turning up rpm for your original speed of 9.4 knots.   Against this current it will only make 9.1 knots.   Line WP is your new course which, if you use, will offset the action of the current.   This is 024° true.

The ETA: The distance from your 0138 fix and the new destination is 14 miles.   The new speed will be 9.1 knots.   A S-D-T problem will indicate 92 minutes to make the voyage.   Ninety-two minutes is 1h 32m which should be added to the 0138 departure time from the fix.   0138 and 0132 = 0310 for an ETA.

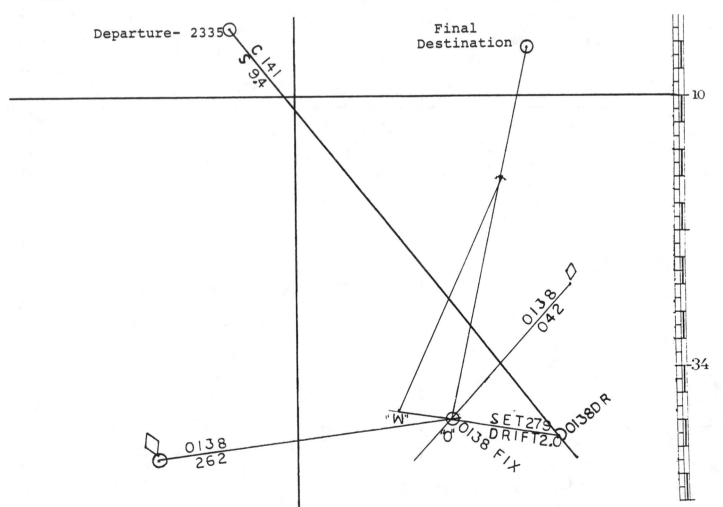

SET & DRIFT PRACTICE

The followng six problems are answered at the bottom of this page and summarized on a reduced chart on the following page. Again, assume all variation at 15° E. Recall, discouragement is forbidden.

1) Departing Sandy Point (far west end of Santa Rosa) at 1835 steering psc 340° with 5° deviation west and making 14.2 knots, you pause at 1943 for a loran fix. This results in a position of 34° 15.0' N & 120° 13.1' W. Find your set and drift. In view of your set & drift, indicate the new course and speed to Brockway Point and your ETA.

2) In your new sailboat you depart Santa Barbara's flashing green bell buoy at 1640 on compass (psc) course of 243°, speed 6.6 knots. If your deviation on this course is 3° west, at what time **should** you first see the Spa Rock Light? When **should** this light be abeam? (Caution: each time you measure the distance, **do it from the S.B. buoy**.) Suspicious of your DR position, nineteen minutes later you swing your bow to take a bearing on the Spa Rock Light. Psc, with deviation at 4° E. the light bears 281°. Swinging your bow again, you take a bearing on the Santa Barbara Light yielding 061° with 6° west deviation. With your new position clear, along with your set and drift, plot a new course to Carrington Point on Santa Rosa Island indicting your new course, adjusted speed calculation and ETA.

3) Setting a course for Santa Barbara Light from West Point Light at 1350 and making 10.2 knots with deviation at 5° E, you stop after 1h 10m to take a fix. Maintaining course, you sight on the West End which yields psc 175°. Coche Point bears psc 115°. In view of these new elements of the weather, what is your true course and ETA to the Santa Barbara Light?

4) On a true course of 290° with deviation at 6° E, Cavern Point Light bears psc 209° at 1330. Your speed is 11.6 knots. At 1410, you shoot the light again; this time the compass bearing is 109°. Indicate your 1410 position.

5) With deviation at 2° W and a speed of 9.3 knots and a compass course of 007°, the Bunny Isle light bears 037° psc at 1512. At 1624, the same light bears 105° true. Indicate your 1624 position.

6) Depart Cavern Point Light at 1647 making 10.3 knots on a compass course of 331° with deviation on this course 4° E. One hour twenty-nine minutes later you take a compass bearing on the Santa Barbara Light which indicates 316°. At the same time, Rincon Point bears psc 056°. Plot the set and drift so you can indicate your new course and ETA to Rincon Point. Keep in mind that since no one said "turning your bow to bear on the object" you must assume a pelorus bearing and **each deviation** used must conform to the heading of the vessel; in this case 4° east.

6) New course-084° true. New speed 8.1 knots. ETA 1935.

5) 1624 position-latitude 34° 14.7' N & longitude 119° 32.5' W.

4) 1410 position-latitude 34° 07.6' N & longitude 119° 39.8' W.

3) New course-048° true. New speed-8.7 knots. Distance 11.0 Mi. ETA 1616.

2) Light at 1915. Set 120°-Drift 0.6. New course=184°-New speed 6.9 knots. ETA 2155.

1) New course-178° true. New speed-15.7 knots. ETA 2036.

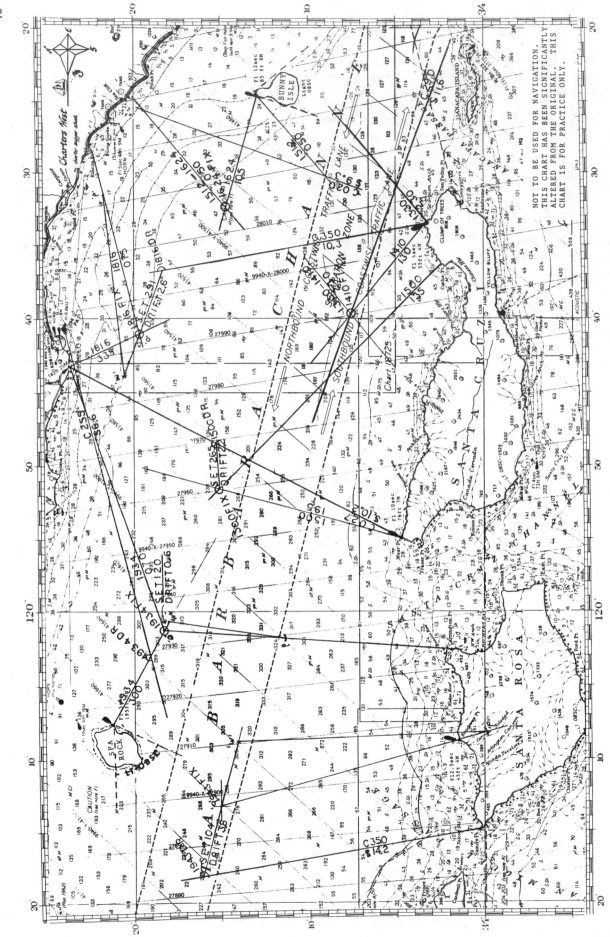

NOT TO BE USED FOR NAVIGATION. THIS CHART HAS BEEN SIGNIFICANTLY ALTERED FROM THE ORIGINAL. THIS CHART IS FOR PRACTICE ONLY.

A DIRTY DOZEN FOR THE ROAD

Here's the big time. The following twelve problems are solved on two reduced charts found on pages 217 & 218. Six on each page. Pages 215 & 216 hold the aids and answers to guide you through the charts. These are very similar to the **type** of problems you will encounter on the real Coast Guard charting test. They encompass all prior concepts on our exercises plus a few variations. You should be able to work the first ten problems in less than three and a half hours maintaining a 90% accuracy. To accomplish this the first time through would be most amazing. But, at least you can use the examples repeatedly to hone your skills. Numerous catch-type glitches are included to frustrate you like the CG exams frequently employ. Don't throw the book across the room when you miss. Study the solutions and discussions and learn **why** it works. Better you screw it up now than with the CG. If you need more practice problems see the special order form in the back of the book.

Two things to remember. Assume all variations herein to be 15° east. A "radar mile" is considered as 2,000 yards.

1) Departing from a point 1.5 miles southwest of the Santa Barbara flashing green bell buoy at 0415 on a compass course of 253° making 11.6 knots and deviation on this course of 3° west, plot your 0532 DR. At this point a Spa Rock Light pelorus bearing yields 275° psc. At the same time, Goleta Point bears 041° psc. From this information determine what speed you will have to maintain to clear Spa Rock's southern-most point by a 1/2 mile.

2) Having departed the Santa Barbara flashing bell buoy at 1515 on a compass course of 131° making 12.5 knots and deviation at 4° east, you take bearings at 1627. Visibility is excellent so you take a compass bearing on the Bunny Isle lighthouse of 081°. Anacapa Island Light bears psc 123°. Utilizing this information and maintaining your present course, state your ETA at the northern edge of the Separation Zone.

3) Depart Carrington Point at 2040 on course 332° true. Making 16.2 knots at what time should you first see the Spa Rock Light?

4) Depart the West Point Light at 2140 knowing your set and drift will be 090° and drift will be 4.5. Turning up engine rpm's to make your usual 10.5 knots, what will be your ETA at the Santa Barbara flashing green bell buoy?

5) Leaving the Santa Barbara flashing green bell buoy at 1230 making 15.6 knots, you are informed that the set, plotted previous to your departure, is 100° with a drift of 2.5 knots. Your destination is Cavern Point. After arriving at Cavern Point, you troll the area fishing for the day then return to Cavern Point. Departing Cavern at 1815, you are bound for Santa Barbara and your afternoon point of departure experiencing the same set and drift.

Give your afternoon ETA at Cavern Point and your evening ETA upon return to Santa Barbara.

6) Underway at 2130 on compass course 071° with deviation at 4° east. The Bunny Isle Light bearing is 131° psc four miles off. What is your position?

7) On a course of 071° psc with deviation at 6° west, the Brockway Point Light bears 126° psc at 2240. Ninety minutes later, making a constant speed of 5.8 knots, the same light shows a compass bearing of 231°. What is your position?

8) On a foggy night at 2035 the range on Goleta Point is 15,600 yards.   At the same time Spa Rock Light shows a range of 18,000 yards while the West Point Light is 28,000 yards off.   Indicate your position.

9) The following radar ranges are taken on the following three points at 0410.   Plot these and indicate your position.

   a) The end of the Punta Gorda Pier -near upper right corner of chart where
      the Fl 5 sec light is located- ranges 12,000 yards.
   b) Bunny Isle Light - 14,000 yards.
   c) Cavern Point - 27,000 yards.

10) The visibility is restricted at 2212.   Your fathometer indicates you are on the forty fathom line.   Swinging your bow to bear on Carrington Point your compass reads 199° and your deviation card shows deviation on this heading of 3° east.   Setting a course for Spa Rock and making 9.2 knots, the meteorological visibility degenerates to 1/2 mile.   At what time would you see the Spa Rock Light under these conditions?   Hint: Go to the Luminous Range Diagram in the appendix.

11) At 1835 you set a course for Bunny Isle Light from West Point Light making 10.3 knots with deviation on this course of 2^O west.   At 1930 Cavern Point Light bears 107° psc.   The Bunny Isle Light bears 047° compass.   Plot your set and drift, indicate your new course and speed and give your ETA at Bunny Isle Light.

12) You are en route to the Santa Barbara Fl G bell buoy departing at 1718, deviation 5° east making 13.2 knots.   If the Santa Barbara radio beacon has a broadcasting range of 10 miles what time **should you** first hear its signal?   At this time you take a radar bearing of 325° true to Goleta Point when the Santa Barbara Light bears 160° psc.   Knowing your new position, what coursee would you steer while maintaining a speed of 12 knots to reach the Bunny Isle Light?

     Still feel a little unsure?   By now, you should have made your appointment with the Coast Guard to take your exam.   Want some more practice plotting problems like those above?   Something to work on the night before the exam?   See the special order form in the back of the book.

AIDS AND ANSWERS TO THE DIRTY DOZEN

1) This a cute variation of set and drift. However, basically the principle is the same and so is the step-by-step procedure. First, plot your new track line so it passes 1/2 mile south of the southern-most point of Spa Rock. Then extend your set-drift line 2.7 miles. Now, all you need is "P". Where is "P" and how do you find it? "P" is still 11.6 miles (your former speed) from "W" on the track line. Draw the 11.6 mile line from "W" to "P". Now measure OP. You should get 10.4 miles, hence the new speed of 10.4 knots. Nothing has changed. The questions was merely asked differently. Your new course ("WP") will be 283°. Incidentally, if it weren't for the drift, this course would run you smack into the middle of Spa Rock.

2) Did you notice that your set is exactly the opposite of your course line? This means the current is working directly against you. You're bucking it straight on. In fact, over the 1h 12m you were underway you lost 3.7 miles of distance because of the current. Over a period of 72 minute underway, that works out to a drift of 3.1. If you turned up rpm to make 12.5 knots and had a drift of 3.1 working **against** you, your speed was really 9.4 knots. (12.5 minus 3.1). At a speed of 9.4 knots with 7.5 miles to go, you would make the Separation Zone in another 48 minutes...or 1715 for an ETA. No fancy "W" "O" and "P" drawings were necessary.

3) This one was conceived to make you watch all around. Assume nothing. Maybe you thought those dotted lines emanating from Spa Rock Light indicated the six mile limit the light could be seen. No way. If you come across one of these seemingly simple things, beware. You won't get in the range of the visibility of the light until you pass by the rock picking up the light on the other side. Note the six mile arc drawn on the solution chart. The light will show up at 2159.

4) Isn't this sweet of some one? They gave you the set and drift before you departed West Point Light. Get that! You don't have to plot set and drift. Assume West Point Light is your **fix**. Well, O.K., call it point "O". Since the set is 090° and the drift is 4.5, draw this line **from** "O" before you head for the Santa Barbara buoy. On the east end of this 090° 4.5 mile line is our old friend "W". And how fast were you expected to head for S.B? 10.5 knots? Then, from "W" spread a 10.5 mile space on your dividers and find "P" on the track line. You should get a new speed of 12.2 knots steering a course of 010°. The distance to S.B.'s buoy is 22.8 knots. Your ETA would be 2332.

5) Same as above, but doubled. There are two separate and distinct problems here. Plot your set and drift from Santa Barbara by finding "W" which is 2.5 miles 100° from the buoy. The new speed to Cavern will be 16.5 knots on a course of 172° true. The distance from the buoy (point "O") to Cavern is 21.6 miles. ETA Cavern will be 1349. On the return trip the distance is the same from Cavern to the buoy. However, your set and drift must be plotted again before you depart. The new speed (OP) is 14.4. The distance is still 21.6 miles. Departing at 1815 on a course of 336°, your ETA will be 90 minutes later, or 1945.

6) First draw the bearing line from Bunny Isle Light. This is 150° true. Four miles from the light -on 150°- is your position. Latitude 34° 16.3' N. & longitude 119° 27.2' W.

7) This is a running fix. Plot the 2240 bearing line 135° true to the light. Next, plot the 0010 bearing line of 240° true. Ninety minutes later is 8.7 miles for a 0010 DR. (Recall: your course line can pass through these two bearings from the light at any distance off the light.) Find 8.7 miles from your 2240 DR. Advance your 2240 135° bearing line to your 0010 DR. To make this advance, draw a 135° bearing line through your 0010 DR on your course line. Where the advanced (2240-0010) 135° line intersects the second bearing line from the light, (240°) is your 0010 position. Latitude 34° 05.2' N & longitude 120° 01.0' W.

8) Each range in yards should be divided by 2,000. For example, the range on Goleta Point was 15,600. Divided by 2,000 this yields a distance of 7.8 miles. Use your drafting compass to swing a 7.8 mile arc. Do the same with the other arcs from Spa Rock and West Point. Where the three intersect –or the center if there is a space in the middle– is your position. In this case: latitude 34° 18.6' N & longitude 119° 57.2' W.

9) Same technique as above. Position: latitude 34° 16.5' N & longitude 119° 31.9' W.

10) The true bearing from Carrington Point as 217°. The forty fathom line is marked as indicated in the General Knowledge section of this volume. This is indicated by dots and dashes. See page 121, numbers 14 and 17. On your chart look for the string of four dots separated by dashes. Where your 217° bearing intersects this line there is a numeral "40" –for forty fathoms– just below and to the right of your position. Starting from here at 2212 you will travel 16.6 miles before sighting the Spa Rock Light. Why 16.6 miles? Because if the meteorological visibility is 1/2 mile on a light with a nominal range of 6 miles, its visibility is then reduced to **one mile**. This **one mile** is not indicated on the right side of the diagram...but on the left side. You will reach this point at 0000 or, if you like, 2400.

11) The course to Bunny is 072° true. Set works out to 114° with drift at 4.8 because the set drift line is 4.4 miles long. The true bearing on Cavern Point was 120°, the one on Bunny was 073° true. New course will be 038° with a new speed of 12.4 knots. The distance to go is 14.0 miles which will take 68 minutes making it 2038 ETA.

12) The true course is 031° as indicated on the answer chart. Your bearing to the Santa Barbara Light at 1815 is 000°. Your set-drift line measures 3.1 miles, which over a 57 minute period of underway time should give you a drift of 3.3. The set is 089°. Since you are now heading for the Bunny Isle Light, draw a course line from your fix (now called point "O") to the light. The problem indicates you must maintain a speed of 12 knots. Thus, measure 12 nautical miles from the fix along the course line and label it "P" like you always do. Then extend the set-drift line 089° for the length of the drift which is 3.3 knots. That gives you point "W". Draw a line from "W" to "P". If line "OP" is your speed, (12 knots), then "WP" must be the course to steer...103°.

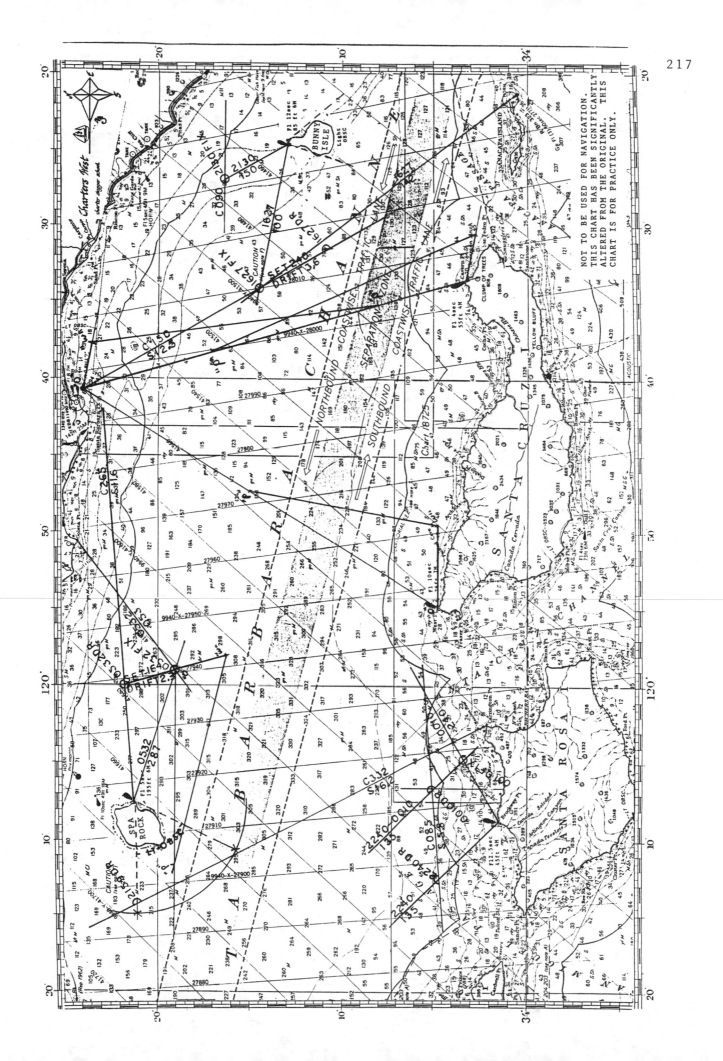

217

NOT TO BE USED FOR NAVIGATION.
THIS CHART HAS BEEN SIGNIFICANTLY
ALTERED FROM THE ORIGINAL. THIS
CHART IS FOR PRACTICE ONLY.

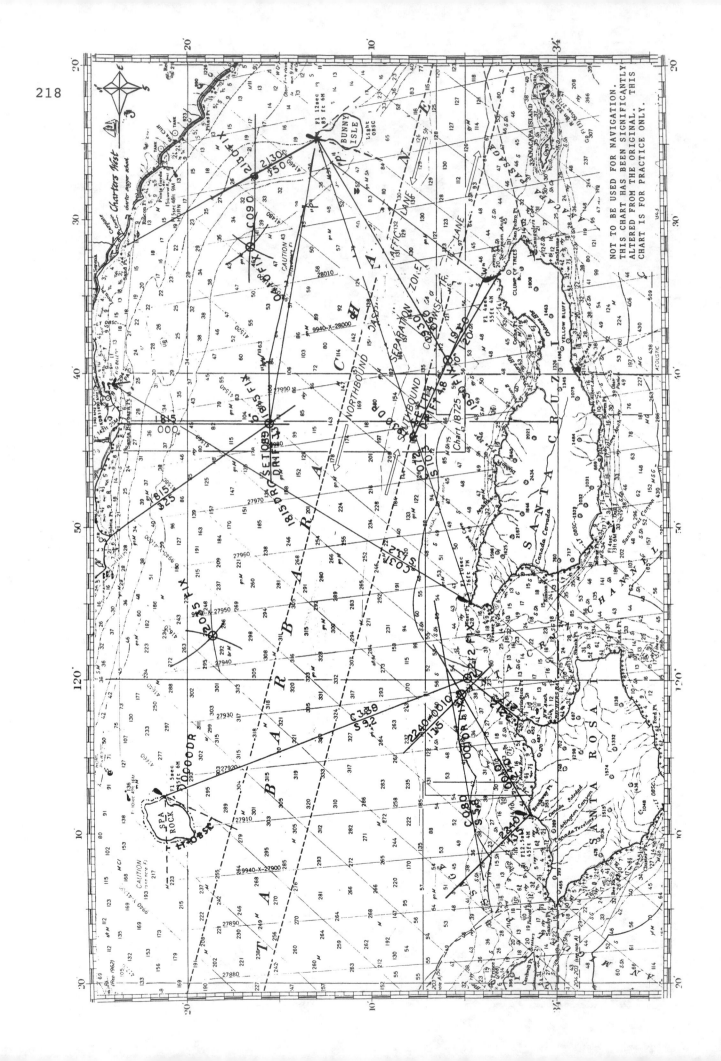

218

NOT TO BE USED FOR NAVIGATION.
THIS CHART HAS BEEN SIGNIFICANTLY
ALTERED FROM THE ORIGINAL. THIS
CHART IS FOR PRACTICE ONLY.

APPENDIX

LUMINOUS RANGE DIAGRAM

This diagram is based on the fact that restricted visibility (fog, etc.) can substantially reduce the distance a light can be seen. The chart comes from page vii in the government publication called the **Light List**. A few offices have thrown in questions regarding this chart, but neglect to tell you where to find the answer. Since all of the current marine publications are stocked in each REC examining room, they can sit back and watch you frantically thumbing pages. How does it work?

Assume a foggy night and you are approaching a light on some shoreline which has a **nominal range** of six miles. This nominal range is found on the chart, so looking this up along the bottom or top line of the chart, assume some official body has broadcast the fact that the current **meteorological visibility** is two nautical miles. Move up from the bottom along the six miles nominal range entry at the bottom of the chart. Keep moving until you encounter the **curved line** indicating two nautical miles. Stop at that precise intersection. Then go horizontally to the right or left to the edge of the chart. What is the approximate number you encounter on the right or left edge? About 2.6 miles.

Try another. The nominal range of the light (ashore) is 20 miles. How far would you see the light when the meteorological visibility is ten miles? **About** eighteen miles. How far would the same light be visible if the meteorological visibility was two miles? **About** 6.2 miles.

Don't worry about taking this page into the examining room with you. Just remember where to find it should the need arise.

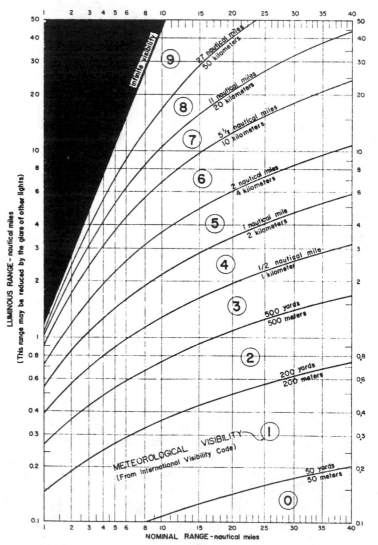

LUMINOUS RANGE DIAGRAM

Approved by OMB
2115-0006

DEPARTMENT OF TRANSPORTATION U.S. COAST GUARD CG-866 (Rev. 6-82)	SEA SERVICE FORM (MILITARY EXPERIENCE) *See Privacy Act Statement on Instruction Sheet*	FILING DATA *(C.G. USE ONLY)*

NAME *(Last)*	*(First)*	Middle Init. *(Suffix)*	SOCIAL SECURITY NO.	BRANCH OF SERVICE

VESSEL NAME:_____ CLASS:_____ TONNAGE OR HORSEPOWER[1]:_____

INCLUSIVE DATES OF SERVICE, FROM: _____ Mo. | Day | Yr. _____ _____ Mo. | Day | Hr.

RANK OR RATE:_____ PERCENTAGE OF UNDERWAY TIME _____ STEAM OR MOTOR[2] _____ WATERS NAV.[3] _____

LIST UNDERWAY WATCHSTANDING DUTIES: _____
_____
_____

LIST OTHER DUTIES:_____
_____
_____

DESCRIBE ANY OTHER QUALIFYING EXPERIENCE: _____
_____
_____

VESSEL NAME:_____ CLASS:_____ TONNAGE OR HORSEPOWER[1]:_____

INCLUSIVE DATES OF SERVICE, FROM: _____ Mo. | Day | Yr. _____ TO: _____ Mo. | Day | Hr.

RANK OR RATE:_____ PERCENTAGE OF UNDERWAY TIME _____ STEAM OR MOTOR[2] _____ WATERS NAV.[3] _____

LIST UNDERWAY WATCHSTANDING DUTIES: _____
_____
_____

LIST OTHER DUTIES:_____
_____
_____

DESCRIBE ANY OTHER QUALIFYING EXPERIENCE: _____
_____
_____

VESSEL NAME:_____ CLASS:_____ TONNAGE OR HORSEPOWER[1]:_____

INCLUSIVE DATES OF SERVICE, FROM: _____ Mo. | Day | Yr. _____ TO: _____ Mo. | Day | Hr.

RANK OR RATE:_____ PERCENTAGE OF UNDERWAY TIME _____ STEAM OR MOTOR[2] _____ WATERS NAV.[3] _____

LIST UNDERWAY WATCHSTANDING DUTIES: _____
_____
_____

LIST OTHER DUTIES:_____
_____
_____

DESCRIBE ANY OTHER QUALIFYING EXPERIENCE:_____
_____

VESSEL NAME: _____ CLASS: _____ TONNAGE OR HORSEPOWER[1]: _____

| | Mo. | Day | Yr. | | | Mo. | Day | Hr. |
INCLUSIVE DATES OF SERVICE, FROM: _____|_____|_____ TO: _____|_____|_____

RANK OR RATE: _____ PERCENTAGE OF UNDERWAY TIME _____ STEAM OR MOTOR[2] _____ WATERS NAV.[3] _____

LIST UNDERWAY WATCHSTANDING DUTIES: _____
_____
_____
_____

LIST OTHER DUTIES: _____
_____
_____
_____

DESCRIBE ANY OTHER QUALIFYING EXPERIENCE: _____
_____
_____
_____

VESSEL NAME: _____ CLASS: _____ TONNAGE OR HORSEPOWER[1]: _____

| | Mo. | Day | Yr. | | | Mo. | Day | Hr. |
INCLUSIVE DATES OF SERVICE, FROM: _____|_____|_____ TO: _____|_____|_____

RANK OR RATE: _____ PERCENTAGE OF UNDERWAY TIME _____ STEAM OR MOTOR[2] _____ WATERS NAV.[3] _____

LIST UNDERWAY WATCHSTANDING DUTIES: _____
_____
_____
_____

LIST OTHER DUTIES: _____
_____
_____
_____

DESCRIBE ANY OTHER QUALIFYING EXPERIENCE: _____
_____
_____
_____

VESSEL NAME: _____ CLASS: _____ TONNAGE OR HORSEPOWER[1]: _____

| | Mo. | Day | Yr. | | | Mo. | Day | Hr. |
INCLUSIVE DATES OF SERVICE, FROM: _____|_____|_____ TO: _____|_____|_____

RANK OR RATE: _____ PERCENTAGE OF UNDERWAY TIME _____ STEAM OR MOTOR[2] _____ WATERS NAV.[3] _____

LIST UNDERWAY WATCHSTANDING DUTIES: _____
_____
_____
_____

LIST OTHER DUTIES: _____
_____
_____
_____

DESCRIBE ANY OTHER QUALIFYING EXPERIENCE: _____
_____
_____

[1] If applying for deck officer's license, give gross tonnage; if applying for engineer's license, give horsepower.
[2] Engineer's ONLY — State whether S - Steam or M - Motor.
[3] O - Ocean; C - Coastwise; GL - Great Lakes; BSL - Bays, Sounds and Lakes other than Great Lakes; R - Rivers.

| DATE SUBMITTED | SIGNATURE OF APPLICANT | PAGE |
| | | _____ OF _____ |

Approved by OMB
2115-0006

DEPARTMENT OF TRANSPORTATION U.S. COAST GUARD CG-866 (Rev. 6-82)	SEA SERVICE FORM (MERCHANT VESSEL SERVICE) See Privacy Act Statement on Instruction Sheet	FILING DATA (C.G. USE ONLY)

NAME (Last)	(First)	Middle Init. (Suffix)	SOCIAL SECURITY NO.	USMMD NUMBER

Name of Vessel	Class of Vessel[1]	Tonnage or HP[2]	Steam or Motor[3]	Waters Nav.[4]	Served As	Date Shipped	Date Discharged	SERVICE		
								Yrs	Mos	Days

[1]Passenger, freight, towing, pleasure, fishing, yachts, uninspected, etc.
[2]If applying for deck officer's license, give gross tonnage; if applying for engineer's license, give horsepower.
[3]Engineer's ONLY — State whether S - Steam or M - Motor.
[4]O - Ocean; C - Coastwise; GL - Great Lakes; BSL - Bays, Sounds and Lakes other than Great Lakes; R - Rivers.

Name of Vessel	Class of Vessel[1]	Tonnage or HP[2]	Steam or Motor[3]	Waters Nav.[4]	Served As	Date Shipped	Date Discharged	SERVICE		
								Yrs	Mos	Days
							TOTAL			

DATE SUBMITTED   SIGNATURE OF APPLICANT   PAGE

_____ OF _____

DEPARTMENT OF TRANSPORTATION U.S. COAST GUARD CG-866 (Rev. 6-82)	SEA SERVICE FORM (SMALL BOAT EXPERIENCE) *See Privacy Act Statement on Instruction Sheet*	

NAME ____ *(Last)* ____ *(First)* ____ Middle Init. *(Suffix)* | SOCIAL SECURITY NO. | FILING DATA *(C.G. USE ONLY)*

VESSEL NAME:_____ OFFICIAL NO. OR STATE REGISTRATION NO. _____ LENGTH OF VESSEL: _____

GROSS TONS:_____ PROPULSION: _____ SERVED AS: _____

VESSEL WAS OPERATED BY THE APPLICANT UPON THE WATERS OF: _____

_____ BETWEEN _____ TO _____
(Name body or bodies of water) *(Geographical Point)* *(Geographical Point)*

NAME OF OWNER OR OWNERS OF BOAT IF OTHER THAN APPLICANT:_____

WRITE IN THE BLOCK UNDER THE APPROPRIATE MONTH THE NUMBER OF DAYS THAT YOU OPERATED OR SERVED ON THE ABOVE NAMED BOAT.

JANUARY *(Year)*	FEBRUARY *(Year)*	MARCH *(Year)*	APRIL *(Year)*	MAY *(Year)*	JUNE *(Year)*

JULY *(Year)*	AUGUST *(Year)*	SEPTEMBER *(Year)*	OCTOBER *(Year)*	NOVEMBER *(Year)*	DECEMBER *(Year)*

VESSEL NAME:_____ OFFICIAL NO. OR STATE REGISTRATION NO. _____ LENGTH OF VESSEL: _____

GROSS TONS:_____ PROPULSION:_____ SERVED AS:_____

VESSEL WAS OPERATED BY THE APPLICANT UPON THE WATERS OF: _____

_____ BETWEEN _____ TO _____
(Name body or bodies of water) *(Geographical Point)* *(Geographical Point)*

NAME OF OWNER OR OWNERS OF BOAT IF OTHER THAN APPLICANT:_____

WRITE IN THE BLOCK UNDER THE APPROPRIATE MONTH THE NUMBER OF DAYS THAT YOU OPERATED OR SERVED ON THE ABOVE NAMED BOAT.

JANUARY *(Year)*	FEBRUARY *(Year)*	MARCH *(Year)*	APRIL *(Year)*	MAY *(Year)*	JUNE *(Year)*

JULY *(Year)*	AUGUST *(Year)*	SEPTEMBER *(Year)*	OCTOBER *(Year)*	NOVEMBER *(Year)*	DECEMBER *(Year)*

VESSEL NAME: _____ OFFICIAL NO. OR STATE REGISTRATION NO. _____ LENGTH OF VESSEL: _____

GROSS TONS: _____ PROPULSION: _____ SERVED AS: _____

VESSEL WAS OPERATED BY THE APPLICANT UPON THE WATERS OF: _____

_____ BETWEEN _____ TO _____
(Name body or bodies of water)   (Geographical Point)   (Geographical Point)

NAME OF OWNER OR OWNERS OF BOAT IF OTHER THAN APPLICANT: _____

WRITE IN THE BLOCK UNDER THE APPROPRIATE MONTH THE NUMBER OF DAYS THAT YOU OPERATED OR SERVED ON THE ABOVE NAMED BOAT.

JANUARY (Year)	FEBRUARY (Year)	MARCH (Year)	APRIL (Year)	MAY (Year)	JUNE (Year)

JULY (Year)	AUGUST (Year)	SEPTEMBER (Year)	OCTOBER (Year)	NOVEMBER (Year)	DECEMBER (Year)

VESSEL NAME: _____ OFFICIAL NO. OR STATE REGISTRATION NO. _____ LENGTH OF VESSEL: _____

GROSS TONS: _____ PROPULSION: _____ SERVED AS: _____

VESSEL WAS OPERATED BY THE APPLICANT UPON THE WATERS OF: _____

_____ BETWEEN _____ TO _____
(Name body or bodies of water)   (Geographical Point)   (Geographical Point)

NAME OF OWNER OR OWNERS OF BOAT IF OTHER THAN APPLICANT:

WRITE IN THE BLOCK UNDER THE APPROPRIATE MONTH THE NUMBER OF DAYS THAT YOU OPERATED OR SERVED ON THE ABOVE NAMED BOAT.

JANUARY (Year)	FEBRUARY (Year)	MARCH (Year)	APRIL (Year)	MAY (Year)	JUNE (Year)

JULY (Year)	AUGUST (Year)	SEPTEMBER (Year)	OCTOBER (Year)	NOVEMBER (Year)	DECEMBER (Year)

DATE SUBMITTED	SIGNATURE OF APPLICANT	PAGE
		_____ of _____

LIST OF U.S. COAST GUARD
REGIONAL EXAMINATION CENTERS (RECs)

ALASKA, Anchorage
(907) 271-5137

U.S. Coast Guard, Marine Safety Office (REC),
701 C Street, Box 17, Anchorage, AK 99513

ALASKA, Juneau
(907) 586-7325

U.S. Coast Guard, Marine Safety Office (REC),
612 Willoughby Ave., Juneau, AK 99801

CALIFORNIA, Alameda
(415) 437-3094

U.S. Coast Guard, Marine Safety Office (REC),
Building 14, Room 109, Government Island,
Alameda, CA 94501

CALIFORNIA, Long Beach
(213) 590-2383

U.S. Coast Guard, Marine Safety Office (REC),
165 N. Pico Avenue, Long Beach, CA 90802

FLORIDA, Miami
(305) 594-4305
     594-4220

U.S. Coast Guard, Marine Safety Office (REC),
8120 NW 53rd Street
Miami, FL 33166

HAWAII, Honolulu
(808) 546-7318

U.S. Coast Guard, Marine Safety Office (REC),
Rm. 1, 433 Ala Moana Blvd., Honolulu, HI 96813

LOUISIANA, New Orleans
(504) 589-6183

U.S. Coast Guard, Marine Inspection Office (REC),
F. Edward Hebert Bldg., 600 South Street,
New Orleans, LA 70130

MARYLAND, Baltimore
(301) 962-5134/5

U.S. Coast Guard, Marine Safety Office (REC),
U.S. Custom House, Baltimore, MD 21202

MASSACHUSETTS, Boston
(617) 523-0139/40

U.S. Coast Guard, Marine Safety Office (REC),
447 Commercial Street, Boston, MA 02114

MISSOURI, St. Louis
(314) 425-4657

U.S. Coast Guard, Marine Safety Office (REC),
210 N. Tucker Blvd., Rm. 1128, St. Louis, MO 63101

NEW YORK, New York
(212) 668-7864
     668-7492
     668-6395

U.S. Coast Guard, Marine Inspection Office (REC),
Battery Park Bldg., New York, NY 10004

OHIO, Toledo
(419) 259-6394

U.S. Coast Guard, Marine Safety Office (REC),
Rm. 501, Federal Bldg., 234 Summit Street,
Toledo, OH 43604

OREGON, Portland
(503) 240-9346

U.S. Coast Guard, Marine Safety Office
6767 N. Basin Ave., Portland, OR 97217

SOUTH CAROLINA, Charleston
(803) 724-4394

U.S. Coast Guard, Marine Safety Office (REC),
196 Tradd Street, P.O. Box 724,
Charleston, SC 29402

TENNESSEE, Memphis
(901) 521-3297/8

U.S. Coast Guard, Marine Safety Office (REC),
100 N. Main St., Suite 1134, Memphis, TN 38103

TEXAS, Houston   U.S. Coast Guard, Marine Inspection Office (REC),
   (713) 229-3559   7300 Wingate Street, Houston, TX 77011

WASHINGTON, Seattle   U.S. Coast Guard, Marine Inspection Office (REC),
   (206) 442-4923   1519 Alaskan Way S., Bldg. 1, Seattle, WA 98134

"MONITORING FACILITIES"

CALIFORNIA, San Diego   U.S. Coast Guard, Marine Safety Office
   (213) 590-2383   2710 Harbor Dr., San Diego, CA 92101

VIRGINIA, Norfolk   U.S. Coast Guard, Marine Safety Office
   (301) 962-5134/5   Norfolk Federal Bldg., 200 Granby Mall,
                         Norfolk, VA 23510

PRACTICE ANSWER FORMS FOR INTERNATIONAL

UNIFIED & GENERAL KNOWLEDGE QUIZZES

1)	28)	55)	82)	109)	136)	163)
2)	29)	56)	83)	110)	137)	164)
3)	30)	57)	84)	111)	138)	165)
4)	31)	58)	85)	112)	139)	166)
5)	32)	59)	86)	113)	140)	167)
6)	33)	60)	87)	114)	141)	168)
7)	34)	61)	88)	115)	142)	169)
8)	35)	62)	89)	116)	143)	170)
9)	36)	63)	90)	117)	144)	171)
10)	37)	64)	91)	118)	145)	172)
11)	38)	65)	92)	119)	146)	173)
12)	39)	66)	93)	120)	147)	174)
13)	40)	67)	94)	121)	148)	175)
14)	41)	68)	95)	122)	149)	176)
15)	42)	69)	96)	123)	150)	177)
16)	43)	70)	97)	124)	151)	178)
17)	44)	71)	98)	125)	152)	179)
18)	45)	72)	99)	126)	153)	180)
19)	46)	73)	100)	127)	154)	
20)	47)	74)	101)	128)	155)	
21)	48)	75)	102)	129)	156)	
22)	49)	76)	103)	130)	157)	
23)	50)	77)	104)	131)	158)	
24)	51)	78)	105)	132)	159)	
25)	52)	79)	106)	133)	160)	
26)	53)	80)	107)	134)	161)	
27)	54)	81)	108)	135)	162)	

PRACTICE ANSWER FORMS FOR SEAMANSHIP SECTIONS

I. SEAMANSHIP

1)	28)	18)	18)	6)	13)	**VI. RULES**
2)	29)	19)	19)	7)	14)	1)
3)	30)	20)	20)	8)	15)	2)
4)	31)	21)	21)	9)	16)	3)
5)	32)	22)	22)	10)	17)	4)
6)	33)	23)	23)	11)	18)	5)
7)	34)	24)	24)	12)	**ENGINES**	6)
8)	35)	25)	25)	13)	1)	7)
9)	36)	26)	26)	14)	2)	8)
10)	**II. WEATHER**	**III. BOATS**	27)	15)	3)	9)
11)	1)	1)	28)	16)	4)	10)
12)	2)	2)	29)	17)	5)	11)
13)	3)	3)	30)	18)	6)	12)
14)	4)	4)	31)	19)	7)	13)
15)	5)	5)	32)	**V. FIRE**	8)	14)
16)	6)	6)	33)	1)	9)	15)
17)	7)	7)	34)	2)	10)	16)
18)	8)	8)	35)	3)	11)	
19)	9)	9)	36)	4)	12)	
20)	10)	10)	37)	5)	13)	
21)	11)	11)	38)	6)	14)	
22)	12)	12)	**IV. FIRST AID**	7)	15)	
23)	13)	13)	1)	8)	16)	
24)	14)	14)	2)	9)	17)	
25)	15)	15)	3)	10)	18)	
26)	16)	16)	4)	11)	19)	
27)	17)	17)	5)	12)		

GLOSSARY

Advection fog – Fog caused by warmer offshore air cooling rapidly over a cold sea and condensing into fog. See Weather section under Seamanship.

All-around light – A 360° light visible on all points of the horizon.

Arc – A geometric term describing **part** of a 360° circle.

Backfire arrestor – A high density mesh covering carburetor air intake preventing flames emerging during a backfire. Required on all U.S. manufactured power craft burning gasoline.

Backing – The movement of on-coming wind in a counter-clockwise direction from the relative heading of a craft. Also called "hauling".

Barometer – A device for measuring atmospheric pressure.

Beam – At a right angle to the keel.

Bearing – A relative, magnetic or true direction of an object **from** one's location.

Bifurcation – Technical term denoting converging channels.

Bollard – A piling which sticks up through the dock to which mooring lines are tied.

Broach – To veer to windward and come broadside to the wind and/or waves.

Broad on the beam – At a right angle to the keel at the widest point of the vessel, generally about half way between bow and stern.

COLREGS – A term applying to the "Convention of the International Regulations for Preventing Collisions at Sea, 1972." Formalized in 1972, becoming effective July 15, 1977. Sometimes referred to as the '72 COLREGS and refer primarily to the International Rules of The Road. On June 1, 1983 fifty-five amendments were added to the '72 COLREGS.

Combustible (liquid) – One having a flashpoint at or above 100° F, e.g. vegetable and lubricating oils.

Compass error – The algebraic sum of the variation and deviation.

Cross signals – An old, now illegal, signal whereby one blast was answered with two blasts and vice versa.

Current – Anything contributing to or affecting the direction of movement of a large body of water.

Danger signal – At least five short blasts on ship's whistle. More appropriately, in maneuvering, a signal of **doubt.**

Demarcation line – A line across harbor entrances, or nearby, indicating the separation line between inland and international waters and the rules applying thereto. Indicated on most large scale charts.

Deviation – Compass error caused by ferrous metals in close proximity to a compass on board ship.

Diabetes - A blood disease wherein victim is unable to burn normal amount of sugar.

Diaphone - An out-of-date air pressure diaphram device which activated a fog horn ashore. Diaphram was pumped up mechanically, then released to activate fog horn.

Down-draft carburetor - Carburetor with air intake facing up. Air is pulled "down" the carburetor. Standard on today's gas powered craft.

Drift - Speed of the current.

Drip Pan - Small pan placed beneath old fashioned up-draft carburetors with air intakes facing down. To catch dripping fuel.

Drogue - A sea-anchor trailing from the stern. To keep stern into oncoming sea and prevent yawing.

Ebb tide - A receding tide. One which is "going out".

ETA - Estimated time of arrival.

Extremis - Term used to imply collision is imminent

Fairway - A navigable channel or traffic pattern, generally within a harbor.

Fix - A known location found by bearings, visual, radar, loran or SatNav.

Flammable (liquid) - One having a flashpoint below 100° F. with a vapor pressure less than 40 psi, e.g. gasoline, alcohol, and acetone.

Flashing - Referring to a buoy light which flashes about 30 times per minute.

Flood tide - Indicating the tide is rising, or "coming in".

Fog horn - A warning of foul ground generated by a horn buoy or lighthouse ashore. Term is no longer used in Rules of The Road as regards ships.

Fog Signal - One of many whistle, bell or gong soundings when underway or at anchor in or near an area of restricted visibility. Generally, the deeper the tone, the larger the vessel.

Give-way craft - The burdened vessel in a meeting, crossing or overtaking situation. Does not have the right-of-way.

Hauling - The moving of an on-coming wind in a counter-clockwise direction relative to the heading of a vessel. Also called "backing".

Hogging line - A line strung beneath the ship from one side to the other. Used to support collision matting (canvass or similar) to prevent taking of water when a hull is stoved.

I.A.L.A. - International Association of Lighthouse Authorities. Refers to the new buoyage system which started in 1983 to be finished by 1989. See "Buoys" under Seamanship chapter in this volume.

Inland - Referring to any navigable bodies of water shoreward from a demarcation line. Western rivers and Great Lakes are separate as regards **some cases** in the Inland Rules of The Road. See VTC below.

Inspected vessels - Vessels inspected by the U.S. Coast Guard and granted a Certificate of Inspection to carry passengers for hire; generally, more than six. Certificate denotes maximum number of passengers vessel may carry and other conditions of operation.

Insulin - An injection given to diabetics victim to aid in balancing of body sugar.

Insulin shock - A reaction from having administered too much insulin.

Knot - A measurement of speed over the water, i.e. how many nautical miles are covered each hour underway.

"L" Vessel - Certificated passenger carrying vessel sixty-five feet or greater in length.

LPG gas - Liquid petroleum gas. Examples are butane and propane. Not allowed on passenger carrying vessels.

LOP - Line of Position. A plotting line on a chart derived from a bearing for the purpose of finding one's position at sea.

Masthead light - A 225° white light high on a mast.

Mayday - Verbal radio distress call.

Nautical mile - Approximately 6076 feet, (6076.1155')

NFPA - The National Fire Prevention Association.

Not under command - "Exceptional circumstances" prevent maneuvering. Adrift.

Occluded - Weather term referring to the coming together of air masses with dissimilar temperatures.

Occulting - A light which is on more than it is off.

Ocean Operator - A Coast Guard licensee holding an Ocean Operator's License to carry passengers for hire on inspected vessels less than 100 gross tons. Tonnage limit **may be** raised and grandfathered to 200 tons July 1, 1986

OinC - Officer in Charge.

OinCMI - Officer in Charge, Marine Inspection.

Parcelling - The taping of a cable, generally after it has been wormed.

PFD - Personal flotation device. A life jacket, cushion or ring/horseshoe buoy.

Piledikes - Poles driven into a riverbed adjacent to the riverbank to prevent errosion by passing current.

Pitchpole - Term applied to any vessel when bow digs into wave and oncoming stern wave forces stern up and over the bow.

Port - To the left. The left side of a vessel.

Psc - Short for "per standard compass".

Quick flashing - A buoy light which flashes 60 fpm.

Radio beacon - A radio shoreline transmission signalling device with frequency and identifying morse code signal indicated on a chart.   Range is generally limited to about ten miles.

RDF - Radio direction finder - A radio signal receiving device equipped with a loop antenna capable of pinpointing direction of any given incoming broadcast.

REC - Regional Examination Center.   Where marine exams are given by the U.S. Coast Guard.   See appendix this volume for locations and phone numbers.

Relative bearing - The direction of some object from the boat's position irrespective of the direction in which the vessel is pointing.   As a comparison: Bearing 3:00 O'Clock would be bearing 090°.   Bearing 9:00 O'Clock would be bearing 270°.

Restricted in ability to maneuver - Special nature of vessel's work severely hampers maneuverability.

Restricted visibility - Vision hampered by fog, mist, falling snow, heavy rain, sandstorm or persumably similar causes.

Rode - Scope of an anchor line.

Running fix - A fix by taking two bearings at different times on the same object.

Running lights - An all-inclusive term referring to lights required on any vessel when underway at night or in restricted visibility.   Frequently misused to indicate sidelights.

"S" vessel - Certificated passenger carrying vessel less than sixty-five feet in length.

Separation zone - A buffer zone between two opposite bound taffic lanes.

Serving - the wrapping of a cable, stanchion or fitting with a preservative type of lanyard or line, (generally marlin).

Set - Direction of current flow.

Sidelights - Lights of a vessel shinning from dead ahead to 22.5° abaft the beam on their respective sides of red to port, green to starboard.

Six-Pac - A slang term for Motorboat Operator's License to Carry Passengers For Hire.   Also referring to a "six-pac boat" meaning a small passenger carrying vessel, less than 100 gross tons, permitted to carry six or less passengers for hire without a Coast Guard Inspection or certificate of inspection.

Slack tide - Standing water between flood and ebb.

Small passenger vessel - A vessel equipped to carry passengers for hire and conforming to the requirements of the U.S. Coast Guard.   Less than 100 gross tons.

Spar - A boom to which lifeboats are secured.   Any long boom, generally wood or aluminum.   From the Coast Guard motto (s)emper (par)atus.   A World War II female Coast (sic) Guardsman.

Stand-on craft - The vessel with the right-of-way in a meeting, crossing or overtaking situation.

Starboard - To the right. The right side of a vessel.

Stern light - A white light shown from stern of craft underway. Shows in an arc of 135º.

Torch - A British term for flashlight.

Towing light - A yellow light shown above the stern light of any tug towing a tow from behind. Also used inland when pushing ahead or alongside in inland waters. 135º of arc.

Trolling - Trailing a fishing line behind a boat.

Up-draft carburetor - An out-of-date version on which the air intake pointed downwards, towards the bilge or nearly so.

Underway - Any craft is underway when not made fast to shore, at anchor or aground.

Underway with way on - Underway and making way through the water. Not adrift.

Unified - Referring to inland waters' rules and their close proximity to those applying in international waters. Enacted into law Dec. 24, 1980, becoming effective Dec. 24, 1981 (effective Great Lakes March 1, 1983).

Uninspected vessels - Those vessels not inspected by U.S. Coast Guard to carry passengers for hire, e.g. six-pac small passenger carrying vessels.

Variation - Part of compass error. Geographic difference between magnetic and true north.

Veering anchor - Method by which a large vessel at anchor on a river can move from side-to-side by turning the rudder hard over. Current reacting against the rudder moves the vessel to one side.

VTC - Vessel traffic control. Special area rules applying to various sections in the Western Rivers.

Way on - Making way through the water.

Western Rivers - Those rivers which empty into the Mississippi River with the exception of the Red River of The North.

Worming - The weaving of treated line (generally marlin) into the groves of a cable to make it flush.

Yaw - The forcing of the stern of a craft from one side to the other. Caused by a following sea and can cause loss of steering ability when stern is raised and rudder is clear or nearly clear of the water.

INDEX

A LIST OF QUESTIONS

I MUST ASK THE LOCAL COAST GUARD

1) _____

2) _____

3) _____

4) _____

5) _____

6) _____

7) _____

8) _____

9) _____

10) _____

11) _____

12) _____

13) _____

14) _____

15) _____

16) _____

17) _____

18) _____

19) _____

20) _____

ORDER FORM

Have copy made
Retain this original

Orders are posted the same day received. Orders of **only** plotting problems and flash cards are shipped first class. Other items listed below are shipped UPS. There is no extra charge for handling and shipping individual orders. If no UPS is available in your location, include $3 for first class mail. California residents must add 6% sales tax.

Send all orders and make checks payable to: Charters West-P.O. Box 675-B, Goleta, CA 93116. Sorry, we have no provisions for phone orders.

THE COAST GUARD LICENSE
FROM SIX PAC TO OCEAN OPERATOR

1) Please ship immediately _____ copies of The Coast Guard License - From Six Pac to Ocean Operator at $21.95 each.

THE RULES OF THE ROAD

2) Please ship immediately _____ copies of The Rules of The Road at $4.95 each.

FLASHCARDS

These flashcards are printed on ten sheets of heavy-duty 8 1/2" x 11" construction paper and are shipped uncut. Colors are to be added by the student with felt pens. This order forms a complement of 82 separate flashcards of the lights, dayshapes and **fog signals.**

3) Please ship me immediately _____ set(s) of the flashcards described here at $6.99 per set.

CHARTING PROBLEMS

This order includes twelve charting problems similar to the "Dirty Dozen For The Road" found on pp. 213-218. A reduced text chart detailing the plots is included.

4) Please ship me immediately _____ set(s) of the Charting Problems-$3.99 ea.

- - - - - - - - - -

Order all three of numbers 2, 3, & 4 above and save $3.18. Pay only $12.75.

ORDER SUMMARY

The Coast Guard License
From Six Pac to
Ocean Operator..........$_____

Rules of The Road.......$_____

Flash Cards.............$_____

Twelve charting problems,
key & reduced chart.....$_____

NEW LICENSE UPDATES:
Read page 11 before
ordering. $2.00........$_____

If items 2, 3, 4
are ordered,
deduct $3.18
         Sub-total...$_____

California residents
add 6% sales tax........$_____

**NO UPS IN MY AREA.
ENCLOSED IS $3.00
FOR FIRST CLASS MAIL....$_____**

(No tax on special
 shipping costs)

    Total enclosed...$_____

Name_____

Address_____

City_____State____Zip_____